Bledsoe County Tennessee

CHANCERY COURT MINUTE BOOK

1836–1847

VOLUME II

WPA RECORDS

Heritage Books
2024

HERITAGE BOOKS

AN IMPRINT OF HERITAGE BOOKS, INC.

Books, CDs, and more—Worldwide

For our listing of thousands of titles see our website
at
www.HeritageBooks.com

A Facsimile Reprint
Published 2024 by
HERITAGE BOOKS, INC.
Publishing Division
5810 Ruatan Street
Berwyn Heights, MD 20740

1938

International Standard Book Number
Paperbound: 978-0-7884-9065-1

WPA RECORDS

The WPA Records are, for the most part, carbon copies of the original that was typed on onion skin paper during the Depression. Since these records were typed on poor machines by people who did not type well either and read by persons not always sure of the older handwritten material, the results are often less that perfect.

We have made every attempt to make as good a copy as can be made from these older papers. Sometimes there are water stains and burned edges around the paper.. This is the results of a fire at the home of one of the workers, Mrs. Penelope Allen, who was over most of the project.

The WPA Records are now very scattered between the State Archives, various Public and Private Libraries and other collections. Some day, there is a hope that all of these can be collected and stored in one place. In spite of their many mistakes and problems, these are still the most complete collection of Tennessee records found anywhere.

NEW INDEX

BLEDSOE COUNTY

CHANCERY COURT MINUTE BOOK
Vol. II 1836-1847

Name	Pages
Benson, Isaac	161-181-188-189-216 230-237-256-271-278 288-323-356
Berah?, Jacob	262
Berry, James	64-159
Bible, Christopher C.	325
Bible, George	71-325
Bible, Philip	325
Billingsley, Camelia	94-174
Billingsley, John	5-224-260-289
Billingsley, John M.	94-174-180
Billingsley, Samuel	174
Blackwell, Julius W.	232
Bledsoe County	1-351 inclusive
Blevins, James	324
Bowman, John	39
Boyd, Elizabeth H.	314
Bradford, Edward	319
Bradford, Martha	319
Bradford, James	100-289-319
Bradford, Thomas	319
Bradley County, Tenn.	99-159
Brannon, Aaron	123-157-174-186 238-250-251
Brannon, Ephraim	175-238-250
Brannon, Jane	175
Bridgman, Benjamin F.	100-127-143 153-160-163 166-201-225 226-227-254 290
Bridgman, John	1-2-5-10-11-22-49- 63-154-170-171-172 178-179-194-231 232-284
Bridgman, Narcissa F.	100
Briggs, Andrew	50
Briggs, W. M.	158
Brock, George	352
Brown, Elizabeth	144-146
Brown, George	13-15-20-24-48-68- 115-147-315
Brown, Jessee	24
Brown, John	6-9-29-37-38-57-59- 68-85-86-102
Brown, Robert A.	35-38-39
Brown, Smith	315
Brown, Thos.	38-297-310-336-348
Brown, William	17-26-36-47-55-61- 83-101-114-142-143 180-214-224-260-261 289-297-310-336-348
Broyles, Ira D.	41-84
Bryson, Adaline	45
Burk, Robert	304
Burnett, Berry	253-263
Burnett, Eliza	292-293-295-347
Burnett, George W.	253-295
Burnette, Thomas	263-265-287-288 292-330-331-347 348
Bushyhead, Jesse	210
Butler, Pleasant H.	16-22-33-53- 60-115-133-134 140-182
Butler?, Tuna? M.	210

- C -

Name	Pages
C. Morgan & Sons	162
Cain, Bersheba T.	30-33-34-50-52
Cain, Eliza	50
Cain, George W.	39-50-52
Cain, ames	8-13-27-30-33 34-50-51
Cain, James M.	39-50
Cain, James Sen.	39-52
Cain, John	13-30-33-39-50 51
Cain, Lucinda	50
Cain, Rebecca	50
Cain, Ruth	50
Caldwell, David	246-277
Caldwell, Vesta	324
Calloway, Thomas H.	53-59-81
Campbell, Elizabeth	106
Campbell, Eliza M.	90-126-131-176 208-209 210-211
Campbell, George W.	149-150-199 200-254
Campbell, Hugh	209
Campbell, John	209-211
Campbell, Margaret Ann	90-209
Campbell, Sarah	209-210
Campbell, T. J.	44
Campbell, William	209-210
Cannon, B. B.	36-71-172-241-348
Cannon, John O.	275-276-303-304
Cannon, Newton	1-2-10
Carpenter, Frey	281-325-342
Carlton, Allen B.	338
Carrole, Hugh	44
Carrol, James M.	108-149-163 267-268-269

Hoge, Susan	341		
Hogue, Martha L.	323-328		
Holding, Green J.	197-345		
Holding, John	345		
Holding, Samuel	345		
Holloway, Edward B.	108-138-163		
	267-268-268-280		
Holloway, Edward B.			
Holloway, John	18-22-37		
Holt, Elisha M.	90-209		
Holt, William L.	210		
Hoodenpyle, Peter	214		
Hoodenpyle, Thos. J.	192		
Hoots? Philip	314		
Hopkins, George W.	276-303-319		
Hopkins, Thomas	68-244-276-230		
Hopkins, Wm.	319		
Horn, John	110-137-143		
	165-176-200-290		
Hornsby, Brinkley	62-77-93-101-103		
Horsely, Ann	319		
Horsely, Robert	319		
Houston, Sam	73		
Hoyle, John	44		
Hudgens, Benjamin	47-48		
Hudleston, Creed	130-178-249		
Hudleston, Willis	130-178-249		
Hughes, Margaret	247-281		
Hughs, Frances	282		
Hughs, Francis	282		
Humble, John	327		
Humble, Mariah	327		
Humes, Jane	121		
Humes, John M.	121-286		
Hunter, Ann C.	127-153		
Hunter, Elmira R.	165-173-192		
Hunter, James A.	127		
Hunter, Joseph C.	127-153		
Hunter, Joshua W.	165-173-221		
Hunter, Martha	127-153		
Hunter, Rebecca	221-222		
Hunter, Samuel H.	127-153-154		
Huston, James	30		
Hutcheson, Alpherd	28-40-43-44		

- I -

Igou? Samuel	9
Illinois (State)	262
Inman, Benjamin R.	30-36-70-85-
	86-98

- J -

Jackson, Andrew	304-319
James, Nancy	327
James, Tyler	327
Jarnajin, Spencer	99-121-128-133
	134-152-154-157
Jasper, Tenn.	18-32-43-58-167
Jefferson County, Tenn.	351
Jasper & Pelham Turnpike Co.	
	310-347
Jenkins, James H.	12-22-32-42-52
Johnson, Alfred	327
Johnson, Benjamin	41-84
Johnson, Celia	327
Johnson, James M.	285
Johnson & Rawlstown	58
Johnson, Samuel M.	384
Johnson, Theodore P/	5-25
Johnson, William	309-349
Jones, Armstead	337 354
Jones, Jeremiah	86
Jones? Johney	64-66
Jones, Lewis	44
Jones , Stephens	95-99
Jones, William	67-80-123

- K -

Keele, Isaac	108
Keeney? James	42-69-99-118
	295-315
Keeney, John	64
Keith, Charles F.	215
Kelley, Alexander	22-31-32-42-55
	89-126-131-152
	176-208-323-326
	328-341-344-347
Kelley, Jane	323-328
Kelley, Stephen	26
Kelley, Valentine	323-328
Kelley, Wm. J.	323-328-341-344
Kelly, James	170-171-172-253-
	323-328-341
Kelly, John	188-227-258-262-
	289-322-323-327
	328-341-344-347
	356
Kelly, Joseph T.	253
Kelly, Nancy Ann	228-341-344
Kelly, Samuel	224

Kelly, Thomas J.	228-316-321
	323-341-352
Kennidy, Allen	47-63-85-107-109-
	121-158
Kersey? Owen	50
Kersey? Ruth	50
Kersey, William	185
Ketner, David	175
Keys, Elizabeth	18-27
Keys, Isaac	18-27
Keys, Riley	210-211
Kimmer, Elizabeth	80
Kimmer, John	8-14-21-80-222
Kincannon? Landon A.	78-89-107-
	115-135-139-
	147
Kinchulow? Bird C.	197
King, Binjamin R.	135-167-214
	238-300-303
	321-343-347
Kirk, John	304
Kirkland, Robert	163
Kirklin, Elisha	6-166-181-254
Kirkman, H & J	187
Kirkpatrick, Eliza	30-36-70-85-98
Knight, Emily John	319
Knox Co. Tenn.	68
Knoxville Register	68
Knoxville, Tenn.	9-21-51-57-68
	80-133-134-230
	259-270-279-296
	29?-317-318-320
	355
Krammer, Charles F.	308

- L -

Labaum? Amy	319
Labaum, Thomas	319
Ladd, Milly	348
Ladd, Noble	252-291
Lamb, Adam	163-170-171-172-178
	179-194-229-239-259
	279
Lamb, Cornelius	282
Lambert, Samuel	351
Langley? Nathaniel	192-223-249
Lassater, Hardy	282
Lassater? Johnie	50
Latham, Thomas	316-321-352
Lea, Luke	64-81-89
Legg, M. W.	29-159
Lenior, A. S.	47-59-63-85-107-109
	121-158

Leuttrell? Caswell	259
Leuty, Burton	56
Leuty, David	180
Leuty, Stanton W.	56
Leuty, Thomas	56
Leuty, Wm. S.	27-28-56-57 -82
Lewis, John	260
Lewis, Wm. L.	319-320
Lines, James C.	170-171-225-226-227
Locke, Franklin	179-180-190-202-203
	212-242-244-276-303
	319
Locke, James H.	173-192-221-222
Locke, John	27-28-31-44-68-74-
	75-82-165-173-192-
	202-203-212-221-242
	243-276-319
Locke, Newton	190-203-212
	212-242-243
	319
Locke, Ralph B.	320
Locke, Robert	173-222
Long, John T.	47-48-52-180-189
Love, Jacob	191-215-261-262- 263
Love, Jefferson B.	119-215-261-262
Love, Joseph N.	262
Love, Mary E.	262
Love, Samuel M.	191-261-262
Love, William N.	191-261-262
Lovelady, John	64
Lowe, Amy	40-80-102-187-
	213-214-248
Lowe, Andrew	40-80-102-214
Lowe, Elizabeth	247
Lowe, James S.	213
Lowe, John	80
Lowe, Moses	80
Lowe, Samuel C.	40-80-197-247
Lowe, Rebecca	213-214
Lowe, William B.	213
Loyd, James	62-77-93-94-104-
	118-141-142-189-
	235-254-279-281
	298-315-316-334
	353
Lupton, John B.	99
Luttrell, George	280
Lyles, Samuel	30

- M -

Majors, Berry	157
Marchbank, Andrew J.	319
Marcum, Reuben	122-146

Shelton, Margaret	191-261-262
Shelton, Ralph	79-89-115-135-147
	197-237
Shelton, Sarah	177-270-284
	293-294
Shelton, Temperance	108
Shelton, Wm. H.	191-262
Sheppurd, Alladin	327
Sheppurd, Hugh	327
Sherley, John	44
Sherley, Thomas	5-12-16-19-22-26
	30-33-34-36-39-
	47-53-54-58-59-
	60-75-81-82-95
	96-97-125-132-
	140-141-161-183
	200
Sherrill, Charles K.	248
Sherill, Craven	32-345
Sherill, Henry	60-147-187-213-214
	248
Sherill, Rebecca	50-147-213-248
Shipley, Nathan	99-188-258
Shipley, Park	258
Shipley, William P.	188-258
Shockley, O.	8013-17-25
Shockley, Richard	39
Shockley, S.	8-13-17-25
Shorter? Alfred	299
Shreak? Ambuuse	222-270-286-301
Shreak, John	243-270-286-301
Shugart, John	245
Siglers, Philþp	15
Skillern, Anderson	38-58-85-99-
	114-128-148-152
	166-175-193-195
	204-243-274-300
	302-324-338-345
Skillern, James V.	30-58-148-166-
	.195-243
Skillern, John	99-114-128-143-
	152-175-188-193
	204-221-303-322
	345-353
Skillern, William	345-353
Smith, David	296-312-314
Smith, Elizabeth	312
Smith, E. M.	178-179-194-195
	229-231-232
Smith, G.W.	312
Smith, James	9
Smith, John	231

Smith, Joseph G.	7-8-38-43-58-83
	95-99-110-114-128
	129-137-143-148-
	153-165-166-176-176
	187-193-195-200-204
	221-234-241-243-274
	278-280-291-300-302
	303-322-324-345-353
Smith, Kinzey	49-144
Smith, Laten K.	25
Smith M.G.	296
Smith, Maajiah?	312-313
Smith, Marcellus	302
Smith, Martha	296-312
Smith, Nancy	313-314
Smith, Robert	64
Smith Samuel A.	322
Smith, Selvana L.	312-313
Smith, Susa?	296
Smith, Thomas	123-157-174-186
	238-250-251
Smith, William	71-121-159-231-
Smith, Williamson	41
Sorrle? W.A.	263-292
Southwestern Rail Road Bank	236
	246-247-255-279-289
	317-318
Sparka, William G.	64-159
Sparta, Tenn.	261
Spergin, Jacob	118
Spergin, Jacob	118
Spergin, Rachel	118
Spicer, Thomas W.	5-12-16-26-30-
	33-34-36-53-54
	58-75-92-96-140
	141-161-183-200-
	245
Spring, David	77-104-118-119-142
	189-235-236-254
	279-316-353
Spring, James B?	101
Spring, Jane M.	77
Spring, Margaret A.	119-235-254
	279-316-334
Spring, Nicholas	235-254-279
	316-331
Spring, Valentine	141-162-175
	195-278-294
	306
SPRINGS	
Rattlesnake	206-246
Standifer, Alfred	281-285
Standifer, James	283-284

- Y -

The End

ORIGINAL INDEX

BLEDSOE COUNTY

CHANCERY COURT MINUTE BOOK
Vol. II 1836-1847

Parties Names   Pages on the Minute Docket

- S -

Skillerns execution & Miller -vs-
J. G. Smith   New Book   360
Skillern Wm. & A. - vs Smith &
Frazier   "   "   360

- A -

Ally vs Ally et al   304-329-334-345-N.B.455
Ally vs Mead   217-266-308
Ally vs Hamby   136
Allison vs Butler et al   46-60-83-99-123-133
Allen. vs Lenoir et al   47-107
Arendale vs Standifer et al   287

- B -

Brown vs Hixson et al   6-9-9
Brown vs Cornett et al   13-15-20-24-48-68-82-103-147-317
Beatty vs Seabourn et al   14-17-23
Beck vs Brown   17-26-36-47-55-61-83-101-114-
                                              142-151
Barbee vs McMurry et al   19-26-46- 64
Bean vs Mead   217-268-300-310- 330
Billingsley vs Brown   182-226-262-291
Bell vs Benson et al   183-191-232-273-290
Billingsley vs Billingsley et Ml   94
Bridgeman vs Bridgeman et al   100
Billingsley, J. M. vs Billingsley   176
Burnett vs Lasseter et al   140-144-157-189
Beatty vs Crutchfield et al   140-144-157-189
Beatty vs Martin et al   143-160-168-203
Bank vs McDonald et al   154-170-220
Benson vs Worthington   161-190-218-258-280
Broyles vs McClure et al   41-84
Brown vs McCulls   299-311-338-350-N.B.370-377-386
Barbee vs Pryor   305-313
Burk vs Groves & Kirk   306
Bank vs Lambeth   35 3-N.B.371
                                              388
Bank vs Gilleum et al   N.B.413
Bridgman admr. vs Griffin et al   N.B.462-508-514-538

Bridgman & Hicks vs Norwood et al   N.B. 470-491-501-516-545-572-588
Bank assignees of Evans vs Swafford et al   N.B.478-434
Bridgman & Hicks vs A. Loyd
et al   N.B.492
Billingsley G. H. vs Smiths
etal   N.B.492-521-545
Boyd et al Exparte   N.B.534
Bridgman J. M. vs Barnett et   N.B.535
Bridgman & Hicks vs Houzy
et al   N.B.547-557-629-661
T? Bank adr Schoolfield   N.B.566
B & Hicks vs White   N. B. 584
Bank Sparta vs Hedgeoth   N. B. 603-604-630
Planters Bank vs Bird Panky
et al   N. B. 608-636-672
Brown vs Clark   N. B. 615
Brown & Wife vs Henson   N. B. 615-638-676
Brown vs Holding   631-677
Bridgman & Agee vs Sloan   636-664-683
Brown vs Dorsey & Swafford   N.B. 640-680-681
Bridgman J.,M. vs Bridgman
B. F. et al   N. B. 679
Bridgman B. F. vs Cumberland
County   681
Burge vs Coleman   683

- C -

Cosbey vs Worthington et al   237-325
Cathey vs Beatty et al   5
Carpenter vs Standifer et al   283
Condra vs Medley   106
Cain vs Cain et al   13-19-30-33034-52-50
Clevland vs Sherley et al   36-53-59-81
Cornett vs Barker et al   12-23
Cornett vs Keyes et al   18-27
Crutchfield vs Vail   84-128
Campbell vs Kelley   89-105-126-131-152-178-210
Carpenter vs Martin   327-344- N. B. 358
Carroll J. M. vs Ally E.   N.B. 456-466-472-487
Cline vs Rogers   N.B. 476-498
Carlock vs Hornbucke   N. B. 509-513-523
Cain G. W. vs Bridgman admr.   N.B. 535
Colville vs Waterhouse   N.B. 539
Clark vs Clark   N.B. 615-632-668

- D -

Davis Admr. vs Hixson Rebeca   N.B. 491
Daville? vs Long et al   47
Dixson vs Hall   68-91-184
Dixson vs Shelton et al   199

Kreamer vs White   et   al   310
Kelley admr   Exparte   365-328-346
Kelley Admr vs Rawlings et al   330-334-343-589
Kelley Admr vs Mitchell & Salmon   N. B.   366-380-403-409
Keys G. W. vs Henson, John   n. b.   467-535-592-561-592-607
Kirklin vs Anderson   N. B.   499-520-541-557
                                                                     586-606-655-683

Kirklin vs L? R? Robertson   N. B.   537-561
Knowles vs Merriman   N.B.   608-672

- L -

Loyd vs Spring   et al   191-237-281-319
Lowe   vs Lowe A. et al   40-80
Lowe A. vs Ormes   et al   102
Lowe A. vs Sherill   et al   147-189-215-250
Lowe S. C vs Holding   et al   199
Langley vs Hale   et al   194-225-251
Love   vs Love   et al   193-217-263
Long vs Chandoin et al   182-192
Lamb vs Rawlings   et al   200-241-261-231
Lowe E. vs Lowe S. C.   249
Ladd   vs James   254-293
Loyd   vs Exparte   256-283-317-N.B. 309
Ladd vs Thompson   350- N.B.360
Loyd Francis vs Loy Albert   N.B.   480-506-509
Lea John vs Bridgman   N.B.   527-532
Lowry vs Clark   N.B.   615-638-666-682

- M -

Mead   vs Stone   et al   18-43-104-194-207
McCullie   vs Pharris et al   24
Mitchell vs Moyres   et al   38-85
Martin vs Rice   et al   64-72-84-108-129-163
Mead vs Prestley   et al   59-67-80-123
Montgomery vs Smith   95-129
Montgomery vs Crutchfield et al   105-124-144-156-313-340
Mitchell vs Mullins   et al   130-164-188
Montgomery vs Wynn   et al   174
Martin vs Gardenhire   et al   182-251-290-302
Mead vs Everett   et al   14-18-21-37-45-62-87
Mead Admrs vs Rucker   et al   313-341-344
Martin vs Easterly   et al   20-25
Montgomery vs Merriman et al   313-340 N.B. 362-397-541
Morgan & Allison vs Thurman et al   342-N.B.362
Montgomery & Frazier   vs Steel et al   N.B.   374-378-395
McReynolds vs Anderson   N.B.   441-452-460-488
Murphy et al vs Murphy et al   N.B.   475
Merriman vs Merriman et al   N.B.   496-512-537-670-674
Miller & Wife vs Beatty   N.B.   560-602-613-655-677
Murry vs Murry   N.Book   573-575-576
Merriman B. vs Mary Merriman   N.B.   589-614

BLEDSOE COUNTY

CHANCERY COURT MINUTE BOOK

VOL II 1836-1847

P-1   June Term 1836

    Be it remembered that at a Chancery Court opened and held for   the
eight district in the Eastern division of the state of Tennessee at   the
court house in the town of Pikeville in the county of Bledsoe and state
of Tennessee before the honorable Thomas L. Williams chancellar and on
the second Monday and the thirteenth day of June in the year of our Lord
one thousand eight hundred and thirty six.
    Scott Terry Esquire of the county of Bledsoe was by the court   ap-
pointed clerk and master of the chancery court of the eighth district of
Eastern division of the state of Tennessee who there upon in open court
took an oath to support the constitution of the United States and   of
Tennessee an oath of office and an oath against duelling where up on the
said Scott Terry together with John Bridgman (Chancery Court June term)
and James A. Whiteside his securties entered into and acknowledged the
following bond in open court (towit)
    Know all men by these presents that we Scott Terry , John Bridgman
and James A. Whiteside are held and firmly bound unto Newton Cannon
Gouvenop in and over the state of Tennessee and his succesors in office
in the sum of ten thousand dollars to which payment will and truly be made
and done we bind our selves and each of our executors and administrators
jointly and severally firmly by these presents signed with our names and
sealed with our seals this thirteenth day of July 1836.
    The conditions of the above obligation is such that whereas the above
bound Scott Terry (Page 2, Monday June 13th 1836) hath been appointed
P-2   clerk and master of the chancery court at Pikeville for the
chancery district composed of the counties of Rhea, Bledsoe and Marion
& Hamilton in the state of Tennessee now if said Scott Terry shall truly
and honestly keep the records of said court discharge the duties of said
office according to law then the above obligation to be void and of no
effect other wise to remain in full force and virtue given the day and
date above written signed sealed and acknowledged in open court this 13th
June 1866.

    Test: Scott Terry (Seal)
    Thomas L. Williams   J. Bridgman (Seal)
                               James A. Whiteside (Seal)

P-2   Know all men by these presents that we Scott Terry , John Bridgman
and James A. Whiteside are held and firmly bound unto Newton Cannon
Gouvenor in and over the state of Tennessee and his successors in office
in the sum of one thousand dollars the judgment of which well and truly
to be made and done we bind ourselves our heirs and executors and administrators jointly and severally firmly by these presents signed with our
names and sealed with our seals this 13th day of June 1836.

P-2   The condition of the above obligation is such taht whereas the a-
bove bound Scott Terry has been appointed clerk and master of the Chancery court at Pikeville for the chancery district composed of the counties
of Rhea- Bledsoe Marion and Hamilton , now if the said Scott Terry shall
faithfully collect and pay in the, manner required by law the fines and
forfeitures that may arise in said court then this obligation to be void
P-3   other wise to remain in full force and virtue Given the day and
date above written signed sealed and acknowledged in open court 13th June
1836

    Test:
    Thos. L. Williams   Scott Terry (Seal)
                                      J. Bridgman (Seal)
                           James A. Whiteside (Seal)

P-3

    Know all men by these presents that we Scott Terry John Bridgmand a
and James A. Whiteside are held and firmly bound unto Newton Cannon Gov-
enor in and over the state of Tennessee and his successors in office in
the sum of five hundred dollars the payment of which well and truly to be
made we bind our selves our heirs executors and administrators   jointly
and severally firmly by these presents signed with our names and sealed
with our seals this 13th day of June 1836

    The condition of the above obligation is such that whereas the above
bound Scott Terry has been appointed clerk and master of the Chancery
Court at Pikeville for the chancery District composed of the counties of
Rhea Bledsoe Marion and Hamilton Now if the said Scott Terry shall duly
collect and pay into the public treasury all such tax and causes as may
arise in said court of chancery at such time and in such manner as is
or may be prescribed by law then the above obligation to be void otherwise to remain in full force and virtue Given under our hand the day and
date above written signed sealed and acknowledged in open court 13th
June 1836

    Test:
    Thos. L. Williams   Scott Terry (Seal)
                                        J. Bridgman (Seal)
                           James A. Whiteside (Seal)
P-4

    George Read   )   On motion of the complaint by his
       vs. J. B.   )   Attorney leave is granted him to
    Benjamin Griffith et al   )   file an ammended bill in this cause
    — — — — — — — — — — — — — — —)   up on the payment of the cost   of
                                    the ammendment.
    All cases not other wise disposed of are continued until the next
term of this court.
    Court then adjourned until court in course.

                                        Thomas L. Williams
                   December Term 1836
P-4
State of Tennessee
    At a chancery court opened and held in the court house in Pikeville

P-4   in the state of Tennessee in the eight districtof the Eastern
division of said state on the 2nd Monday of December and the 12th   day
of said month 1836 by the Honorable Thos. L. Williams chancellor.

P-4
Richard Walker	)	O&P Bill
vs.	)	Cause the parties and with their con-
Daniel Graham et al	)	sent and by the assent of the court
	)	this cause is continued until the next
		term of this court.

P-5
Thomas W. Spicer	)	O & P Bill
vs	)	
Thomas Sherley	)	On the motion of the respondent by
	)	his counsel the term of six weeks is
		allowed him answer complaints bill.

P-5
George D. Foster	)	I nj. Bill
vs	)	
Theodore P. Johnson	)	Came the parties by their counsel and
	)	this cause is remanded to the rules .

P-5
Samuel Cathey	)	Be it remembered that on Monday the 12th
Edward Seaborn &	)	day of December 1836 came on the above
Joseph Seaborn	)	cause before the Honorable Thomas L.
vs	)	Williams Chancellar & C at Pikeville in
Hugh Beaty &	)	the county of Bledsoe and it appearing
John M. Beaty	)	to the satisfaction of the court, that
	)	the matters in dispute in this cause had
		heretofore been refered by the parties

to the final arbritrament and determination of John Billingsley ,   John
Bridgman and Charles Maysey who having had the matters in cnotrovercy?
before them and having returned their award into court and the same being
inspected by the court and it appearing to the satisfaction of the Court
that the said award had been complyed with except as to the payment of
the cost in the suit and the said arbitrators having awarded that Samuel
Cathey, Edward Seaburn and Hugh Beaty should each pay one third of the
cost of this suit it is therefore ordered and adjugded by the court that
P-6   the complaintahts bill be dismissed and that the said Samuel
Cathey Edward Seaburn and Hugh Beaty pay one third of the costs each in
this expended for which execution may issue.

P-6
John Brown	)	O & Inj. B.
vs	)	
William Hixon &	)	Be it remembered that on Monday the 12th
Elisha Kirklin	)	day of December 1836 and first day of the
	)	present term came on to be heard the
		foregoing cause before the Honorable

Thos. L. Williams Chancellar & C on the bill of plea and the cause being
argued and freely understood by the court.
    It is ordered adjudged and decreed by the court that the dependants

P-6   plea be allowed and that the injunction in this cause be desol-
ved and the complantants Bill be dismissed and it is futher ordered adjudged and decreed by the court the defendant recover against the complaintant John Brown and William Rogers and Thomas Coulter his securities for the persecution of this suit the sum of five hundred and eighty
six dollars 57 1/2 cents the amount of the award and the judgment of the
county court of Hamilton County together with six per cent interest from
the rendition of said to this day and also the defendant recover against
the complaintant John Brown and William Rogers and Thomas Coulter his
securities the sum of sebventy six dollars 92 cents the amount of the
arbritrators upon the suit at law originating in the Circuit court of
Bledsoe County together with six per cent interest thereon from the
making of said award to this day and it is futher ordered and adjudged
by the court that the complaintant John Brown William Rogers and Thomas
Coulter his said securities pay the cost in his behalf expended from
which execution may issue.

December Term 1836

P-7

James Hickson   )   Ing- Bill
     vs   )
Joseph G. Smith   )   Came the parties of their counsil and
_ _ _ _ _ _ _ _ _ _ _)   the respondant by his council moved the
                          court to dissolve the injuction in this
cause and after the Bill and answer being read and inspected by the court
an argument being had of council It is considered by the court that the
complaintant injunction be dissloved and it is futher ordered adjudged and
decreed by the coubt that the repondant recover against the complaintant
the sum of one hundred and thirty eifght dollars and fifty cents the same
being the amount of the judgment rendered against the complaintant in
favor of the respondant in the circuit court for the county of Bledsoe
at the november term of said court and on the fifteenth day of said month
1836 together with the futher sum of six per cent interest thereon from
the rendition of said judgment to this day together with the costs in
this behalf expended for which eviction may issue and it is futher ordered by the court that the said respondant enter into bond with such security as the clark and master of the court may deems sufficient conditioned that in the event said complaintant should prosecute his said Bill
of complaint with effect he should refund back to said complaintant the
said sum of one hundred and thirty eight dollars and fifty eight with
lawful interest and that execution shall not issue until on complyrance
with this order.

P-8

O & S Shockley   )   Came the parties of their council
     vs   )   and upon motion of respondant it ord-
James Cain et al   )   e red bynthe court that the complain-
)   tant give good and sufficient security
_ _ _ _ _ _ _ _ _ _ _)   for the prosecution of their suit on
)   or before the first day of the next
of this court or that his suit shall stand dismissed.

P-8

James Hixon	) O & Inj- Bill
vs	)
Joseph G. Smith	) On motion of the complainant leave is
	) granted him to amend his Bill filed in
	) this cause upon the payment of the cost

of said amendment.

P-8

James Nelson et al	) It appearing to the satisfaction of com-
vs	) plainants council is confined to his bed
John Kimmer et al	) and not able from indisposition to appear
	) for said complainant It is ordered by
	) the court that this cause be continued

until the next term of this court ordered by the court that the clerk and
master furnish hereafter three Dockets one for the court one for   the
bar and one for himself with the orders rules & C had in each suit   dis-
tinctly placed upon each Docket opposite tothe name of the case.
Court adjourned until to-morrow morning 9 oclock.

Thos. L. Williams

P-9

Tuesday December 13th 1836-

Court ret pursuant to adjornment.

John Brown	) Came the complainant by his council and lea-
vs	) ve is granted to him with the original
Hixon & Kirklin	) obligation filed in this cause up on a cer-
	) tificate thereof being retained in office.
	) Come the complainant by his council and prays

an appeal to the supreme court at Knoxville and it being a case in which
the chancellar is of the opinion that the matters is doubtful and   dif-
ficult and aught to be reheard in the supreme court said appeal is allowed
upon the complainants giving bond with security for the payment with the
costs in chancery and the costs in supreme court and there upon the complainant together with Samuel Igow and James Smith his securities entered into bond for the prosecution of said appeal.
Court then adjourned until Court in course.

Thos. L' Williams

December Term 1836

Be it remembered that at a chancery court opened and held for the
eighth chancery district at the court house in the town of Pikeville on
the second monday and twelvth day of June in the year of our Lord   one
thousand eight hundred and thirty seven - Present on the bench the
Honorable Thomas L. Williams Esquire chancellor & C.

Scott Terry Esquire tendered to the court his resignation as   clerk
and master of the chancery court which was excepted by said court- There
up on the court proceeded to the appointment of a clerk and master after

P-9   examination had it is considered by the court that Thomas N.
Frazier be appointed clerk and master of said court who there up on en-
tered into bond and security in the words and figgers following towit.
P-10

Know all men by these presents that we Thomas N. Frazier   Samuel
Frazier , Samuel L. Story and John Bridgman are held and firmly bound
unto Newton Cannon Governor in and over the state of Tennessee and   his
successens in office in the sum of ten thousand dollars to which payment
well and truly be made selves and each of our heirs executors and administrators jointly and severally firmly by these presents signed with our
names and sealed with our seals this 12th day of June 1837- The condition
of the above obligation is such that t where as the above bound Thomas
N. Frazier hath been appointed clerk and master of the Chancery Court at
Pikeville for the chancery District composed of the counties of   Rhea,
Bledsoe, Marion and Hamilton in the state of Tennessee. Now if the said
Thos. N. Frazier shall truly and honestly keep the records of said court
and discharge the duties of said office according to law then the above
bond to be void and of no effect otherwise to remain in full force and
virtue Given the day and date above written.

signed sealed and acknowledged in open court 12th June 1837.

Test: Thos. N. Frazier (Seal)
Thomas L. Williams   Samuel Frazier (Seal)
Chancellor   Samuel L. Story (Seal)
                                               J. Bridgman (Seal)

P-10

December Term 1836

Know all men by these presents that we, Thomas N. Frazier, Samuel
Frazier, Samuel L. Story and John Bridgman are held and firmly bound unto
Newton Cannon Governor in and over the state of Tennessee and his sucessors in office in the sum of one housand Dollars the payment of   which
well and truly be made and done we bind ourselves our heirs executors and
administrators jointly and severally firmly by these presents signed with
our names and sealed with our seals this 12th day if June 1837.

The condition of the above obligation is such that whereas the above
bound Thomas N. Frazier has been appointed clerk and master of the chancery court at Pikeville for the chancery district composed of the counties
of Rhea, Bledsoe, Marion and Hamilton-
P-11

Monday June 12th 1837-

Now if the said Thomas N. Frazier shall faithfully collect and pay
in the manner required by law the fines and forfeitures that may arise
in said court then the above obligation to be void otherwise to remain in
full force and virtue.

Given the day and date above written- Signed sealed and acknowledged
in open court the 12th June 1837.

                                        Thomas N. Frazier (Seal)

Test: (Continued)

P-11   Samuel Frazier (Seal)
    Thomas L. Williams   Samuel L. Story (Seal)
                                                 J. Bridgman (Seal)

    Know all men by these presents That we Thomas N. Frazier, Samuel
Frazier, Samuel L. Story and John Bridgman are held and firmly bound unto Newton Cannon Governor in and over the state of Tennessee and his
sucessors in office in the sum of five hundred dollars the payment of
which well and truly be made we bind ourselves our and each of   our
heirs executors and administrators jointly and severally firmly by these
presents signed with our names and sealed with our seals the 12th day of
June 1837.

P-11

    The conditions of the above obligation is such that whereas the a-
bove bound Thomas N. Frazier has been appointed clerk and master of the
chancery court at Pikeville for the Chancery District composed of the
Counties of Rhea, Bledsoe , Marion and Hamilton . Now if the said Thomas
N. Frazier shall duly collect and pay into the public treasury all such
tax or causes may arise in said court of chancery at such times and in
such manner as is or may be prescribed by law then the above obligation
to be void otherwise to reamin in full force and virtue- Given the day
and date above written- signed seale d and acknowledged in open court
12th June 1837.

    Test
    Thomas L. Williams   Thos. N. Frazier (Seal)
    Chancellar   Samuel Frazier (Seal)
                                                Samuel L. Story (Seal)
                                                 J. Bridgman (Seal)

P-11   June term 1837

    Know all men by these presents that we Thos. N. Frazier, Samuel
Frazier, Samuel L. Story and John Bridgman are held and firmly bound unto
Newton Cannon Governor in and over the state of Tennessee and his   successors in office in the sum of five hundred dollars the payment of which
well and truly be made we bind ourselves our and each of our heirs executors and administrators jointly and severally firmly by the presents signed
with our names and sealed with our seals this 12th day of June 1837 .

    Test:
    Thomas L. Williams
    Chancellar   Thos. N. Frazier (Seal)
                                                S'amuel Frazier (Seal)
                                                Samuel L. Story (Seal)
                                                 J. Bridgman (Seal)

P-12
    Where upon Thomas N. Frazier appeared in open court and was duly
qualified according to law as clerk and master of said court and   also
took the oath against duelling.

P-12   June term 1837

    James H. Jinkins   )   On motion of the complainants by his
            vs   )   counsel he is allowed to with draw the
    Mitchell & Kelly   )   original motrgage mentioned in the plea-
)   dings in this cause for the purpose of
                                     proving its execution by the mortgagers
the clerk and master taking a certified copy of the same filing it among
the papers in this case.

P-12

    John Carnett   )   Came   the parties by their attorney and
            vs   )   the motion heretofore made to dissolve
    Charles & Joel Barker)))   the injuction in this cause being consid-
            &   )   ered and fully understood by the court
    James Russell   )   it is ordered and adjudged by the court
)   that the defendant James Russell on ser-
                                     vice of a copy of this decree deposit the
funds mentioned in complainants bill with the clerk and master of this
court and that the injunction in this cause be dissolved and it is futher
ordered and adjudged by the court that the clerk and master pay over the
funds to the defendants Charles & Joel Barker or either of them   upon
the said Charles & Joel Barker entering into bond and security to refund
the same on the final hearing of this cause if the decree there should be
against them .

P-12

    Thomas W. Spicer   )   For sufficient reasons appearing to the
            vs   )   court from the affidavit of the defend-
    Thomas Sherley   )   ent this cause is remanded to the rules
)   for futher evidence .

P-13

    Richard Walker   )   Came to the parties by their attorney and
            vs   )   it appearing to the satisfaction of the
    Daniel Graham et al   )   court from the inspection of the record
)   in this cause that two terms had elasped
)   with out the complainants taking any steps
in this cause - It is there fore ordered and adjudged by the court that
the complainants bill be dismissed and that this complainant pay   the
costs in this behalf expended for which execution may issue.

P-13

    George Brown   )   It appearing to the satisfaction of the
            vs   )   court from the report of the clerk and
    Mary Carnett et al   )   master that this cause was transfered to
)   this court at last term it is ordered
                                     by the court that this cause be retained
upon the Docket.

    P-13Owin & Samuel Shookley)   Ordered by the court that this cause
            vs   )   be dismissed unless complainants give
    James Kain et al   )   security for the prosecution of this

P-13   suit on or before the 1st day of the next term.

P-14

Richard Waterhouse et al)	Came the defendant by his attorney
vs)	and a motion is allowed him to dis-
James Swan)	miss this suit for want of prosecut-
)	ion and said rule is continued on
	affidavit of complainant and a

certiorari awarded returnable to next term for more perfect transcript of
this cause.

P-14

Samuel B. Mead)	It is ordered by the court that unless
vs)	the article of compromise is produced
Everett & Alley)	by one of the parties at the next term
)	of court as the suit its self futher
	prosecuted at the next term that this

cause shall be dismissed.

P-14

John M. & Hugh Beaty)	Motion to dissolve came the parties by
vs))	their attorneys and the said motion
Blackwell and Seaburn)	being considered by the court it is
)	ordered by the court that the defendant
	be allowed to prosecute their suit at

law to judgment only.

P-14

James Nelson et al)	For reasons appearing to the satisfac-
vs)	tion of the court from the affidaivt
John Kimmer)	of the complainant this case is con-
)	tinued and remanded to the rules for
	futher evidence.

P-14

John L. Yarnell)	Motion to dissolve the defendant
vs)	having filed his answer It is ordered
Richard Waterhouse)	by the court that this the injunction
)	in this case be dissolved.

P-15

George Brown)	Came Samuel Cathey into open court
vs)	and acknowledges himself security to
Mary Carnett et al)	the plaintiff for the prosecution
)	of this suit and that if the comple-
	inant shall fail to pay condemnation

of the court that he the said Samuel Cathey will do it for him.

P-15

William Hall)	Be it remembered that on Monday
vs)	the 12th day of June 1837 and the
William Lowery et al)	first day of the present term came
)	on to be heard the foregoing case

P-16   before the Honorable Thomas L. Williams Chancellar & C on   the
bill taken for confessed and exhibits and it appearing to the satisfaction
of the court that the legal title to a certain tract of land lying   in
Bledsoe county Tennessee Lot No. 4 containing three hundred and fifteen
acres bounded and described as follows, towit beginning at two black caks
on the south east side of a high ridge in the line of a forty nine and a
half acre tract laid off for Josiah R. Allen thence south fifty east with
said line one hundred and eighty poles to a black oak and post oak corner
to said tract in a line of Philip Siglers former tract then north forty
east with said line sixty seven poles to two hickory saplings in a barrow
hollow corner to said Siglers said tract then north seventy five East
with another line of said Siglers 46 poles to a post oak thence north 15
west one hundred poles to two small post oaks then north forty East Forty
poles to two maples then north 40 west up Rock creek two hundred and ten
poles to a stake in the northwestern boundry line of said lot then south
40 west with said lot line two hundred poles to a stake then south 50 East
eighty four poles to the beginning was at the time of fileing the original
bill in this case the defendants but the equitable right and title was and
is in the complainants It is therefore ordered adjudged and decreed that
the legal title to the land and premises before described That be diverted
P-16   out of the defendants and vested in the complainants William Hall
his heirs and assign forever and that the complainants pay the cost   of
this suit for which execution may issue.

    And then the court adjourned until court in course.

                                            Thos. L. Williams

P-16
                    December term Monday 11th 1837

    Be it remembered that at a chancery court opened and held for the
eighth district (Chancery) in the Eastern Division of Tennessee at the
court house in the town of Pikeville on the second monday and 11th day of
December in the year of our Lord one thousand eight hundred and thirty
seven Present on the bench the Honorable Thomas L. Williams Chancellar &
C.

P-16
    Thomas W. Spicer   )   This day came the parties by their coun-
         vs   )   sel and for reasons appearing to be sat-
    Thomas Sherley   )   isfaction of the court from the affidavit
)   of the respondant this case is remanded
    _____)   to the rules and the futher time of four
months be allowed the parties to take testimony.

P-16
    Thomas M. Spicer   )
         vs   )   O Bill
    Sherley & Butler   )
)   Be it remembered that on this 11th day
    _____)   of December 1837 this case came on to
                                   be heard and determined on the bill
and answers and the proofs taken in the case and after argument   of
councel and mature deliberation of the court it is ordered and decreed

that an account in this case be take n that Samuel L. Story be appointed
a joint commissioner with the clerk and master to take said account and
report same to the next term of court that in taking said account commissioner call the parties complainant and respondant before them and examine
them on oath. Be it futher ordered and decreed that the said commissioner
is stating said account shall ascert ain and state the amount of the
Capital stock paid in by each party of sales made the net profits of the
partnership dealing how much came to the hands of each party and be it
futher ordered and decreed that the said parties exhibit and produce before said commissioners all books papers notes accounts and vouchers
touching and relating to their said partnership dealings within the knowledge and under the controll of such party.

P-17

Aaron Schoolfield	)	I" Bill
vs	)	
Asa Crandle	)	This day came the complainant by his
	)	counsel and described his bill in this

case to be dismissed That the respon-
dent go hence with out day and recover of the complainant his costs by
him about his defense in this behalf expended for which execution may
issue.

P-17

Richard Waterhouse	)	Executors of Richard	)	
Blackstone Waterhouse	)	G. Waterhouse Deceased	)	Original Bill
vs			)	
James Swan			)	

This day came the complainants by their council and directed his
bill in this cause to be dismissed.
It is therefore ordered adjudged and decreed by the court that said
bill be dismissed that the defendants go hence thereof woth out day and
recover of the plaintiffs on costs in this behalf expended for which
execution may issue.

P-17

Owen & Samuel Stockley	)	This day came the respondant by
vs	)	their counsel and it appearing to
James Cain and others	)	the satisfaction of the court for
	)	the prosecution of this suit in
		pursuance of an order made at the

last term of this court. It is ordered adjudged and decreed by the court
that the complainants bill be dismissed that the respondants go hence and
recover of the complainants all costs in this behalf expended for an
execution may issue.

P-17

John M. & Hugh Beaty	)	This day came the parties by their
vs	)	counsel and by consent and with the
Edward Seaburn et al	)	assent of the court this case is
	)	remanded to the rules.

P-18   December term 1837

David Beck)	This day came the parties by their counsel
vs)	and by mutual consent and with the assent
William Brown)	of the court this case is remanded to the
)	rules.

P-18

Archibald White)	O Bill
vs)	Decree
John Holloway)	
&)	This the 12th day of December 1837 came
Thompson Gardenhire)	on the above case before the Honorable
)	Thomas L. Williams Chancellar to be
	heard and determined upon the bill

answers application and proofs when the court was pleased to order and did
direct that the clerk and master ascertain and report what property
respondants or either of them obtained from complainant the value thereof
How much either of them procured title there to It is futher ordered that
the clerk report have at the term of next court and the equity of the case
is reversed until the final hearing.

P-18

John Carnett)	Decree
vs)	
Isaac Keys &)	Be it remembered that on this 12th
Elizabeth Keys his wife)	day of December 1837 came on this
&)	case to be heard before the Honorable
Samuel B. Heard)	Thomas L. Williams Chancellor upon
)	the bill taken for confessed as to
	Keys and wife the answer of defend-

ant Mead and replication there to when the court was pleased to order and
did order and decree that the clerk and master report whether defendants
Keys and wife are able to make complainants a good and sufficient title
for the land named in the bill and it is futher ordered that he also report what sums have been paid by complainant for said land and that he
report hereof at the next term of court.

P-18

Samuel B. Mead)	Came this complainant by his council
vs)	and on his motion it is ordered by
Commissioner of Jasper)	the court that the order of publica-
)	tion heretofore made in this case be
	revived.

Samuel B. Mead)	
vs)	This day came the respondant
John C. Evoutt Erasmus Alley)	by their council and it ap-
Samuel L. Chum)	pearing to the satisfaction
&)	of the court that the articles
Wm. N. Gillespie)	of compromise have not been
)	produced by either of the

P-18   parties in this case and that this case has not futher been prosecuted in pursuance of an order made at the last term of court -

It is therefore ordered adjudge d and decreed by the court that the complainants bill (P-19) be dismissed that the respondants go hence without day and recover of the complainant all cost in this be half expended for which an execution may issue.

P-19

Terry Kiddle	)
vs	)
Anslem L. Dearing	)
	)

This day came the respondant by his counsel an on motion of the respondant by his counsel and it appearing to the satisfaction of the court from an inspection of the record in this case that two terms has elapsed with out the complainant having taken any steps in this case It is there fore ordered and adjudged and decreed that the complainant bill be dismissed and that the complainant pay all costs in this behalf expended for which an execution may issue.

P-19

John Cain	)
vs	)
James Cain et al	)
	)

Came the parties by their and it appearing to the satisfaction of the court that five months has not elapsed since the filing of the complainants replication in this case - It is ordered by the court that the same be remanded to the rules.

P-19

Barbees Heirs	)
vs	)
William McMurry et al	)
	)

Came the respond and by this counsel and moved the court to dismiss the complainants bill for want of prosecution and it appearing to the satisfaction of the court from an inspection of the record that this case was transfered from the circuit of Marion county to this court and filed at the present term it is ordered that the motinn be over ruled.

P-19

Thomas Sherley	)
vs	)
Henry J. Williams et al	)
	)

This day came the parties of t their counsel and for the reason appearing to the satisfaction of the court from affidavit of T. Nixon Vandyke Esq. a rule is granted the complainant to case William W. Williams one of the respondants in this case and Benj. R. Montgomery Esq. to produce the exhibits marked A & C in the complainant bill in this case or show case why the same are not produced and for subsequent reasons appearing to the satisfaction of the court from the affidavits of the said William and Montgomery It is ordered by the court that said rule be discharged and by consent this case is remanded to the rules.

P-20

George Brown	)
vs	)
(Continued)	

This day came the parties and the oath? of Mary Carnett one of the respondants in

P-20 Mary Carnett   )
 John Carnett Jr.   )
 John Carnett Sr.   )
 James Russell   )
)

THIS CASE IS SUGGESTED BY solicitors
for the defendants.
  Court then adjourned until tomorrow
at 8 oclock A.M.

             Thos. L. Williams

      Tuedsay Bec. 12 1837.

P-20
  Court met persuant to adjournment present on the bench the Honorable Thos. L. Williams Esq. Chancellor & C.

Joseph Marten   )
  vs   )
Easterly & Smith   )
)

In this case it is ordered by the court
that unless the articles of compromise
be produced or the suit itsself futher
prosecuted at the next term of this court
this case to stand dismissed.

P-20
 Nelson & Wife   )
  vs   )
 John Kimmer   )
)

Be it remembered that on the 12th day of
December 1837 came on the foregoing case
to be heard and determined before the
Honorable Thos. L. Williams Chancellor & C
an th4 bill answer replication and proof
and after argument of counsel and mature deliberation of the court it is
ordered by the court that the injunction in this case be dissolved and
that the complainants bill be dismissed and it is futher ordered   adjudged and decreed by the court that the opmplainants pay the costs of
this suit for which execution may issue.
  The following rule is ordered by the court and ordered to be entered upon thencourt to wit.
  In all cases where suits pending in this court are compromised and
terms of compromise are not satisfactory made known to the court at the
term of which the compromise is made The suit compromised shall be dismissed at the term succeeding such compromise at the costs of the complainants.

P-21
 Samuel B. Meade   )
  vs   )
 Everett & Alley   )
)

Came the parties by their counsel and
the order in this case entered on
yesterday to strike this case from
the docket is set aside and the said
case is reinstated on the docket and
it is futher ordered by the court that if the terms of compromise in this
case are not produced at the next term of this court that the said ,case
shall stand dismissed at the cost of complainant.

P-21
 Nelson & Wife   )
  vs   )
 Kemmer   )
)

In this case the complainants prays an
appeal to the next supreme court to be
held at the court in the term of Knoxville and it is allowed him upon   his

P-21 giving security or taking the --------? oath before the clerk & master as required by law within one month from this date-

Court adjourned until court in course.

Thomas L. Williams

Monday September term 1838

P-21 Be it remembered that at a chancery court opened and held for the eighth chancery district in the eastern division of Tennessee at the court house in the town of Pikeville on the second monday and 10th day of September in the year of our Lord one thousand eight hundred and thirty eight present on the bench the Honorable Thos. L. Williams Chancellor & C.

P-22

James & Jenkins	)	Came the parties of this counsel and
vs	)	from sufficient reasons appearing to
William C. Mitchell	)	the satisfaction of this court this
&	)	case is continued until the next term
Alexander Kelly	)	and remanded to the rules.

P-22

Archibald White	)	Came the parties of their counsel and
vs	)	by consent and with the assent of the
Thompson Gardenhire	)	court this case is continued u til the
&	)	next term.
John Holloway	)	

P-22

Thomas W. Spicer	)	Be it remembered that on Monday the
vs	)	first day of the September term 1838
Thomas Sherley	)	of the Chancery court at Pikeville the
&	)	above case came on to.be heard before
Pleasant H. Butler	))	the honorable Thos. L Williams & C
	)	upon the exception taken to the report
		of the clerk and master in this case

and by the consent of the parties and with the assent of the court that said account be retaken before the clerk and master and John Bridgman Esq and that said clerk and said commissioner in taking said account operation and report the amount capital furnished by each party the amount of profits of said firm and the amount which each party is entitled of the profits pro- rata and that the parties respectfully produce all the books vouchers and invoices of said firm to the commissioner aforesaid and that said commissioner make report hereof at the next term.

P-23

John M.,Beaty	)	Be it remembered that at a chancery court
&	)	opened and held for the eighth district at
Hugh Beaty	)	the court house in the town of Pikeville in
vs		the county of Bledsoe and state of Tennessee

P-23 Julius W. Blackwell)
      &   )
Edward Seaburn)
)

on the second Monday of September 1838 and the 10th day of said month before the Honorable Thomas L. Williams Chancellar & C came on the above case to be heard abd determined upon answers and depositions taken in the case and after argument of counsel and mature deliberation of the court it is adjudged and decreed by the court that the judgment recovered at law by defendant Julius W. Blackwell who said in the name of Edward Seaburn for use of said Julius W. Blackwell in the circuit court of Bledsoe County in the state of Tennessee at the July term 1837 of said circuit court founded upon a writing obligatory executed by complainants to defendants Seaburn for the sum of two hundred and fourteen dollars and bearing date 5th day of September 1836 and due twelve months after date and bearing interest from th e date be perpetually enjoined that the clerk of said Circuit court issue no execution upon said judgment and it is futher ordered by the court that the defendant Edward Seabourn pay all costs in this behalf expended both in law and equity , for which an execution may issue.

P-23

September Term 1838

John Carnett)
   vs   )
Charles Barker)
Joel Barker)
James Russell)
)

Be it remembered that this case came on to be heard and determined before the honorable Thomas L. Williams Chancellor upon the bills answer and deposition on Monday the firsd day of the September term 1838 of the chancery court at Pikeville and after argument and mature deliberation of the court.

P-24 It is ordered and decreed by the court that the complainants bill be dismissed that the defendant Russell pay to the defendant Barker the amount of money collected by him for said Barker on the judgment at Law with legal interest thereon until,paid within one month from this time failing in which an execution may issue against said Russell there for and it is further ordered that the complainant Cornett pay all costs in this behalf expended for which execution may issue.

P-24

George Brown)
   vs   )
Mary Cornett & John Cornett Jr.)
     &   )
John Cornett et al)
)

This day came the parties by their solicitors and for reasons appearing to the satisfaction of the court from the affidavit of John Cornett r. one of the defendants in this case and upon failure therein it is ordered that the clerk take said bill pro confesso and set the same for hearing as to the said John Carnett Sr. Ex parti and it is further ordered by the court that the said John Carnett pay all the costs in this behalf expended up to and including the fileing of his answer for which an execution may issue.

P-24

Thomas McCallie)   This day came the complainant by his solicitor

P-24 vs   ) and directed his bill in this case to be
 Peter L. Harris &   ) dismissed it is there upon ordered to be
 Jesse Brown   ) adjudged and decreed by the court that
) the said bill be dismissed that the de-
 — — — — — — — — — —) fendant go hence there of with out day

and recover of the complaint all costs in this behalf expended for which
an execution may issue.

P-24

 Richard Waterhouse & Blackstone Waterhouse) This day came the
 Executors of Richard G. Waterhouse   ) complainant by his
      vs   ) solicitor and di-
 James Swan   ) rected his bill in
) this case to be
 — — — — — — — — — — — — — — — — — — —) dismissed It is

therefore ordered adjudged and decreed by the court that the said bill be
dismissed that the defendant go hence there of without day and recover of
P-25 complainant all costs in this behalf expended for which an execution may issue.

P-25

 Joseph Martin   ) This day came the parties by their soli-
   vs   ) citors and produced a written agreement
 Latin R. Smith   ) to dismiss this case in the words and
   &   ) figures following (to wit) Know all men
 Isaac Easterly   ) by these presents that we Claibourn Gant
              the legal assingee of Joseph Martin and
 — — — — — — — — — Latin R. Smith do mutually hereby agree to

dismiss a certain suit between Joseph Martin complainant and Latin R.
Smith respondant in the chancery court at Pikeville and we do futher agree
that we will each pay half the costs expended in said case. Given under
our hands and seals this the 25th day of March 1838.

                   Latin R. Smith (Seal)
                   Claiburn Gant (Seal)
P-25

  Where upon it is ordered adjudged and decreed by the court that said
suit be dismissed that the said Claiburn Gant and Latin R. Smith pay each
one half of the costs in this behalf expended for which execution may issue.

P-25

 George D. Foster   ) Be it remembered that on this day came
   vs   ) on the above case to be heard and de-
 Theodore P. Johnson) termined before the honorable Thomas
) L. Williams & C upon the bill answer
 — — — — — — — — — — replication and proff and upon agree-

ment of council and mature deliberation of the court It is ordered adjudged and decreed by the court that the complainants bill be dismissed
that the defendant go hence thereof with out day and recover of complainant all costs in this behalf expended for which execution may
issue.

P-25 Owin & Samuel Stookley) On motion against James Cain by
vs) his solicitors leave is given him
James Cain & Others) to withdraw his original deeds which
) were filed as exhibits in this case.

P-26
David Beck) This day came the parties by their solicitors
vs) and from reasons appearing to the satis-
William Brown) faction of the court from the affidavit of
) the respondent This case is continued and
remanded to the rules .

P-26
John L. Yarnel) This day came the respondent by his
vs) counsel and on his motion to dismiss
Richard Waterhouse) said case for want of prosecution and
and) it appearing to the satisfaction of
Stephen Kelly) the court from an inspection of the
) record that two terms had elapsed,
with out any steps having been taken
in this cause- It is ordered adjudged and decreed by the court that the
complainants bill be dismissed and that the respondent go hence woth out
day and recover of the complainant all cost in this behalf expended for
which an execution may issue.

P-26
Jefferson Barbe et al) Came the parties of their solicitors
vs) and the complainant by his counsel
William McMurry et al) leave of the court being first had
) and obtained withdrew his exceptions
to the respondants McMurry's ans-
wer and was allowed to file a replication thereto.

P-26
Thomas W. Spicer) Be it remembered that this case came on
vs) to be heard upon bill answer replication
Thomas Sherley) and proofs in this case on the 10th day
) of September 1838 before the honorable
Thomas L. Williams Chancellor when the
court was not satisfied as to the extent of the partnership between complainants and defendant where upon the court doth order that an issue be
made up and tried on Monday of next chancery court to ascertain the extent of the said partnership mentioned in complainants bill and denied by
defendant.

P-27
John Carnett) This the 10th day of September 1838, came
vs) on this cause before the Honorable Thomas
Isaac Keys &) L. Williams Chancellor to be finally heard
Samuel,B. Mead) and determined upon the pleading interloc-
) tury decree and the report of the clerk
and master said report not being excepted
to is in all things confined it does not appear said Isaac Keys and his
wife Elizabeth Keys have any title to the tract of land named in the bill

P-27   and which was sold by them to the complainant so that they can make title thereto it appears from said report that the complainant has paid about said land the sum of one hundred and forty two dollars it is therefore ordered and decreed that the Isaac Keys refund to complainant the sum of one hundred and forty two dollars with interest there on from August 1828 being the amount paid by said Carnett for said land It is futher ordered that Samuel Mead pay the costs in this case in this court and also the costs of the suit at law and that execution therefore as at law.

P-27

William N. Gillespie)	This the 10th day of September 1838
Sidney Ann Gillespie)	came on this case to be heard before
vs)	the honorable Thomas L. Williams Chan-
John Locke)	cellor upon the bill answers replica-
Peletiah Chitton)	tion & C when the court was pleased to
and Others)	order and did order and decree that the
)	clerk and master state an account in this
	case and show the account of the estate

of William L. Lenty? deceased that has come to the hands of John Locke and Ideleah Chitton (Page 28)   as his executors and when how much they have received for interest and what demand and when and to whom and   how they have disbursed said monies and when and to whom and on what account also how much said executor have received for rent or how much received by any other person and when and by whom on the real estate of said Lenty and on the real estate purchased by them as executors under the will of said Lenty when received and what desposition they have made of it also that said clerk show when any portion of said real estate was assigned to complainant the amount of rent upon such real estate for the year in which it was assigned and by whom and by whom the same was received That   he also state and show the amount of personall property belonging to the estate of said William L. Lenty deceased at the time of his death and what disposition has been ,made of the same - That he also state and show the amount of bad debts due said estate specifying cash and also the amount of debt if any such that might have been collected- It is furthered ordered that this account be taken in the town of Washington in Rhea County all matters of equity reserved till the final hearing - The clerk make report to the next term .

P-28

William Vernon)	Be it remembered that at a chan-
Administrator of)	cery court opened and held at the
Anderson Vernon Deceased)	court house in the town of Pike-
vs))	ville on the 10th day of Sept-
Alphard Hutcheson et al)	ember 1838 it appearing to the
)	court that William Vernon ad-

ministrator of Anderson Vernon deceased on his own behalf as well as the widow heirs legals and distributes of the estate of Anderson Vernon deceased against Alford Hutcheson and the other creditors of said estate had filed his bill under the provisions of the act of the general   assembly of the state of Tennessee passed the 26th day of January 1838 chapter 61 in which he sets forth that the assets of said estate in the hands of said administrator are insufficient to pay the debts owing by   said estate . That there is no real estate that the personal estate of said

P-28 deceased exceeds the value of five hundred dollars therefore on motion of the complainant by the counsel it is ordered by the court that publication be made three successive weeks in the Knoxville Register a nwe paprt printed in the town of Knoxville Tennessee and (Page 29) successive weeks in the Athens Currier a news paper published in the town of Athens Tennessee requiring all persons interested or having claims against said estate to come forward and exhibit the same and have themselves made parties to said bill on or before the nest term of this court that distribution of said estate may be made pro rata.

P-29

James White	)	This day came the parties by their counsel and
vs	)	from sufficient reasons offering to the satis-
John Cornet	)	faction of the court from the affidavit of M. W
	)	Legg it is ordered by the court that an attach-

ment ni si issue against the defendant John Cornet Returnable to the next term of court.

And then the court adjourned until tomorrow at 5 oclock.

Thos. L. Williams

P-29

Tuesday Sept. 11 1838

Court met pursuant to adjournment present the same Chancellor as on yesterday.

| William Vernon Administrator of Anderson Vernon Deceased vs Matthew Simmons & Others |))))) | On application of the respondant Matthew Simmons two months time given him to file his answer in this case. |

P-29

| David Rankin vs John Brown & Others |)))) | In this case defendant are allowed ten m months to file their issues & C. Count adjourned until court in course. |

Thos. L Williams

P-30

March Term 1839

Be it remembered that at a chancery court opened and held for the eighth chancery district in the Eastern division of Tennessee at the court house in the town of Pikeville on the second monday and 11th day of March in the year of our lord one thousand eight hundred and thirty nine present on the beanch the honorable Thos. L. Williams.

P-30

| Benj. Thurman vs |))) | This day came Eliza Kirkpatrick by his solicitor and on application time given him until the first monday in April to file his answer |

P-30

William McDaniel &   )   in this case.
Eliza Kirkpatrick   )
)
_____)

P-30

Thomas W. Spicer   )   This day came the parties by their solici-
        vs   )   tors and there upon came a jury of   good
Thomas Sherley   )   and lawful men towit John Acuff, Jesse
)   Walker, James Huston, James H. Roberson,
_____)   Wm. Thomas, William S. Dalton, William Green
John Bridgman Wm. B. Whiteside, James V. Skillern William Hall and Andrew
I. McCulley who being elected and sworn will and truly to try the issue
of pact made up at the last term of this court in this case and ascertain
the extent of the partnership mentioned in the complainants bill and de-
nied by the defendant upon their oaths say that they find the firm of
Sherley and Spicer commenced in Jasper 1827 and thay they continued until
March 1834 and that they traded in negroes, horses, cattle bacon corn
passessory , claims , goods, ware and merchandise.

P-30

John Cain   )   This day came James P. Thompson Esq. and
        vs   )   produced in open court a transcript of
James Cain & Others   )   the record of Warren County Court   ap-
)   pointing   Bursheba P. Cain special ad-
_____),   ministratrix of John Cain deceased to prosecute the suit and on his motion it is ordered by the court that said
suit be received in the name of the said Bersheba P. Cain as special   ad-
minis trix of the said John Cain deceased and that the cause be set   for
hearing.
        It is ordered by the court that Samuel Lyles be fined the sum of one
dollar for a contempt.

P-31

William N. Gillespie   )   Came the   complainants   by
        and   )   their solicitor and from suf-
Sidney Ann Gillespie   )   ficient reasons disclosed in
        vs   )   the affidavit of Wm. Gillespie
John Locke   )   one of the complainants   the
Palitiah Chitton and others   )   report heretofore made by the
)   clerk and master in this
_____)   cause is set aside and on ac-
count is ordered to be taken by said clerk and master according to the
Doembal? order made in this case at the last term of court and that   said
account be taken at the office of the clerk and master.

P-31

James H. Jenkins   )   Be it remembered that on monday the 11th
        vs   )   day of March 1839 came on the above
Alexander Kelly   )   cause to be heard and determined before
        &   )   the honorable Thomas L. Williams Chance-
William Cattitchell   )   lor upon the bill answer of defendant Kelly
)   order pro confesso as to defendant
_____)   Mitchell replication and proof and after
argument of counsel it appears to the satisfaction of the court   that

P-31   defendant Mitchell executed to the complainant a mortgage inden-
tuer on the 14th day of April 1830 to secure the complainant in the sum
of four hundred dollars and that the defendant Kelly had purchased of his
codefendant Mitchell the tract of land in the pleadings mentioned   with
full notice of the lein of complainant on said land but because it does not
appear to the court here; what amount is due the complainant on the said
mortgage indenture - It is ordered by the court that the clerk and master
take and state on account of the amount due the complainant by the   defendant and that he report thereof n tomorrow morning all other matters
and things are reserved until the coming of the report.

     And the court there adjourned until tomorrow morning 1/2 after   8
oclock.

                                                  Thos L. Williams
P-32
                         March 12 1839

     Court met persuant to adjournment present on the bench the Honorable
Thomas L. Williams Chancellor.

P-32
     James H. Jenkins   )   Be it remembered that on this 12th day
           vs   )   of March 1839 this case came on to be
     William C. Mitchell   )   heard and was heard before the Honor-
           &   )   able Thomas L. Williams Chancellor up-
     Alex Kelly   )   on report of the clerk and master to
)   whom it was refered to take and state
     _ _ _ _ _ _ _ _ _ _ _ _ _)   an account of the amount due the com-
plainant by the defendant Mitchell on the mortgage indenture in the
pleadings mentioned and to report during the present term of the court w
 hich report being unexpected to is in all things the words and figures
following to wit The clerk and master to whom it was referred by a de-
crulal order of the court made on the 11th of March 1839 to take and
state an account of the money due the complainant Jenkens on the mortgage
executed to complainant by the defendant Mitchell respectfully reports
that it appears from the note and mortgage executed on the 14th of April
1830 by the defendant to the complainant that the defendant Mitchall was
indebted to the complainant to the sum of $ 400.00 principle debt bearing
interestm from the date which has accrued to the sum of $ 213.50 up to
this date making in all $ 613.50 all & C.
     Thereupon the court thinks fit to order adjudge and decree and it is
accordingly ordered adjudged and decreed by the court that the clerk and
master of this court proceed to sell the land in the pleadings mentioned
after giving forty days notice in the Hamilton Gazette a paper published
as Ross landing of the time and place of sale the land to be sold at the
court house in the town of Jasper Tenn for cash unless defendant   shall
pay unto the office of the clerk and master the debt and interest aforesaid of $ 613.50 within five months It is further ordered adjudged and
decreed that the deed of conveyance executed by Mitchell to his   co-
defendant Kelly in the pleadings be cancelled and declared void as against
the complainant it is further ordered that the costs of this suit be paid
out of the proceeds of the sale of the land and if not so paid that the
defendant pay the same and that execution issue for the same as at   law

P-32   all other matters reserved until the coming in of the report of the clerk and master.

It is ordered by the court that Craven Sherrill be fined the sum of one dollar for a contempt for failing his presence order in court.

P-33

Thomas W. Spicer)	Be it remembered that on this 12th day

Thomas W. Spicer)
        vs   )
Thomas Sherley   )
        &   )
Pleasant H. Butler)
_____)

Be it remembered that on this 12th day of March 1839 this case came on to be heard upon exceptions field to the report made in this case by the clerk and master and John Bridgman as special c commissioner where it appeared to the court that said report is defective for uncertainty for want of specification and reference to proof upon which the same is founded and for other cases appearent on the face of same. It is thereofre the opinion of the court that said exception are well taken and that the said report be set aside and the whole matter of said account be again referred to the clerk and master and to the said John Bridgman as special commissioner with directions to retake the whole of said account and that in taking the same the said commissioner call the parties before them with power to examine both complainant and defendant upon interrogations and hear all such other testimony of witness as the said parties may produce before them and shall also have power to require the parties to produce all the books paper accounts notes receipts and other paper vouchers which may be necessary in taking Said account it is further ordered that in taking said account the said commissioner in stating the same shall ascertain and report the amount of capital stock paid in by each party the amount of purchase and sedes made the net profits and loss of said partnership dealings how much came to the hands of each party and from whom received and how applied and also take said account that said partnership and so that no two or more of said parties shall have credit separately for the same sum or sums of money and in producing the book papers and accounts said parties shall as required produce all such books and papers as may be within possession of each respectfully It is further ordered and decreed that in taking said account the proof and testimony upon which each item is allowed or disallowed and founded shall be specifically referred to and the same filed with the account taken and the same may be reported all matters not now decreed are reserved.

P-33

B.P.Cain Administrator   )
of John Cain   )P-34
        vs   )
James Cain and others   )
_____)

On affidavit of James Cain leave is granted to the defendant to take the deposition of James M. Cain a defendant in the case subject to all legal exceptions at the hearing said case not to be remanded to the rules.

P-34

Bersheeba P. Cain Administrator)
of John Cain   )
        vs   )
James Cain & Others   )
_____)

Order

In this case it appearing to the satisfaction of the court from the affidavit of complainant that the securities

P-34   in the original bond given for the appearance and production   of
the negroes to abide the finall decree in this case are insufficient   it
is ordered adjudged and decreed by the court that process of no   exact
issue directed to the sheriff commanding him to take into possession   the
negroes in the pleadings mentioned and them safely keep until further
order of this court unless defendant give other and sufficient security
for the forth coming of said negroes to abide the final decree of the
court.

March Term 1839

P-34

Thos. W. Spicer   )   Be it remembered that this case came on to
        vs   )   to be heard on the 12th day of March   1839
Thomas Sherley   )   before the Honorable Thomas L. Williams
  B _____)   Chancellor & C upon bill answer replication
                              interluctory decree order proof and ver-
dict of the jury here to fore impounded to try the issue of fact made be a
former order in this casehand upon agreement of solicitor on both sides
and it appearing by the verdict of the jury which is here by ratified and
confirmed as the decree and judgment of this court that the complainant
and defendant entered into a partnership under the firm and style of Sherley and Spineu (Spicer) at Jasper in the year 1827 and that the said partnership continued until March 1834 and that they traded in negroes horses
cattle bacon corn passessory claims to lands real estate goods wares and
merchandise where upon it is ordered adjudged and decreed by the court
that the clerk and master state on account of all said partnership dealing
for said time in all the kinds of property aforesaid and of debts owing
to said firm showing the profits and less of all said business and of all
the debts and credits to which the complainant and defendant are respectively entitled and showing the amount of all the receipts and disbursements
of said firm and of said parties respectively and the amount of the pro-
P-35   ceeds of the sale or sales of said property made by said firm on
or b either of said parties have come to the hands of either of said
parties and when so received and whether the sums has been retained and
been applied by either of said parties to their private individual use or
whether applied to the use of said firm and that said report also   show
whether any of said partnership property has been sold by said parties or
either of them since March 1834 or whether any partnership debts and money
have been collected by said parties or either of them since March 1834 and
whether the proceeds of such sales or collections have been accounted for
and applied to the credit of said firm or applied and retained to   the
individual use of either of said parties and what said sums and it is also
hereby ordered that the defendant or complainant shall produce to the Clerk
and Master when required by the clerk and master or on the requisition of
the opposite party the book of account receipts notes and all paper evidences of the dealings of said firm pertaining to all the foregoing matters it is also ordered that interrogations at the instance of either party
or the clerk and master may put to both or either the complainant or defendant it is further ordered and decreed that both the complainant and
defendant respectively be enjoined from selling or disposing of any interest and title legal or equitable which they may have in partnership to
any land town lots or real estate where so ever situated in this   state
and from disposing of any negro negroes or other personall property   and
from selling transfering or disposing of any bound notes debts   and

P-35   accounts due to said firm until the final hearing of this case It
is also ordered and decreed that each of the said parties pay one half
of the costs of this case and all matters not now decreed are reserved.

March 1839

P-35

David Rankin   )
   vs   )
John Brown   )
Robert A. Brown &)
others   )

For reasons appearing to the satisfaction of the court from the affidavit of
Robert A. Brown ofe of the defendants
in this case it is ordered that the rule
entered against him taking the bill for
confessed be set aside as to him and that
he be allowed to answer the same.

P-35

James White   )
   vs   )
John Cowart   )

This day came Spencer Journegan Esq. &nsuggests
to the court that the compliments in this case
has departed this life.

P-36

David Beck   )
   vs   )
Wm. Brown   )

For reasons appearing to the satisfaction of the
court from the affidavit of the defendant it is
ordered that this case be remanded to the rules
for the purpose of taking the deposition
       Aron York-Elijah Sexton and
       Van Allen

P-36

Cyntha Tucker)
   vs   )
George Tucker)
Wm. McCoy   )

This day came William McCoy by his solicitor
who having heretofore filed his answer in this
case and moved the court for a disolution of
the injunction in this case as to him and the
said motion being considered of by the court
it is ordered that said motion be over ruled.

P-36

Benjamin R. Inman)
   vs   )
William McDaniel)
   &   )
Eliza Kirkpatrick))

This day came the parties by their solicitors and the complainants exception to the
respondants William McDaniel answer being
argued and considered of by the court it is
ordered that said exceptions be sustained
and by consent time is given said McDowell
until the first Monday in April next to file

his answer.

P-36

Eli Colvard   )
   &   )
Thomas H. Calloway   )
   vs   )
Thomas Sherley & Others)

This day came Thomas Sherley by his
solicitors and filed his demurer to
the complainants bill in this case
which being argued and considered
of by the court it is ordered that
said demurrer be over ruled and that
the said Sherley file his answer to

said bill and by consent time is allowed him until the first Monday   in
July to answer said bill.

P-36

        Thomas W. Spicer   )   This day came the parties by their sol-
            vs   )   icitors and filed the following argument
        Samuel I. Poe   )   in writing towit State of Tennessee Chan-
)   cery Court at Pikeville Thow. W. Spicer
    _____)   vs Samiel I. Poe. Thomas W. Spicer com-
plainant in this case do hereby order the dismission of this case as the
matter in controversy on which said bill was instituted is fully adjusted

        Test: Thos. W.Spicer
        Asakel Rawlings

    I Samuel Poe respondant to the bill filed in the above stated case
do assume and take up on myself the payment of the court costs accrued
or that may legally accrue in said case.

        Asakel Rawlings   Samuel I.Poe
        B.B. Cannon

P-37   It is therefore considered by the court that this suit be dismissed and that the complainant recover of the respondnat the costs in
this behalf Expended for which an execution may issue.

P-37

        Samuel B. Mead   )   This day came the parties by their solicit-
            vs   )   ors and the respondant J.C.Everett having
        John C. Everett   )   heretofore filed his answer by his counsel
)   moved the court for a disolution of the
    _____)   injunction in this case which said motion
being considered by the court it is ordered that the same be over ruled.

P-37

        George W. Williams   )   This day came the parties by this sol-
            &   )   icitor and the respondant demurrer to
        Silas Williams   )   the complainants bill filed in this case
            vs   )   being argued and fully considered of
        John Brown   )   by the court - It is ordered that the
)   said dumurrer be sustained and it is
    _____)   therefore ordered by the court that
the complainants amend their said bill on or before the first Monday in
May next.

P-37

        Archibald White   )   Be it remembered that on the 12th day
            vs   )   of March 1839 in the Chancery Court
        Thompson Gardenhire   )   at Pikeville came on the above cause to
            &   )   be heard and determined before the Hon-
        John Holloway   )   orable Thomas L. Williams Chancellor
)   on the bill answers replication proofs
    _____)   and report of the clerk and master and

P-37   after argument of counsel and mature deliberation of the court it
is ordered adjudged and decreed by the court that the complaint bill be
dismissed and that the respondnat pay the costs of said bill. It is there
fore considered by the court that the complainants recover recover of the
respondant all costs in this behalf expended for which an execution may
issue.

From which judgment of the court The complainant by his counsel
prays an appeal to the next term of the supreme court to be held at Knoxville and it is allowed (Page 38) him upon his giving bond and securtiy
P-38   or taking the pauper oath as required by law within two months
from date

P-38

Anderson Skillern et al	)
vs	)
Joseph G. Smith et al	)

By consent of the parties time is
allowed the respondant Joseph G.
Smith until the next term of this
court to file his answer in this
case.

P-38

James Hixon	)
vs	)
Joseph G. Smith	)

In this case it is ordered by the court
that the clerk and master report the
steps which have been taken in this case
and report to the court instanter.

P-38

Solomon P. Mitchell	)
&	)
Edward H. Travis	)
vs	)
John Moyrs	)
and	)
John Brown	)

Came the parties of their counsel and
the respondant having heretofore filed
their answers by their solicitors moved
the court to dissolve the injunction
in this case and after the bill and
answers being read and inspected by the
court and argument of council being had
there on It is considered by the court
that said injunction be dissolved and
it is further ordered by the court that before these defendants or either
of these receive any of the money specified in the bill that the   defendant receiving the same or any part thereof shall give bond with
security to be approved of by the clerk & master of this court to refund
the same on the final hearing of this case.

P-38

David Rankin	)
vs	)
Robert H. Brown &	)
Jas. M/ White	)
&	)
his wife	)

This day came the parties of their
solicitors and filed a written argument
in the words and figures following towit
Rankin Vs Brown we agree this case be
dismissed - Each party paying one half
the costs March 12 1839.

Test:
Wm. J. Standefer

D. Rankin
B.H.Brown

P-38 Where upon it is considered by the court that the complainants
bill be dismissed and that the respondant recover of the complainant one
half of the costs expended (Page 39) and that the complainant recover
P-39 of the respondant Robert H. Brown the other half of the costs
in this behalf expended for which execution may issue.

P-39

    Thomas Sherley   )   By consent of the parties this
        vs   )   case is continued until the next
    Henry J. Williams et al   )   term of court.
)

                                      B.R.Montgomery Esq.

P-39

    James White   )   This day came John Cowart the respondant who
        vs   )   has been arrested on an attchment vise for
    John Cowart   )   contempt in disobeying an injunction here-
)   tofore issued in this case and it appearing
                     to the satisfaction of the court from the
off. of the defendant the evidence produced in the case that he has not
been guilty of a contempt It is therefore ordered by the court that he be
discharged from said attachment.

P-39

    Henry Whiteside   )   This day came the parties by their
        vs   )   counsel and the respondant having here
    Gatewood Qualls   )   tofore filed his answer moved the court
)   to dissolve the injunction in this case
                     and the bill and answer being read and
inspected by the court an argument of counsel being had thereof It is
ordered by the court that the injunction in this case be dissolved and it
is futher ordered by the court that before the defendant is allowed to
issue an execution at law for the judgment specified in the bill that he
shall give bond with security to be approved by the clerk and master of
this court to refund the amount of said judgment andnthe interest thereon
The final hearing of this case should it be decreed against him.

P-39

    James Cain Sr   )   Came the plaintiff by their attorney
    James M . Cain   )   and it appearing to the court scire
    George W. Cain   )   facias has been made known to the
    John Cain &   )   defendant and that he does not appear
    Richard Shockley   )   and plead to said sciro facias but makes
        vs   )   defalt It is therefore considered by
    John Bowman   )   the court that the plaintiff have ex-
)   ecution against the defendant for the
                     sum of twenty six dollars and six
cents for costs in the scia facias mentioned together with the costs by
P-40 them in suing forth and prosecuting the scira facias.

P-40

    William Vernon Adm.   )   This the 12th day of March 1839 came
    of Anderson Vernon Decd.)   on this case to be heard before the

P-40   vs   ) HonorableThomas L. Williams Chancellor
    Alfred Hutcheson et al   ) upon the bill in this case it appear-
) ing to the satisfaction of the court
) that publication had been made in pur-
_ _ _ _ _ _ _ _ _ _ _ _ _ _ _ _
suante of a previous order of this court - The court was pleased to order
and did order and decree that the clerk and master state an account   in
this case and show the amount of the personal estate and assets of the
said Anderson Vernen deceased that has or can come to the hands of the
said administrator and also to show the amount of the claims against said
estate which have been filed by each creditor and of what character they
are and also the whole amount of all the claims so filed and also that
the distribution show of said estate after deducting the costs of this
suit to which each creditor will be entitled distributing the same pro
rata and report to next court.

P-40

    Andrew Low   ) This day came the parties by their
    Samuel C. Low   ) counsel and the respondant Amy Low
    Moses Low et al   ) having heretofore filed the answer by
            vs   ) her counsel moved the court to   dis-
    Amy Low & C.B. Hill   ) solve the injunction in this case and
) the bill and answer being read and
_ _ _ _ _ _ _ _ _ _ _ _ _ _ _ _   ) inspected by the court and argument
of counsel being had there on It is considered by the court that   the
injunction in this case be dissolved so far as to premit the said Amy Low
to prosecute her petition for dower in the circuit court of   Bledsoe
County to a judgment and no further u ntil a final hearing in this case.
P-41   Ordered by the court that the   fine introduced against   Craven
Sherrell be released with out cost.
    Court adjourned until court in course.

                                        Thos. L. Williams

                            Sept. 1839

P-41   Be it remembered that at a chancery court opened and held   for
the eighth chancery district in the Eastern division of Tennessee at the
court house in the town of Pikeville on the second Monday and the 9th
day of September in the year of our Lord one thousand eight hundred and
thirty nine there was present on the bench the Honorable

                                        Thos. L. Williams
                                        Chancellor & C

P-41
    George Reed   ) This day came the respondant by
            vs   ) their counsel and moved the court
    Benjamin Griffith Williams   ) to dismiss the case for want of
            &   ) prosecution and it appearing to
    Smith I. Rea & C.M.Rea   ) the satisfaction of the court
) from inspection of the record
_ _ _ _ _ _ _ _ _ _ _ _ _ _ _ _   ) that two terms had elapsed with
out any steps having been taken in th is case. It is ordered adjudged and
decreed by the court that the complainant bill be dismissed and that the

P-41   respondents go hence without day and recover of the complainant
all costs in this behalf expended for which an execution may issue .

P-41

Ira D. Broyles)	This day came the parties by
&)	their solicitors and the ans-
Benjamin Johnson)	wer of William Garrett having
vs)	been here to fore filed in
William Garrett Greenbery)	this case the said respondent
Garrett & Holbert McClure)	by their counsel moved the
and Holbert McClure)	court to dissolve the injun-
)	ction and the bill and ans-
	wer being read and inspected

by the court and argument of counsel heard thereon - It is ordered by the
court that said injunction be dissolved and it is further ordered by the
court that before the defendant Holbert McClure is allowed to issue an
execution at law on the judgment specified in the bill - He shall give
bond with security to be approved of by the clerk and master of this court
to refund the amount of said judgment and the interest thereon the final
hearing of this case should it be cleared against him.

P-42

James H. Jenkins)	Be it remembered that this case came
William C. Mitchell)	on to be heard upon the report of the
vs)	clerk and master heretofore are filed
Alexander Kelly)	in this case which is as follows to-
)	wit The clerk and master in obedence
	to a decrutal order made in this case

at the last term directing the sale of the land in the pleadings mentioned
if complainants debt was not paid into office within five months from that
time- Respectfully reports that said money was not paid in the office
within five months from that time Respectfully reports that said money
was not paid in the office within the time above specified and that the
clerk and master advertise said land to be sold at the court house   in
Jasper on the 12th day of October 1839- There not being time to advertise
and sell said land after the expiration of five months and reports there
of to this term said report not being excepted to it is ordered adjudged
and decreed that the clerk and master proceed to sell said land according
to said notice on the directions of the decrse heretofore made and report
here of at the next term of this court.

P-42   Sept. 9, 1839

James Keeney &)	By consent of the parties of the defend-
William Gardenhire)	ants in this case are allowed until the
vs)	first Monday November next to file their
Samuel Williams)	answer.
and others)	

P-42

George W. & C. C. Trabue)	By consent of the parties we with
vs)	the assent of the assent of the court

P-42 Butler & Rawlings   )   THIS CASE is continued until the next term
)   of this court .
)

P-42
    Harvey L. Douglass   )   By consent of the parties and with the
            &   )   assent of the court this case is con-
    Larkin F. Wood   )   tinued until the next term.
        vs   )
    Butler & Rawlings   )
)

P-43
    James Henson   )   This day came the complainant by his sol-
        vs   )   icitor Benj. R. Montgomery Esq. and direc-
    Joseph G. Smith   )   ted his bill to be dismissed - It is there
)   fore ordered adjudged and decreed by the
                              court that the said bill be dismissed and
that the defendant go hence and recover of the complainant all costs in
this behalf expended for which an execution may issue.

P-43
Samuel B. Mead   )   This day came the complainant by his
    vs   )   solicitor Samuel Frazier Esq. and
Martin Wyrick   )   suggested the death of Martin Wyrick
David Oatis and   )   and David Oates two of the defendants
the other commissioners   )   on the role and from sufficient rea-
of the town of Jasper   )   sons appearing to the satisfaction
)   of the court this case is continued
                              and remanded to the rules.

P-43
    William Vernon   )   Be it remembered that this day t
    Administrator of   )   this case coming on to be finally
    Anderson Vernon Deceased)   heard and determined before the
        vs   )   Honorable Thomas L. Williams
    Alfred Hutcheson & others)   Chancellor for the Eastern divis-
)   ion of Tennessee presiding in
                              chancery at Pikeville this 9th day
of September A. D. 1839 upon the bill judgment pro-confesso and the report of the clerk and master and because it appearing to the satisfaction
of the court by the report of the clerk and master that the Estate of
the complainant intestate is insolvent and unable to pay the whole amount
of this debt against the same and that these will remain in the hands of
P-44   of the complainant after paying all costs attending said administration and the costs of this suit which amounts to the sum of one hundred and twenty dollars and seven cents the amount of seven hundred and
fifteen dollars and eleven cents and that the following persons are entitled to the following pro rata sums

Alfred Hutcheson sum of $ 188.78¢
Matthew Simmons   "   "   62.45
William Vernon   "   "   200.00
    "   "   2nd claim   71.00

P-44

Robert Vernon	sum of		$ 66.25
Scott Terry	" "		13.50
John Hayle	" "		22.00
John Anderson	" "		18.93½
Samuel Frazier	" "		2.50
Davis Waterhouse	" "		5665
John Crawford			1.68½
Isly Collier	" "		5.00
James Grigsby	" "		1.25
Smith & Spring	" "		3.31
Lewis Jones	" "		3.75
Samuel Gamble	" "		3.10
John Sherley	" "		9.67
Hugh Carroll	" "		1.71
John Dugin	" "		11.00
T.J.Campbell and John Locke			
for the use of Jesse Pau			20.00

It is hterefore ordered and adjudged and decreed by the court that
the complainant pay the same into the clerk and master of this court andt
that if he fail to do so that the clerk and master issue execution a-
gainst said complainnant for the sum of seven hundred and fifteen dollars
P-45 and eleven cents together with said sum of one hundred and
twenty dollars and seven cents the amount of the costs of this suit and
that the clerk and master pay to the several claimants this said several
pro rato allowance.

P-45

Samuel B. Mead)
vs)
John C. Everett)
_____)

Be it remembered that on the 9th day of
September 1839 came on this case to be heard
before the Honorable Thos. L. Williams
Chancellor upon the bill answer and replication and also upon the cross bill filed
in this case by the defendant Everetts answer and replication there to
when the court was pleased to order and did order and decree that the clerk
nad master state an account in this case and show the amount of claims
of the defendant Everett which are coming to him of and from the said
Samuel B. Mead and also show the amount of claims of the said complainant
Mead which he proposes to staff against the claims of the said Everett
and show the diffsnce in any between the said claims and report there of
to the next term of this court.

P-45

Cyntha Tucker)
vs)
George Tucker)
&)
William McCoy)
_____)

This 9th day of September this case came
on to be finally heard and determined before the Honorable Thos. L. Williams
Chancellor upon the bill answer of defendant William McCoy and replication thereto
and the proofs in the case and a judgment
pro-confesso as to the defendant George
Tucker . It appears to the satisfaction of the court that about the year
1836 the complainant was married to defendant George Tucker with whom
she lived till about twelve or eighteen months past in the County of

P-45   Marion in the state of Tennessee that about the time aforesaid
the defendant Tucker contracted an improper intimacy with one Adaline
Bryson as charged in said bill with whom he committed the crime of adultry and with whom he has eloped to parts unknown that on his marriage with
P-46   complainant he received by her considerable property and among
such a negro gilr named Clarissa that is now in possession of with some
other small articles also in her posission . It also appears defendant
William McCoy is indebted to defendant Tucker and has of his effects in
his hands upon this state of the case the Honorable Chancellor is pleased
to order and does order adjugded abd decree that the bonds of Matrimony
between complainant and said George Tucker be and the same are dissolved
and the said Cyntha restored to all the rights of a fine sale that all
the right and title to said negro girl Clarissa divested out of said
George Tucker and vested in said Cynatha Tucker and her heirs forever and
that she also have and enjoy as her own property all and every other
article or articles of property in her possession belonging to said George
Tucker and that she be substituted in the place of said George Tucker as
to the amount due him from the defendant William McCoy may have in his
possession belonging to said George Tucker and that she be vested with t
the right there to. It is further ordered and decreed that clerk & master
ascertain the amount due by defendant McCoy to the defendant Tucker and
also what may be in his hands belonging to said defendant Tucker and report here of to the next term of court and that he have power to call
witnesses before him and their testimony take up on said inquiry. It is
further ordered that defendants Tucke r and Mc Coy pay costs of   this
case and that execution issue there fore as at law.

P-46

Jefferson Barbee et al.   )   From sufficient reasons appearing
         vs   )   to the satisfaction of the court
William McMurry et al.   )   this case is continued and re-
)   manded to the rules.

Monday Sept. 1839

P-46

Crutcher & Allison   )   By consent of the parties and with
         vs   )   the assent of the court this case is
Butler & Allison   )   continued until the next term.

P-47

Jacob Beck   )   For sufficient reasons appearing to   the
         vs   )   satisfaction of the court from the affidavit
William Brown   )   Abra. Mays? this case is remanded to   the
)   rules for five months and it is ordered by
)   the court that the defendant pay all costs
which have accrued in this case from the time said case could by the
rules of this court have been set for hearing up to and inclusive   of
this term.

P-47   Monday Sept. 1839

P-47

Michael R. Allen) This day came the parties by their
Vs) solicitor and the answers of Allen
Allen Kennedy A. S. Lenon) Kennedy A. S. Lenon and R. A.
Reynolds A. Ramsey et al) Ramsey (having here to been filed
) in this case the said respondants
) by their counsel moved the court

to decease the injunction and the bill and answer having been read   and
inspected by the court and argument of counsel there on had - It   is
ordered adjudged and decreed by the court that said injunction be
dissolved.

Monday September 9, 1839.

P-47

Thomas Sherley) By consent of the complainant and the
) defendant counsel B. R. Montgomery Esq.
Henry J. Williams et-al) this case is continued until the next
) term of this court and remanded to the
) rules.

P-47

James White) This day come the defendant by his counsel and
vs) the complainant death having been suggested on
John Cowart) the record at the last term and it appearing
) that no steps has been taken to revise said case
) according to the rules of the court. It is
there ordered that said case abate.

P-47

William M. Davis and) This day came the parties by their sol-
Benjmin K. Hudgens) icitor and filed in court a written
vs) agreement in the words and figures fol-
George W. Williams) lowing to wit Thos. N. Frazier Esq. Clerk
A. M. Rawlings and) of the Chancery Court at Pikeville,
John P. Lewy) Tennessee. The suit pending in court
P-48   ) of which you are clerk and master in
                    which William M. Davis and Benjamin K.

Hudgens are complainants and John P. Long, Aron M. Rawlings and George W.
Williams and Ailey Copa are defendant been compromised an the following
terms viz complainants agree to dismiss their suit and defendant Long,
Rwalings and William assume and because it appear that said answer does
not sufficiently show the consideration given by defendant John Cornett
Jr. for the land purchased of defendant Russell for the land spoken of
in bill or on before the rule day in November next. The court then adjourned until tomorrow morning at 8 o'clock.

P-49

Kinzey Smith Adm. of) Decree-
Joseph Yates deceased) This day the 10th day of Sept. 1839
vs) came on this case to be finally heard
John Bridgman) before the Honorable Thomas   L.
) Williams Chancellar upon the bill
) answer replication there to and proof
It appears to the staisfaction of the court that the negro man horse

35

P-49 September 10th 1839.
money and other articles named in the pleadings received by defendant
Bridgman from Joseph Yates deceased were received by him as an indemnity
as appearance bail for said yates and aught to be surrendered to the complainant. It is there fore ordered and decreed by the court that defend-
and Bridgman deliver to complainant with in three months from this time
the negro boy John named in the pleadings and if not delivered defendant
to be charged with the value of said boy that the clerk and Master state
an account in this case charging defendant with the amount of one hundred and nine dollars as received by him from Joseph Yates deceased the
value of the here of said negro boy the value of the horse and other
articles received by defendant and crediting him with what ever he may
have paid for Yates or on his account also with any sum said yates may
owe him for services and after such deductions charge defendant and crediting him with wthever he may have paid for Yates or an his account also
with any sum said Yates may owe him for services and after such deduction
charge defendant interest up on the balance from the time for the dam-
and made by complainant stated in the time and if the negro boy be not
delivered with in the time given that his value be added to said account
It is further ordered and decreed that defendant pay the amount ascertain-
ed by the Master to complainant and that he also pay the costs of this
case.

September 10the 1839

P-50

Bersheba P. Cain)
Administrator)
vs)
James Cain Ser)
George W. Cain it-al)
)

Be it remembered that the depositions
of James Cain Sr. Rebecca Cain and
John Lassater came up on exceptions being filed by complainant to the reading
of them as evidence for defendants when
it appeared to the satisfaction of the
court that the exceptions were well

taken and that said depositions are incompetent in as much as said witness are intrusted in the event of this suit where upon the court refused
to permit said depositions to be read on the hearing.

P-50

Bersheba Pl Cain)
Special Administrator of)
John Cain deceased)
against)
James Cain Senior)
)

Be it remembered that now at the September term 1839 of the Chancery court
at Pikeville this case came all to be
heard before Chancellor Williams all
bill the answers of the defendants
replication there to exhibits and
proofs in the case and in presence of

solicitors on both sides when it appeared to the satisfaction of the court
here that previous to the year 1826 James Cain ser. was largely indebted to complainant intestate that about the first of April 1838 said James
Cain ser. sold his land in Warren County to William M. Roberson being
greatly embarrassed in his pecuniary affairs at the time that he received
from said Roberson in part pay for said land two negro women Sophia or
Sophy and Hannah who have born since the following issue to with Malinda,
Bob, Mary Violet or Violent and executed at the request of said James
Cain ser. the hire of sale to defendants as the sons and daughters of
said James Cain

September 10 1939

P-51

That after the date of said bill of sale James the father was indebted to John Cain complainant interstate said bill of sale dated the 1st of
April 1828 It farther appeared to the court that on the 19th of August
1835 Complainant intestate recovered a judgment against defendant James
Cain and in the Circuit court of Marion for eight hundred and fifty seven
dollars and eighty seven cents besides cost of suit and that said James
Cain is indebted to complainant in another sum of one hundred and seventy
two dollars 38/100 by account with interest for march 1835 to the present
time up on the whole case this court is satisfied that the afore said
negroes being bought by James Cain the father with his own property and
subject in equity to the payment and satisfaction of the before described
debts against him and that the other and that the other defendants his
title communicated by the bill of sale from Robinson is void for fraud
in law in fact where upon the court thinks fit to order adjudge and
decree that the defendants forth with deliver over to the clerk and
Master of this court the before described negro slaves to be sold by
him at the court house foor in the town of Pikeville to the highest
bidder for cash of so many of them as will be sufficient to pay up the
aforesaid debts of complainant with interest till paid the costs at law
and the cost of this suit together with the amount of any other debts
against said James Cain which may be proved to the satisfaction the
master of the creditors of said Cain the master shall advertise the times
and place of sale at three of the most public places in the county of
Bledsoe and of which shall be the court house door on the coming in of
the report of the report of the Master which will be made to the next
term of this court the title will be decreed to the purchaser all other
matters are reserved till the coming in of the Master report.

From which judgment said decree of the court the respondant passed
an appeal to the next supreme court to be held at Knoxville and it is
allowed them upon their entering into hand with security to be approved
of the master to prosecute said appeal and the other conditions here in
after to be stated.

September term 1839

P-52

Bersheba P. Cain)
Special Administrator)Q
vs.)
James Cain senior and)
George W. Cain and others)
_ _ _ _ _ _ _ _ _ _ _ _ _ _)

On a motion of the complain by her
solicitor and because it appers
to the satisfaction of court that
bond here to fore given by the
defendants for the forth coming
of the negroes mentioned in the
pleading to abide by the decree
rendered in this case it is insufficient. It is ordered by the court
here that unless the defendant give good and sufficient security to the
master for the forth coming of said negroes to abide by an satisfy what
ever decree may be rendered by the superior court on the appeal project
with in ten days after the adjournment of this court that in that event
the appeal shall not operate as supercedeent but the master shall forth
with execute the decree rendered in this drect case and in the event the
defendent shall refuse to deliver up the negroes the master shall issue

P-52

execution as at law against the goods and chattels lands and tenements of all the defendants for the amount specified in the decree.

P-52

Claibourn C. Price	)	This day came the parties by their sol-
vs	)	icitors and filed a written agreement
A. M. Rwlings	)	in this case in the words and figures
George W. Williams and	)	following tewit Thomas N. Frazier Esq
John I. Long	)	clerk of the Chancery court at Pikeville
	)	Tennessee.

The suit pending in the court of which you and clerk and master in which Claibourn C. Price is complainant and A ron M. Rwlings, John I. Long and George W. Williams and defendants has this day been compromised on the following terms viz The complainant agrees to dismiss his suit and defendant Long, Rawlings and Williams assume the payment of the cost you will please Have the same on the terms and conditions here agreed on April 2nd 1839.

C. C. Price
A. M. Rawlings
Jno. I. Long

Where upon it is considered by the court that the complainant bill be dismissed and that the defendant pay all cost in this behalf expended for which an execution may issue.

P-53

Eli Cleveland and	)	This day came the parties by their
Thomas H. Calloway	)	solicitors and the answer of Thomas
vs	)	Sherley and others and of the def-
Thomas Shelby and others	)	endant to the original and supple-
	)	ment bill having here to fore have
	)	been filed and notice given to the

complainant of this motion to disolve this injunction granted the complainant against the said defendant Thomas Sherley which motion being agreed as the complainants solicitor the respondant and fully understood by the court here it is considered by the court that the said injunction be dissolved and the said respondant proceed.

P-53

Thomas W. Spicer	)	Be it remembered that at the September
vs.	)	1839 of the chancery court at Pikeville
Thomas Sherley and	)	this case came on to be heard and det-
Pleasant Butler	)	ermined before chancellor Williams on the
	)	exceptions to the extent of the master
	)	made pursuant to an interstate entry decree

pronounced here in at the next term of this court when the matters of said exception being heard and fully understood by the court the Chancellor thinks fit to order adjudge and decree that the same be disabled and the masters repart is in all things confirmed and it appears to the court

P-54

from the report of the master that the whole amount of debts now due and owing to the firm and property belonging to said firm amount to the sum of four four thousand six hundred ans seventeen dollars and thirty two cents it is ordered by the court that the defendant procede with reasonable diligence to collect said debts and report and pay over to the clerk and master of this court from court to court as having as he may collect the same it is further ordered by the court that the costs of this suit be equally divided amongst all the parties respectively.

P-54

| Thomas W. Spicer vs Thomas Sherley) | Be it remembered that at the September term 1839 of the chancery court at Pikeville the case again came on to be heard before the Honorable Thomas L. Williams Chancellor and made persuant to an interloctury pron- |

ounced here on to the last term of this court when the matters there of being heard and fully understood by the court the Chancellor thinks fit to order adjudge and decree that 1st and 7th exceptions to said report be disallowed and the fourth be disolowed except as to the sum of four dollars to which sum the master is directed to examine the complainant on inter- ogatives and that the second third fifth and sixth exceptions to said report be and the same are here by allowed and that the matters there of are again referred to the master to take additional proof and report here of to thenext term of this court the masters report is in all other things confirmed except as to the boy reported to be dead before fixing the bill in this case the question as to the defendant liability? for him being reserved and because it appears to the court from the report afore said of the master that the defendant is in arrears to the complainant at least the sum of three hundred and fifty dollars on the partner ship dealings it is ordered and decreed by the court that the defendant pay said sum of three hundred and fifty dollars into the hand of the master to the use of complainant in three months after the adjournment of this court and in the event of his failure to do so that execution issue for the same as law It is further ordered that the defendant pay all the costs of this suit.

P-55

| Jacob Beck vs William Brown) | This day came the parties by their counsel and it is ordered by the court that defendant Brown shall take andfille in office all depositions which he wishes to take in the case on or before the rule day in December next. |

P-55

| James H. Jenkins vs Alexander Kelly and William C. Mitcholl) | Be it remembered that on this 10th day of September 1839 the defendant Alexander Kelly paid to the complainants solicitor James P. Thompson the sum of six hundred |

P-55

and thirty one dollars and ninety cents the full amount of his debt and
interest the cost of suit remain unpaid where upon the court doth order
adjudged and decree that the clerk and master desist from selling said
land unless to secure the payment of the costs of this suit.

The court then adjourned until seven oclock tomorrow morning.

Thos. L. Williams

P-56

Court met pursuant to adjournment present on the bench the Honorable
Thomas L. Williams chancellar.

The record of yesterday having been read and signed the court proceeded to business.

Wed. Sept. 11, 1839

P-56

William N. Gillespie &	) Decree
Sidney Ann Gillespie	) This the 10th day of September
his wife	) 1839 came on this case to be
	) finally heard and determined
vs	) the Honorable Thomas L.
	) Williams Chancellac & C up
John Locke & Piletiah Chilton	) on the bills answers a repli-
Executers of William S. Lenty	) cation and the report of the
Thomas Lenty & Burton Lenty	) clerk and master the report
heirs legatees and devises of	) being unexpected to in in
William S. Lenty deceased	) all things confirmed from

said report it appears that there came to the said executors in available
funds the sum of twenty one thousand nine hundred and twenty two dollars
sixty nine and three fourths cents and that they delivered of said   sum
in due course of administration twenty thousand four hundred and seventy
six dollars seventy nine and one half cents leaving a balance off their in
hands of fourteen hundred and forty five dollars ninety and one fourth
cents said report also show said executors are chargeable with the   sum
of nine hundred and sixty five dollars and ninety two cents for two notes
and interest due by executor Chilton making in all their in their hands
to be accounted for the sum of two thousand four hundred and eleven dollars eighty two and due fourth cents ($2411.82¼) It further appears the
rents and profits of the real estate named in the bill never came to the
hands of said executors but that the same were received by defendant
Mary Lenty for herself and as guardian of the minor heirs of said William A. Lenty deceased and have been applied to the support of the said
widow and children and schooling said children according to the will of
the of said William S. Lenty deceased up on the fore going facts the
chancellor is pleased to order and and does order and adjudge and decree
that complainants bill as to said widow and heirs be dismissed that out
of the sum in the hands of said executors They bbe allowed one thousand
P-57 and ninety six dollars and thirteen cents being five per cent upon
the amount by them received for receiving and disbursing said funds and
also a reasonable compensation for attention and labor bestowed on the
estate of said William S. Lenty beyond the receipt and disbursement of
said funds that this branch of the case be referred to the clerk and

P-57   master to hear testimony ascertain and report what will be   such
reasonable compensation showing the services for which he shall make   an
allowance all other matters are reserved for final decree upon the coming
in of said report.

Wed. Sept. 11th 1839

P-57

George W. Rice   )   Be it remembered that at the September
     vs   )   term of the chancery court at Pikeville
Samuel William   )   this case came on to be heard and   the
     &   )   defendants demurrer to complainants bill
James Craige   )   when the matters of law involved in the
)   said demurrer being argued on both sides
------------------)   by solicitors and fully understood by
the court the chancellar thinks fit to order adjudged and decree that
said demurrer be allowed and that complainants bill be dismissed Where upon a motion of the complainant by his solicitor an appeal is granted him
to the next supreme court of errors held at Pikeville and that said appeal
be granted him without giving security and it is further ordered that the
complainant pay the costs of this suit for which execution may issue.

Wed. Sept. 11 1839

P-57

George W. Williams)   This day came the parties by their
     &   )   solicitors and the defendants demur-
Siles Williams   )   rer to the complainants original and
Samuel Williams   )   amended bill in this case came   on
     vs   )   to be heard and after argument of
John Brown   )   counsel and mature deliberation   of
)   the court where upon it was ordered
------------------)   adjudged and decreed by the court
P-58   that the demurrer be sustained and that the complainants bill be
dismissed and that the defendant for him and recover of the complainant
all costs in the behalf expended for which execution may issue.

Wed. Sept. 11 , 1839

P-58

Joseph G. Smith   )   Be it remembered that on the 11th   day
     vs   )   of September 1839 this case came on to
Anderson Skillern   )   be tried on a motion made by Sol.   of
     &   )   defendant James V. Skillern from the
James Skillern   )   ne-exeat allowed in this case and the
)   said motion argued by Sol. and under-
------------------)   stood by the court it is ordered   and
adjudged by the court that the said James V. Skillern be discharged from
from said ne-exeat and it is further ordered by the court that   the court
that the clerk and master deliver the books papers notes and accounts
surrendered by the said James V. Skillern in obedience to the order   in
this behalf to Joseph G. Smith the complainant for collection   taking
the receipt of the said Joseph G. Smith therefore.

Sept. 11th 1839-

P-58

Thomas W. Sherley
vs
Thomas Spicer

On the petition of defendant this day exhibited to the court it is considered that it be referred to the master to take additional proof and the following items 1st did defendant pay to Sherley and West of Nashville towards the extinguishment of the debts of the firm of Sherley and Spicer any sum of money out of his own individual funds and if so how much and when 2nd Was the property the house and lot in Jasper sold under an execution in favor of Johnson & Robinson & Co of Nashville the individual property of Sherley or was it the property of the firm of Sherley and Spicer 3. What did it sell for what was it worth who was the purchaser has the sum been redeemed and if so by whom and at what price and that the masters report here of at the next term of court- where upon came the defendant Thomas Sherley and paid to the complainant counsel James P. Thompson three hundred and fifty dollars for the complainants use and which said soliciter agrees shall be a compliance with the order heretofore made in this case requireing the P-59 defendant ot pay said sum of three hundred and fifty dollars unto the office of the clerk and master.

P-59

George W. and
S. Williams
vs
John Brown

The argument of the defendants demurrer to the compliants bill in this case is continued until the next term of this court.

P-59

Samuel B. Mead
vs
Samuel Prestly
James Prigmore et-al

This day came on the defendant demurrer to the complainants bill to be heard and determined and upon argument of counsel and mature deliberation of the court. It is ordered and adjuged by the court that the defendant demurrer be overruled and upon motion of the defendants by their solicitor nine months be allowed them to file their answer to said bill.

P-59

Eli Clevland &
Thomas H. Holloway
vs
Thomas Sherley

This day came the parties of their solicitors and from sufficient reasons appearing to the satisfaction of the court the order heretofore made in this case disolving the injunction is remanded and said motion to dissolve be continued over until the next term of this court for further argument A new bond was required which was given.

Elizabeth White & others
vs
Allen Kennedy Albert S. Swan
& R.A.Ramsey

The motion heretofore made to dissolve the injunction in this case is discharged. Court

P-59   adjourned until court in course.

Thos. L. Williams

Monday March 1840
P-60

De it remembered that at a chancery court opened and held for the
chancery district in the ---- division of Tennessee at the court house
in the town of Pikeville on the 2nd monday and 9th day of March in the
year of our Lord one thousand eight hundred and forty - There was present
on the bench honorable Thos. L. Williams Chancellar & C.

On application on John M. Lee Esq. he was du ly qualified as   a
practing attorney in this court.

P-60

Thomas Sherley	
vs	)
Henry J. Williams	)
Edward S. Williams	)
&	)
Wm. W. Williams	)

This day came the parties by their solicitors and by the consent of the
parties is continued until the next
term of this court.

P-60

George W & C.C. Trabue	)
vs	)
PleasantHButler	)
&	)
Asakel Rawlings	)

By consent of the parties by their
solicitors and with the consent of
the court this case is continued
un til the next term.

P-60

Harvey L. Douglass	)
&	)
Larkin F. Wood	)
vs	)
Pleasant H. Butler	)
& Asakel Rawlings	)

This day came the parties by their c
counsel and by their consent   and
with the assent of the court this
case is continued until the next term.

P-60

Foster G. Crutcher	)
&	)
Alex Allison	)
vs	)
Pleasant H. Butler	)
&	)
Asakel Rawlings	)

This day came the parties by their
counsel and by their consent and with
the assent of the court this case is
continued until the next term of this
court.

Monday March term 1840.

P-61 Cytha Tucker   )
       vs   )
  George Tucker   )
  William McCary   )
)

This day came the parties by their solicit‑ors and it appeared to the satisfaction oft the court that an account had not been made or taken in conformity with a decretal order pronounced in this case at the last term it is there fore ordered adjudged and decreed by the court that the order made at the last term be revised and that the clerk and master report there on at the next term of court.

P-61

  David Beck   )
   against   )
  William Brown   )
)

'This case coming on to be heard and deter‑mined upon the bill answer replication and proof and an issue being made by the parties under the direction of the honorable court to asscertain the fact whether the complain‑ant and respondant were partners as charged in complainant bill and dismissed in respondants answer and a jury be empanneled and having found that the complainant and respondant were part‑ners as charged in complainants bill by the court that the clerk and master take and state an account assertain what amount was advanced by each partner and what paid out and expended by each, what what amount received by each and the balance now due from respondant to complainant and that he have power hear testimony adduced by the parties on oath tou‑ching their partnership dealing and that the said clerk and master report here of at the next term of this court.

P-62

  Jno. O. Thompson)
       vs   )
  Brinkly Harnsby   )
)

This day came the parties by their soli‑citors and the respondants answer having beenhere to fore filed in this case the said respondant by his counsel moved to dissolve the injunction.

March term 1840

P-62

  Joseph F. Read & his wife)
  James M. Read   )
     vs   )
  James Loyd   )

Came to the parties by their soli‑citors and mutually agree to take depositions of Benjamin F. Hudson administrator in this case.

P-62

  Samuel B. Meed   )
       vs   )
  John O. Everett   )
  Erasmus Ally et-al)
)

This day came the parties by their sol‑icitor and it appearing to the satisfact‑ion of the court that an account in con‑formity with a decreetal order made in this case at the last term. It is there fore ordered adjudged and decreed by the court that the order made at the last term be revived and that the clerk and master report there on at the next term of this court.

The court then adjourned until 8 o'clock tomorrow morning

Thos. L. Williams

Tuesday March term 1840

Court met pursuant to adjournment-Present on the bench the Honorable

Thos. L. Williams Chancellor and C

P-62

Lewis Patterson)
vs)
Catherine Jane Patterson)
Sabina Ann Patterson)
Rhoda Jane Patterson and)
Sophrona Patterson)
by their guardian)
Robert McRee)

Be it remembered that this came
and to be finally heard and determined before Chancellor Williams
at the March term 1840 of the
Chancery court at Pikeville, Tennessee on Monday the first day of
said term and 9th day of the month
of March afore said upon the bill
answers replication exhibits and
proof there upon the court does

order adjudge and decree that all the right title claim and demand which
the dependants their heirs and C. have in and to the following tract of
land towit beginning at a white oak and two spanish oaks thence North
there by five East one hundred and fifty poles to a black oak and sour
wood thence south thirty five west one hundred and fifty poles to a
white oak and dog wood thence one hundred and sixty poles to the beginning containing one hundred and fifty acres and lying in the county of
Hamilton in said state being the same land conveyed by Robert Patterson
to John Patterson by deed hearing date the 16th day of July 1821. It
being the same land mentioned in complainants bill. Be divested and of
the defendants Catherine Jane Patterson, Salina Ann Patterson, Rhoda Jane
Patterson and Sophronia Patterson their heirs and C and he vested in the
complainant Lewis Patterson and his heirs as an estate in fee simple for
ever allowing to the minor heirs respectively six months to impeach the
decree after coming of age and it is further ordered by the court that the
complainant pay the costs in the behalf expended for which as execution
may issue as at law.

P 63

Kinsey Smith)
Administrator of)
Joseph Yates)
deceased)
vs)
John Bridgman)

Decree

On this the 9th day of March 1840 came on the
above stated before the Honorable Thos. L.
Williams Chancellor for final decree up on
the report of the master said report being
unexpected is in all things confirmed from
which said report is appears there remaining
in the hands of defendant that should be paid

over to complainant the sum of one hundred and thirteen dollars ninety
and half cents. It is there fore ordered and decreed by the court that
complainant have execution against the defendant for the said sum.

P- 64

Joseph Martin)
vs)
George W. Rice)

Came the respondent by his solicitor and for
reasons appearing to the satisfaction of the
court from the affidavit of the respondent the
judgment for confessed here to fore entered in
this case is set aside and the respondent per-

mitted to file his answers and the respondents answer being filed in the
case the said respondent by his counsel moved for a desolution of the

March term 1840

P-64

injunction ceased in this case.

Elizabeth White and the heirs of James White, deceased vs Allen Kennedy and A. L. Lenoir and R. A. Ramsey	This day came the parties by their solicitors and from sufficient reasons desclosed to the court from the depositions of A. S. Lenoir one of the defendants in this case. This case is continued and remanded to the rules to take the depositions Asakel

Rawlings, Cornelus Mulgan, John Lowlady, A. T. Prowel, Robert Smith, John Keeney, B. R. Montgomery, Luke Lea, James Berry and William G. Sparks to be read as evidence of the hearing of this case, Jefferson Barby, Rebecca Barley widow of Matthew Barley deceased Jeptha Barby Cyntha Barby Narcissa Barby Coliun Barby Polly Barby and ----- Barby minor heirs of Matthew Barby deceased under the age of twenty one years by their next friend.

P-64

Jefferson Barby vs Joby Jones John Cunningham sr. John D. Cunningham and William McMurry	Be it remembered that this case came on to be heard this the 9th day of march 1840 and was heard before the Honorable Thos. L. Williams Chancellor upon bill answers replication and proofs when it appeared to this court satisfaction of the court that complainants ancester Matthew

Barby paid and otherwise became and became liable for John Cunningham Sr in the sum of nine hundred and fifty dollars that the creditors of John Senior obtained judgment execution against him that David Rankin caused
P-65 an execution to issue upon the judgement be obtained against John Sr. for the sum of one hundred and thirty three dollars and seventy one cents and that Fifa issued upon said judgment and was levied up on seven hundred and fourteen acres of land belonging to defendant John Sr. that said land was sold by the sheriff of Marion County on the 10th day of February 1829 that on 22nd day of February 1830 that Obidiah Bean a creditor of John redeemed said land from said Rankin who had hid it off at the sale aforesaid and hid upon the land the amount of his judgment a and other claims that about 10 months after Bean redeemed with in two years of the sale complainants ancestors redeemed said land the amount specified in the clerks receipt including the judgment which he obtained against said Cunningham and Matthew Barbe and others at further approval to the court that Defendant Cunningham put Matthew Barbe in possession of said seven hundred and fourteen acres of land in his life time that John Senior after the sale sold his right or redemption to Matthew or sold the land and that the redemption and posession of land was aquiesed in by John Senior until after the death of Matthew and that complainants held possession under their ancestors undisturbed until 1833 and it further appeared that John Cunningham Senior made

P-66

a colourable deed of conveyance to defendant William McMurry and Joby
Jones for one hundred and fourteen acres of said seven hundred and fourteen acres in November 1833 that he also made another colourable deed
to said defendant 163½ acres of said land that on the 10th day of October John made another deed to said defendant McMurry and Joby Jones for
300 acres more of said seven hundred and fourteen acres for the pretended consideration of two thousand dollars It further appeared that
defendant William McMurry and Joby Jones instituted an action of equt-
ment? against complainant for the possession of said land say seven hundred and fourteen acres and that at the October term of the Circuit court
for Marion county received jedgment in said action against complainants
and it is further appeared that on the 5th day of January 1836 James
Jones sherrif of Marion county made an exdcuted his deed to David Rankin
for said seven hundred and fourteen acres of land by Moles & Cannady by
virture of his office and in accordance to said sale that on the same day
David Rankin executed his deed of conveyance for all of said land to
Obediah Bean who had redeemed the same by mates and Connady that on the
same day that Obediah Bean by his deed duly made and executed of same
date say say 5th day of January 1835 conveyed saidnland to compensate
all of what deeds have been duly proved and registered and it further
appeared on the 13th of January 1835 co plainants obtained an injunction
restraining defendants from taking out a writ of possession on said judgment in egectment and upon the whole case the court is satisfied that th e
case afore said was fully dedeemed by Mathew Barbe with in two years from
the sale, and that the defendants McMurry and Jones took no title by their
P-67 deed where upon the court thought fit to order adjudge and decree
and it is according ordered adjudged and decreed that the defendant possession and said judgments in ejectment and it is further ordered adjudged and decreed that 714 of land was redeemed by complainants ancestors
and that complainants be quartered in the peaceable posession of said
tract of land and it is further ordered adjudged and adjudged that
defendants McMurry and Jones take no title under the purchase from their
co defendant John Cunningham Sr. and that the defendants pay the costs
of this suit and likewise the costs of the suit at law for all of
which execution may issur as at law from which judgment and decree of
the court the defendant by their counsel pray an appeal to the next term
of the supreme court held at Knoxville upon the defendant giving bond
and security to be approved of by the master conditioned to prosecute
said appeal with effect and that said bond be given with in one month
from the adjournment by this court and the court then adjourned until
tomorrow morning at 8 o'clock.

Thos. L. Williams

Wednesday March term 1840

P-67

Samuel B. Mead)	This day came the parties by their solicit-
vs)	ors and the answer of Samuel Prestly one
Samuel Priestly)	of the defendant having been here to fore
William Jones)	filed the said Prestly by his counsel
James Prigmore)	moved the court to dissolve the injunction
-----------------)	in this case.

P-68

Juhall Dixon	This day came the complainant by his counsel and
vs	it appearing to the satisfaction of the court from
William Hale	the allegations in the bill that the defendant is
	not an inhabitant of this state it is there upon
	ordered and adjudged and decreed by the court

that publication be made for four succes ine? weeks in the Knoxville
Register and Weekly Times a newspaper printed in the town of Knoxville
and county of Knox requiring the said defendant William S. Hall to appear
at the next term of the court and answer plead or demur to the hill of
complaint or the same will be taken for confessed and set for hearing en
parte

P-68

George Brown	This day came the parties by their
vs	soliciters and by consent this
Mary Carnett Jr. and	case is remanded to the rules and
James Russell	continued.

P-68

George and Silas Williams & Co.	This day came Spencer
vs	Jounajin solicitor for res-
John Brown	pondants and suggested up
	on record the death of res-
	pondant.

P-68

Thomas Hopkins and others	This day came on to be argued the
heirs to	demurrer of the respondent to the
Thomas Hopkins deceased	complainants bill where up on it
vs	was ordered and adjudged that said
John Looke	demurrer he sustained and that the
	complainants have leave to amend
	their original bill

and then the court adjourned until 8 o'clock tomorrow morning

Thos. L. Williams

March term 1840

P-69

Henry Whiteside	This day came the complainant by his counsel
&	and produced in open court a written agreement
Gatewood Qualls	compromising this case which is in the words
	and figures following towit In this case we
	the undersigned parties agree to compromise

the suit on the following terms towit Said Whiteside is to dismiss his
bill and pay the costs in equity and the said Qualls is to pay the costs
at law for the judgment enjoined by the bill in equity- Given under

P-69
our hands this 4th day of October 1839

Henry Whiteside
Gatewood Qualls

Test
Thos. N. Frazier Clerk and M.

Where upon it is ordered adjudged and decreed by the court that said
bill be dismissed and the defendant and the defendant be hence discharged
and that the complainant pay all costs in this behalf expended for which
and exection for which and execution may issue as at law and that the
complainant recover of the defendant the costs of the suit at law here to
fore enjoined by this bill for which execution may issue at law.

March term 1840

P-69

James Kinsey and   )
William Gardenhire   )
        vs   )
George W. Williams   )
and others   )
)
-------------------------)

This day came on this case to be heard
and determined on this the 12th of March 1840 before Chanceller Williams up
on a motion to dissolve the injunction
in this case and the same being conside r-
ed of by the court it is ordered adjudged and decreed by the court that said
injunction be dissolved and that the defendant in the use and occupation
of the premises in dispute do no actin which injury to the estate by
committing waste shall accrue.

P-69

Benjamin R. Inman   )
        vs   )
William McDaniel and   )
Eliza Kinrkpatrick   )
)
-------------------------)

This the eleventh day of March 1840 came
on this case to be heard upon the bill
answer replication and proof before the
Honorable Thos. L. Williams Chancellor
it appeared to the court that complain-
and settled upon the south west quarter
of section twenty one in the fourth town ship in range second west of
the basis line in the Ocoa District in what is now the county of Hamilton
about the month of October 1834 that he was in the actual possession and
residing upon said quarter at the time of the survey of the Ocoa District
and at the passage of the law to dispose of the lands in said District
   That respondent William McDaniel and Eliza Kirkpatrick were in the actual possession and resided upon said of land at the same time It further
appeared that complainant on the 21st day of January 1839 had his occupant right upon siad quarter proved according to the provisions of law
preparatory to an entry there of that he proposed to make a joint entry
with defendant McDaniel which was declined That the complainant then
had said land divided by commissioners appointed according to the provis-
uibs of the act of assumbly entitled an act to dispose of the lands in the
Ocoa district and on the 31st of January 1839 applied to the entry taker
of the Ocoa District to be permitted to make a joint entry with defendant
McDaniel of said quarter and then learned the whole quarter had been entered by defendant McDaniel in his own right and as of Eliza Kirkpatrick
P-70 which entry it appears he made when he knew said quarter was about
to be divided and with a view to present complainant making an entry

P-70   either jointly or alone and also to appropriate the whole quarter
to him self in distribution of the occupant right of complaint It further
appeared that defendant McDaniel had purchased the occupants right of de-
fendnat(P-71)   Eliza Kirkpatrick upon the fore going state of facts in
P-71   this case The Chancellor did declare and does adjudge and decree
that complainant and defendant were each entitled to an occupant right and
preference of entry upon said quarter each to an equal part to be divided
according to quality and quanity that defendant McDaniel is entitled to
two shares and complainant the other share to be laid off so as to include
his dwelling house and his portion of land adjoining it is farther ordered
and decreed that the title acquired by defendant McDaniel to said quarter
be in trust for complainant to the extent of complainants third of said
quaeter and that McDaniel sold the same for the benefit of complainant
til said quarter section can be divided and a final decree made It is
further ordered that Benjamin B. Conner and William Smith of Hamilton
County divide said quarter pursuant to this decree and the provisions of
an act entitled an act to dispose of the lands in Ocoa District and report to the next term of that a final decree maybbe rendered and it is
further decreed that defendant McDaniel pay the costs of this suit.

                              March term 1840

P-71
    Thompson Gardenhire   )   Be it remembered that at a chancery court
         vs   )   held at the court house in the twon of
    William McMurry   )   Pikeville and county of Bledsoe and state
    William R. Sheed and   )   of Tennessee and this the 11th day of
    George Bible   )   March 1840 before the Honorable Thos.
)   L. Williams Chancellor came on the above
P-72   case to be heard and determined up on
the bill and judgment Pro Confesso against the defendants and it appeared to the court that the consideration for which a note executes by a
complainant to defendants McMurry and Sheed and by them transferred to
defendant Bible had wholly failed If court thinks fit to order adjudge
and decree that the judgment recovered on said note in the circuit court
of Marion County Tennessee for the sum of fifty dollars Be perpetually
enjoined and that execution an said judgment and it is further ordered
adjudged and decreed that the defendant pay all costs of this suit at
law for which an execution may issue as at law.

P-72
    Joseph Martin   )   Be it that this case came on to be heard
         vs   )   upon bill and answer on motion to dissolve the
    George W. Rice   )   injunction when it appeared to the satisfact-
)   ion(when it appeared to the satisfaction ion)
)   of the court that the equity of complainants
bill was sufficiently answered where upon the court doth order that said
injinction be dissolved and it further appeared to the court that
Thompson Gardenhire and Edward Seabourn are securities in this injunction bond for complainant, There upon the court doth order adjudge and
decree that defendant recover against and his securities afore said the
sum of five hundred and forty eight dollars and ninety cents it being

P-72   the amount of the judgment and interest up to the 12th of March
1840 and that execution issue against the complainants and his said securities for the same as at law and it is further ordered abd decreed
P-73   that no execution issue on said judgment until the defendant
George W. Rice shall give bond with security to be approved of by   the
master to refund said money on the final hearing if it shall be   so
decreed.

March 1840

P-73

William Rice and	)	Be it remembered that this case came on
George W. Rice	)	to be heard before the Honorable Thomas
vs	)	S. Williams Chancellor by consent of both
Elijah C. Rice	)	parties up on bill and answer an this 11th
	)	day of March 1840 when it appeared to the

court that complainant became liable for
and have paid for John ᴿice the sum of 443.00 on the 13th day of August
1839 to John Mitchell Chairman as security of said John as Chairman of
the Sam Houston academy that said liability commenced on the 8th of January 1836 It further appeared that John Rice executed a mortgage on the
property mentioned in said deed to secure an indemnity complainant from
the liability John was permitted to keep the possession of said property

It further appeared that John departed this life in September 1839
intestate and that ᴱlijah administered on his estate in Nov. 1839 and
it appeared that defendant has possession of all of said property that
came to his hands since the death of John-but because it does not appear
to the satisfaction of the court whether the mortgage debt has been paid
by John or what the amount of said debt is- ᴵt is there fore ordered that
the clerk take and state on account of said dant and report by tomorrow
morning all other matters are reserved until the coming in of the report

P-74

Be it remembered that this case came on again to be heard on the
12th of March 1840 upon the report of the clerk and M. heretofore ordered in this case which is as follows towit-the clerk and master to whom
was referred to inquire what sums were due on the mortgage By leave to
report that from the note on file in this case there was $443.00 due 13th
of October 1839 down to this time being $10.05¢ making a balande due
of four hundred and fifty four dollars and five cents all of which is
respeoively sub-mitted and said report being unexcepted to is in all
things confirmed where upon the court thought fit order adjudge and decree
as it is ordered adjudged and decreed-That said mortgage be fore closed
by a sale of all the property contained in said mortgage after giving
twenty days notice of the time and place for cash at the residence of
said defendant Elijah and of said defendant that the proceeds be applied to the payment first of this ease in this suit expended and secondly to the payment of complainants debt of four hundred and fifty
four dollars and five cents and that John Cummons be appointed special
comissioner to sell said property and that he report to the next term
of this court what he has done.

March 10th 1840

P-74   March 10th 1840

William N. Gillespie)
&)
His wife Sidney Ann Gillespie)
vs)
John Locke & Peletiah Chilton)
Executers of William S. Lettey)
Deceased)
)

This 10th day of March 1840 came on this case to be finally heard and determined before the Honorable Thos. L. Williams Chancellar upon the coming in of the report of the clerk & master.

P-75

The report being unexcepted to is in all things confirmed from said report it appears that John Locke is entitled to the sum of nine hundred and seventy five dollars as compensation for services by him as executor bestowed on said estate beyond the receipt and disbursment of the monies belonging to said estate from February 1829 up to March 1840 and that the other executor Peletiah Chilton is entitled to the sum of four hundred and twenty five dollars for services by him rendered beyond the receipt and disbursments (p-75)of monies from the spring 1829 up to November 1834 at which time he is entitled to a credit on the two notes due from him to said estate five hundred and forty eight dollars and six cents being 2 1/2, per cent on the monies received and disbursed and also the sum of four hundred and twenty five dollars for services by him bestowed as aforesaid which would leave a balance of two hundred and ninjy five dollars due said Chilton after discharging the principal and interest of his said two notes up to November 1834.

It is therefore ordered adjudged and decreed by the court that the complainants bill be dismissed and that complainant pay one half of the costs in this suit expended and that the defendant John Locke and Peletibh Chilton pay the other half of the costs in this behalf expended for which execution may respectively issue as at law.

P-75

Thomas W. Spicer)
vs)
Thomas Sherley)
)

Be it remembered that this case came on again tombe heard upon the report of the clerk and master here ye fore ordered at the last term of this court and the same being seen and examined before exceptions

P-76 taken there to by both parties and the court not being satisfied there with the court thought fit to allow said exceptions and to revive the order of refinance made in this case at the last term of this court and the court doth hefe by direct the clerk and master to take additional proof up on the following items referred at the last term and none other that the parties produce all the books papers receipts notes and all other evidence in relation to the matters referred and that the deposition of William I° Standefer and the deposition of all the persons named in Sherlies last examination be produced before clerk and master and that the defendant Sherley be compelled to file the notes executed by Fields to the firm of Sherley and Spicer for improvement in the Cherokee Nation and that the clerk and master report there of at the next term of this court.

March term 1840

P-76

Nathan Sweat & others)
vs)
John & William Henson)

Upon exceptions being taken to the
answer of John Henson which being
heard and examined by the court It is
considered that all of said exceptions
are well taken It was there fore order-
ed by the court that the said defendant be compelled to file a full and
exceptions and that the defendants answer the matters of said exceptions
on or before the first Monday in June next or that said bill be taken as
confessed

March term 1840

P-77

John O. Thompson)
vs)
Brinkley Hornsby)

This day came the parties by their soliciters and the rule here to fore granted dissolve the injunction in the case being heard
and considered of by the court and it appearing to the satisfaction of the court that
equity in the bill is sufficiently answered It is therefore ordered adjudged and decreed that said injunction be dissolved and it is further o
ordered that the defendant have no execution up on this judgment at law
until he gave bond with sufficient suceuity to refund the amount of said
judgment at law with interest there on up on the final hearing should it
be so decreed.

March term

P-77

Joseph F. Reid and his wife)
James M. Reid))
vs)
James Loyd Gardner and co.)

Be it remembered that this case
came on to be heard and determined upon consent of both parties by their soliciters before
the Honorable Thos. L. Williams
Chancellor this the 11th day of
March 1840 when it appeared to the satisfaction of the court that David
Spring departed this life but before his death made and published his
last will and testament that he left a widow and four children that complainant Jane M. Spring was one of his divisens that he left the slaves
mentioned in the bill except those given his wife who is entitled to one
fifth of the slaves and land that the executors appointed by said will
have been removed that the defendant James Loyd has been appointed as-
minist4ator to the will annexed in place of those removed and that said
Loyd was appointed guardian of complainant Jane as well as the other
children that the defendant has possession of the property of said Jane
and the other children except what has been paid to the complainant Reid
P-78   and it further appeared that Reid intemarried with Jane some
twelve or fourteen months since that complainants have moved to the state
of North Carolina that complainant Reid is greatly in debt nearly enough to absorbe the whole amount of Janes estate both real and personal
that he has created debts and liabilities since his intermarriage with
Jane to the amount of near fifteen hundred dollars and that Janes estate
is not worth more than eighteen hundred dollars it further appeared that
defendant had paid to Reid all the personal estate he was entitled to and

P-78   ever paid him some thirty dollars that at the end of this year h
there would be twenty dollars coming to him and that complainant Reid
has sold his interest in the personal estate of Jane to B.R. Montgomery
for fifteen hundred dollars that Montgomery has paid three hundred   and
sixty seven dollars to said Reid and it further appeared that complainant Reid in order to enable said Montgomery to get possession of   the
slaves of complainant Jane executed a power of attorney to Alexander H.
Montgomery authorizing him against other things to sue for and receive
from defendant Loyd complainant Jane distributive share of her farthers
estate but because it does not appear with in the three hundred and sixty
dollars paid by B.R.Montgomery was applied to the benefit of complainant
Joseph is able and has property sufficient settle in complainant Jane a
like amount for her use and benefit and for the use of her children nor
does it appear that complainant Joseph ever propose to make a settlement
on Jane of property in equal value and quanity to her interest on   said
estate where upon the court thinks fit to order adjudged and decree that
the clerk and master inquire if said sum of money received of Montgomery
was expended to the use and support of complainant Jane and secondly that
he receive proposals from complainant Joseph as to his ability and
willingness to settle on complainant Jane an estate of like value   and
P-79   to her separate use and maintainance of that now belonging   to
said complainant Jane and and report thereof to the next term of this
court all other matters reserved until the coming in said report.

March term 1840

P-79

Asa Shelton)	Came the complainant by their s
&)	solicitor and it appearing from
Ralph Shelton)	the complainants bill that the
Administrator)	same had been filed under the
Landon A. Kincannon)	provisions of the act of as-
and the other creditors of)	sembly of the state of Tennessee
David A. Shelton Deceased)	passed the 26th of January 1838,
P-80)	in which they set forth the

assets of the estate in the
hands of the complainants are insufficient to pay the debts owing by deceased exceeds the value of five hundred dollars therefore on motion of
hte complainants by their counsel It ordered and decreed by the court
that publication be made for four successive weeks in the Knoxville
Register and Weekly Times a news paper published in the town of Knoxville
Tennessee requiring all persons interested or having claims against the
said estate to come in and exhibit the same and have themselves made
parties to said bill on or before the next term of this court to be held
at Pikeville on the 2nd Monday of September next or the bill will be
taken for confessed and the assets be distributed Pro rata.

P-80

Andrew Lowe)	Be it remembered that this case came
Samuel C. Lowe)	on to be heard and finally determined
John Kimmer and his)	upon the bill answer replication and
Wife Elizabeth)	profits in the case when it appeared
Moses Lowe Henry Sherrell)	to the satisfaction of the court

P-80

and his wife Rebecca and	)
John Lowe	)
vs	)
Anny Low & C.B.Hill	)
	)
	)

that the   obligations in complainants bill and proof there   on showed no grounds of releif for the complainants it was there fore ordered adjudged and   decreed by the court that the

complainants bill be dismissed and that the defendants go hence   discharged and recover of the complainants all costs in this behalf   expended for which an execution may issue at law.

P-80

Samuel B. Mead	)
vs	)
Samuel Prestly	)
William Jones &	)
James Prigmore	)
	)

This day came on the rule heretofore   entered (Page 81) to dissolve the injunction in this case ot be disposed of the bill and answer having been read and considered of by the court and because it appears to the court that the equity in the bill had been sufficiently answered it is ordered   adjudged and decreed by the court that said injunction be dissolved upon the defendant giving bond and sufficient security to refund the amount of the judgmane at law with interest there on on the final hearing if it shall be so decreed .

March term 1840

P-81

Eli Clevland	)
Thomas H. Calloway	)
vs	)
Thomas Sherley Luke Lea	)
& Pleasant M. R. Edwards	)
	)

This case coming on to be finally heard and determined before the Honorable Thomas L. Williams Chancellar presiding at Pikeville on this 13th day of March 1840 upon bill answer replication and proofs in said case and because

it appears to the chancellar that the complainants in this case have no interest in the land and it further appears to the satisfaction of the court that the respondant Thomas Sherley paid to the state of Tennessee on the entry taker seven dollars and fifty cents per acre and had entered the same before the complainants made any offer to or tender to enter said land and it further appeared to the satisfaction of the court that the complainant did not offer or tender to any more that seven dollars and fifty cents per acre and the Chancellor is therefore pleased to order adjudged and decree that the complainants bill be dismissed and that the complainants pay all the costs of this suit expended for which an   execution may issue as at law.

P-82   for which said decree the complainants prayed an appeal to the next term of the supreme court at Knoxville and to them it is granted without security for costs.

March term 1840

P-82

William N. Gillespie
and Wife
  vs
John Locke & Pelatiah Chilton
executors of William S. Lonty

)
)
)
)
)
)

This day came the complainants and prayed an appeal
in this case to the next term
of the surpreme court to be
held at Knoxville and to
 them it is granted upon
William N. Gillespie in

two months from this term entering into bond and security for costs.
Court adjourned until next term in course.

Thomas L. Williams

Monday September term 1840

P-82

Be it remembered that at a chancery court opened and held for the
eighth chancery district in the fourth division of Tennessee at the
court house in the town of Pikeville, on the second monday and fourteenth
day of September in the year of our Lord one thousand eight hundred and
forty- There was present on the bench The Honorable Thomas L. Williams
Chancellar & C.

P-82

George Brown
  vs
John Carnett Sr.
John Carnett Jr.
& James Russell

)
)
)
)
)
)

This day came the parties by their
solicitors and by the consent and with
the assent of the court this case is c
continued until the next term.

P-82

Thomas Sherley
  vs
Henry J. Williams
Edward H. Williams et. al.

)
)
)
)
)

This day came the parties by their
solicitors and by their consent
and with the assent of the court
this case is continued.

P-83

Anderson Skillern
John Skillern &
Henry Miller
  vs
James A. Whiteside
& Joseph G. Smith

)
)
)
)
)
)

This day came the parties by their solicitor and by their consent and with the
assent of the court this case is continued and remanded to the rules.

September Term 1840.

P-83

George W. & C.C. Trabue)
vs)
Butler and Rawlings)
)

This day came the parties by their solicitors and with the assent of the court this case is continued until the next term.

P-83

David Beck)
vs)
William Brown)
)

This day came the parties by their solicitors and it appearing to the satisfaction of the court from the report of the master filed in the case that no account has been taken . It is there fore ordered that the interlectury decree rendered at the last term ordering an account be revived and that the clerk and master proceed to take an account in said case according to the according to the directions of said decree and report thereof at the next term of this court.

P-83

Douglass & Wood)
vs)
Butler & Rawlings)
)

Came the parties by their solicitors and and by their consent and with the assent of the court this case is continued until the next term of this court.

P-83

Crutcher & Allison)
vs)
Butler & Rawlings)
)

Came the parties by their solicitors and b y their mutual consent and by the assent of the court this case is continued.

P-84

Ira D. Broyles and)
Benjamin Johnson)
vs)
William Garret)
&)
Holbert McClower)
)

Be it remembered that on this the 14th day of September 1840 came on this case to be heard and determined before the Honorable Thos. L. Williams Chancellar upon the bill and answers of the defend- when it appeared to the satisfaction of the court that the complainants are entitled to no releif. It is there fore ordered adjudged and decreed by the court that the complainants bill be dismissed and that the defendant go hence with out day and recover of the complainants all costs in the behalf expended for which execution may issue as at law.

P-84

Cyntha Tucker)
vs)
George Tucker)
and)
William McCoy)
)

Came James F. Bradford Esq. solicitor for the complainant and suggested the death of the complainant upon the rolls

Monday Sept. 1840

P-84

    Thomas Crutchfield)
          vs)
    John Vail)
)

Came the parties by their solicitors and by consent and with the assent of the court this case is continued and re-manded to the rules.

P-84

    Joseph Martkin)
          vs)
    George W. Rice)

Came the parties by their solicitors and by their consent and with the assent of the court this case is continued and remanded to the rules .

P-84

    Patience Reed)
          vs)
    David Reed)

Came the parties by their solicitors and by their mutual consent time is allowed the defendant until the third monday in Nov. next to file his answer in this case.

P-85

    Benjamin R. Inman)
          vs)
    William McDaniel)
          &)
    Eliza Kirkpatrick)

Came the parties by their solicitors and it appearing to the satisfaction of the court that no report has been made by the commissioners appointed to divide the land mentioned in the pleadings It is there fore ordered by the court that the order made in this case at the last term ofnthe court be revived and that the commissioners there in named proceed to divide the land mentioned in the pleadings according to the directions contained in the decree rendered at the last term of the court and report there of at the next term of this court.

P-85

    William Rice)
          &)
    George W. Rice)
          vs)
    Elijah C. Rice)

Came James P. Thompson solicitor for the complainants and suggested to the court the death of William Rice one of the complainants in this case.

P-85

    Elizabeth White &)
    the heirs of)
    James White)
          vs)
    Allen Kennedy)
    A.S. Lenoir &)
    R.A.Ramsey)

Came the parties by their counsel and this case is continued as an affidavits of the complainants .

P-85   September Term 1840

    Solomon P. Mitchhell   )
    Edward H. Travis   )   Bemit remembered that this case came on
        vs   )   to be finally heard and determined before
    John Moyer and   )   the Honorable Thos. L Williams Chancellar
    John Brown   )   on this the 14th day of September 1840
)   upon the bill answers and replication wh
    _____   when it appeared to the satisfaction oft
the court that the complainant had been the security fornthe defendant
John Moyer and liable as charged in said bill and it further appeared to
the satisfaction of the court that the judgment mentioned in said bill was
recovered by t e defendant John Moyer against Jeremiah Jones had amounted
to the sum of four hundred and ninty dollarshand sixty three cents and
that the sum of one hundred dollars had been honestly assigned to   Levi
Truhitt and seventy dollars of said judgment honestly assigned to
Solemon Pittichell leaving three hundred and twenty dollars and sixty
three cents assigned to respondent John Brown and that one hundred and th-
P-86   irty two dollars of said judgment so assigned was for a full
fair and valuable consideration leaving the sum of one hundred   and
eig ty eight dollars and sixty three cents for which there was no consideration given.The court is there fore is pleased to order adjudged and decree that the defendant John Brown pay into the office of clerk and master
of this court the said sum of one hundred and eighty eight dollars and
sixty three cents out of which the clerk and master shall first satisfy
the costs of this suit and the balance pay over to the satis action   of
the debt of the Latimores mentioned in the complainants bill recovered
against said complainants and the defendants John Moyer for which   said
sum of one hundred and eighty eight dollars and sixty three cents.   execution may issue at law.

P-86
    Benjamin R. Inman   )   Be it remembered that on this the 14th
        vs   )   day of September 1840 this case came
    Abraham Thomas   )   on to be finally heard and determined
)   before Chancellar Williams at Pikeville
    _____   in the state of Tennessee on the bill
answer replication and proofs and because it appears to the satisfaction
of the court that the matters in dispute between the parties touching a
division of a quarter section of land mentioned in complainants   bill
P-87   had been submitted to the arbitation of refferes and umpire and
that that an award w s duly made in the premises and which award is   un-
impeachable by proof .
    The court orders and decrees that the complainant is not entitled
to a   ------ of the said quarter section of land as prayed for in his
bill but that the parties hold respectivelt as awarded by the umpire
William R. Standefer in the division of said quarter section of land but
because it further appears to the satisfaction of the court from   said
award that the complainant is entitled to a decree against the defendant
for the sum of two hundred and eighty dollars being the amount,   over
paid by him entering the quarter section of land in said award specified.
It is therefore ordered and decreed by the court that the compalinant
have a decree against the defendant for that sum for which execution
may issue as at law nd that each party pay their own costs in   this

P-87   behalf expended for which execution may also respectively   as at
law.

P-87

Samuel Ballard	)
vs	)
John C. Everett	)
Erasmus Ally	)
Samuel L. Chum	)
&	)
William N. Gillespie	)
	)

Be it remembered this case came on
to be finally heard and determined
before the honorable Thos.   L.
Williams chancellar presiding at
Pikeville upon the original bill
crop bill answers and replication
there to the proof and report   of
the clerk and master being unexpected to is in all things confirmed a
and because it appears to the court from said report that the balance
between the complainant and the defendant amounts to the sum of sixty six
dollars and eighty seven cents in favor of the complainant.

It is there fore ordered adjudged and decreed by the court that the
P-88   respondant John C. Everett pay to the complainant the said sum
of sixty six dollars and eighty seven cents and pay the costs of the
original and cross bill and that if the same is not paid into the office
of the clerk and master that execution issue as at law.

P-88

William C. Wilson	)
vs	)
James Clepper	)
	)

Be it remembered that this case came
on to be finally heard and determined
before the Honorable Thos. L. Williams
Chancellar on this the 14th day of
September 1840 upon the bill answers
replication and proofs in the case and because it appears to the satisfaction of the court that the complainant is entitled to no relief   in
the premises It is there fore ordered and adjudged and decreed by the
court that the compalinant bill be dismissed and that the defendant   go
hence with out day and recever of the complainant all costs in this   behalf expended except the costs expended in taking testimony on part   of
the defendant and that the defendant pay said last mentioned costs for
all of which execution may respectively issue as at law.

P-88

Ephraim M. Evans	)
vs	)
Alexander H. Montgomery	)
&	)
Euphe P. Story	)
	)

Came the parties by their solicitors and by their mutual consent
time is allowed the defendants
until the third monday of November
next to file their answer in this
case.

P-89

Ralph Shelton	)
&	)
Asa Shelton	)
vs	)

Be it remembered that this case came on a-
gain to be heard before the Honorable Thos.
L. Williams Chancellar this 14th day of
September 1840 when it appeared to the
satisfaction of the court that replication

P-89

Landon A. Kenanon)
Abner B. Roberson)
& others)
)
_ _ _ _ _ _ _ _ _ _ _ _ _)

had been made according to the decretal
order made in the case at the last term
of the court notifying the creditors
of the said David S. Shelton to come
in and file their claims as directed by
law where upon the court thought fit to order and decree that the clerk
and master take and state an account of the assets of said estate personal as well as real if any that in taking said account he charge complainants with all assets which have come to their hands and credit them with
any and all advances made by them to other creditors of said estate also
all necessary expenses incurred in the case of their administration and
also a reasonable compensation for their trouble and labour in adminis-
tering said estate and that the clerk and master in taking said accounts
assertain the amount of debits due from said estate to others designating
to whom when due whether by note judgment or upon account or otherwise
and that the clerk and master report here of to the next term of this
court, all other matters reserved until the coming in of the report.

P-89

Alexander Kelly
          Administrator of David Oats

Petition Exparte

        Be it remembered that this case came on to be heard before   the
Honorable Thos. L. Williams Chancellar This the 14th day of September
1840 when it appeared from the petition of complainant and that on the
P-90   15th day of August 1834 David Oats was appointed by the supreme
court of errors and appeals to carry into effect the last will and testament of Eliphus M. Holt That David Oats gave bond and security and took
upon himself the execution of said trust that by said will the negroes
were devised in trust for the support and maintainance of Eliza M.
Campbell and her infant children Mary Jane Campbell and Margarett Ann
Campbell that David Oats obtained in his life time the following slaves
to wit Dick, Dinah, Letty, Failding, Richmond Caroline, Harrett Milly and
an infant named not now recollected . It further appeared from said petition that the said David in his life-time had made considerable disbursement in the discharge of the trust that he had received for the ——————
of said negroes for the year 1840 ending first of January 1841— that the
funds were much encumbered when said negroes came to his hands it further
appeared that expenses had been incurred such as medical bills & c whilst
David was in the discharge of said trust That David died some two years
since that complainant is his surviving administrator that petitioner
has received said negroes since the death of David and it further appears
that Daniel R. Rawlings is a competent person to be appointed in the room
and stead of the said David to represent the interest of the said Eliza
and the children it further appears that David has never settled for the
monies advanced and expenses incurred nor accounted for the hire of said
negroes with any person where upon the court thought fit to order   adjudged and decree that the clerk and master take and state an account of
all monies advanced by said David in executing said trust also also   the
expenses incurred and likewise make all just allowances for compensation

and trouble to said David and also to complainant and that the clerk
charge said David with the hire received of or by reason of his   duty
as trustee and that the said David R. Rawlings be made a defendant   provided he is willing to take upon himself the duties of a trustee in place
P-91   of said David and that he superintend the taking of his account
and that the clerk and master in taking said account charge petetieners
interest with all such sums as he has received or might have received and
credit him with all reasonable disbursements incurred in the discharge
of the trusts and report hereof at the next term all other matters reserved until the coming in of the report.

P-91

Juball Dixon) Be it remembered that this case came on
vs) to be heard and determined upon this the
William S. Hall) 14th day of September 1840 before   the
) Honorable Thos. L. Williams Chancellar up
-----------------------) on the bill taken pro-confesso against

the defendant when it appeared to the satisfaction of the court that the
complainant sold to defendant the said several tracts of land mentioned
in the pleadings for the sum of four hundred and twenty five dollars which
sum is due and unpaid that said sum fell due on the 10th of January 1839
and that the complainant conveyed said lands to the defendant where up on
the court thinks fit to order adjudge and decree the clerk and Master expense to public Sale said several trac s of alnd upon a credit of one and
two years after having advertised the time and place of said sale at least
forty day s the purchaser giving bond and security for the p urshase mony
of and a lieu retained on said lands for the same and and that where said
purchase money is paid the clerk and master to make a legal deed or transfer to the purchaser and that the costs of this suit be paid by the complainant in the first instance and hv have execution over against the
defendant and that the clerk and master report here of at the next term
of this court all other matters reserved until the coming in of said report.

P-91

Thomas W. Spicer) Be it remembered that this case came on
vs) again to be heard before the Honorable
Thomas Sherley) Thos. L. Williams chancellor on this the
) 14th day of Sep ember 1840 upon the report
-----------------------) of the clerk and master here to fore order-

ed to be made which report being unaccepted to The same is in all things
confirmed where it appeared to the satisfaction of the court that the def
endant Thomas Sherley has retained and has in his hands the sum of thirte
teenth hundred and thirty two dollars and eighteen cents of the partnership effects over and above his share of the profits and that said sum
P-92   should have been paid to complainant on the 3rd day of August 1836
and it further appeared that the defendant has failed to file the claims
on the Indians being partnersh ip effects amounting to about the sum of
thirteen hundred do lars where up on the court thinks fit to order adjudge and decree and it is accordinly ordered adjudged and decreed that

P-92

September 1840

the complainant recover of the defendant the said sum of thirteen hundred
thirty two dollars and eighteen cents together with the interest there on
from the 3rd day of August 1836 the time fo filing the bill up to this
time It being about the sum of three hundred and twenty four dollars and
twenty four cents making in all the sum of sixteen hundred and fifty
eight dollars and fortys two cents, subject to a credit of three hundred
and fifty dollars here to fore paid by the defendant, and it is further
ordered that the defendant pay the costs of this suit and that the complainant have his execution for the aforesaid sum and the costs in this
behalf expended as at law.

P-93

Joseph F. Reid and
Clarinda Jane his wife
vs
James Loyd

Be it remembered that this case came
on again to be heard before the honor
able Thos. L. Williams Chancellor up
on this 14th day of September 1840
up on the report of the clerk and mas-
tor here to fore ordered in this case
which is in all things confirmed except as to the money advanced by Montgomery when it appeared to the satisfaction of the court that the complain-
and Joseph F. Reid is wholly unable to make a complainant settlement upon
his wife Jane in liew of her estate that Jane is in destitute circumstances
and it further appeared that complainant Jane in person asks of this cout
to settle upon her self the estate devised to her by her father by the
intervention of a trustee. Which estate consists of aportion of the negroes in the pleadings mentioned and lands and it further appeared that
complainant Jane is desirious to file a cross bill in this case in order
to have her estate up on her self for her own use and that of her children and to be in no wise under the controle of complainant Joseph F. and
that said negroes be divided and that the tract of land be sold or par-
titioned as will best subsence the interest of all the devises in said h
hire and it further appeared that complainant Joseph F. is an improvident
man and not fit to have the management of said property where upon the
court thinks fit to order and decree that the defendant James Loyd have
the possession of said negroes, till the further order of this court and
it is further ordered and decreed that the assignment made to B. R. Montgomery by complainant Joseph F. be declared void and of none effect and e
because it does not appear whether the amount advanced by B. R. Montgomery
was applied to the support and maintainance of Jane It is ordered that the
P-94 master inquire as to that facg and report there of to the next term
and it is further ordered that complainant Jane be allowed to file her
cross bill in order to a partition or sale of said land and for the
purposes of taking an account with defendant Jasper Loyd and for the purpose of selling her estate and her for the use of herself and children
and it is further ordered that the defendant James pay to the complainant Jane the sum of fifty dollars for the purpose of her support for
the next six months in such way and at such times as her necessities may
demand all other matters are reserved until the coming in of said report

September term 1840

P-94

Camelia Billingsley	)
vs	)
John M. Billingsley	)
	)

This day came the parties in proper person and produced to the court a written agreement comprimising this suit which is in the words and figures following towit Pikeville July 30th 1840 Know all men by these presents that we Camelia Billingsley and John M. Billingsley hereby mutually agree to compromise a certain suit in equity now pending in the district chancery court held at Pikeville upon the following terms towit I the said Camelia Billingsley being the complainant in said suit do hereby agree to dismiss said suit at the September term 1840 of said court, And I the said John M. Billingsley being the defendant in said suit do hereby agree to pay costs of said suit expended. In testimony hwere of we have hereunto set our hands this day and date above written.

Test:

    Thos. N. Frazier
    Clerk and Master

                                        Camelia Billingsley
                                        John Billingsley

It is therefore ordered and decreed by the court that said suit be dismissed and that the defendant John M. Billingsley pay the costs in this be half expended for which execution may issue as at law.

P-95

Stephen Jones	)
vs	)
Nehemiah McGee	)
Wyly Bell McGee et al.	)
	)

This day came ch the defendants Nehemiah McGee and Wyly Bell McGee demurrer to the complainants bill It is there fore ordered adjudged and decreed that the defendants Demurrer be ever ruled and on motion the defendants are permitted to file their answer.

P-95

Benjamin R. Montgomery	)
vs	)
Joseph G. Smith	)
	)

Be it remembered that this case came on to be heard upon the bill and answer and on a motion to dissolve the injunction in this case and because it appeared to the satisfaction of the court that the equity of the complainants bill is sufficiently answered. It is there fore ordered adjudged and decreed by the court that said injunction be dissolved and it further appearing to the satisfaction of the court that Thomas Sherley is security for the complainant in the injunction.

It is therefore ordered adjudged and decreed by the court that the defendant recover of the compalinant and his security aforesaid the sum of sixty two dollars and eighty eight cents it being the balance due on the original judgment enjoined and interedt there on up to date the 14th of Sept. 1840. For which asid sum execution may issue against the complainant and his said security as at law and it further ordered that no

P-95   execution issue on said judgment until the defendant Joseph   G.
Smith give bond with approved security to refund said money on the final
hearing if the same shall be so decreed on the final hearing.

P-96

   John O. Thompson   )
        vs   )
   Brinkley Hornsby   )
)

Be it remembered that this came on to be
finally heard and determined on the 14th
of Sept. 1840 before the Honorable Thos.
L. Williams Chancellor upon bill answer
replication and proofs in the case and be-
cause it appears to the satisfaction of the court that the complainant is
entitled to the relief prayed for in his bill and that there was a mistake
as to the hundred dollars having been advanced by the defendant as charged
in the bill. It is therefore ordered adjudged and decreed by the court
that that the defendant Brinkley Hornsby and John Holland and   John
Pardee the securities to the refunding bond pay to the complainant   the
sum of one hundred dollars toget er with the interest there on from the
26th day of Aprile 1839 the time at which judgment complained of was rendered before the justice up,until the time the same shall be paid and that
the complainant have his execution for the same as at law and it is further
ordered ans decreed by the court that the complainant and defendant each
pay his own costs in this behalf expended for which execution may respectively issue as at law - From which said decree The defendant by his solicitor prays an appeal to the next term of the supreme court to be held
at Knoxville and the same is allowed him upon the defendant giving   bond
with approved security to prosecute said appeal with effect or in case be
fail to pay the costs and perform the conditions of this decree within
one month from the adjournment of this court.

September 1840

P-96

   Thomas W. Spicer   )
        vs   )
   Thomas Sherley   )
)

Came the parties by their solicitor and
it is ordered by the court that the defendant file with the clerk and master of th
this court that all the books notes and
vouchers in any wise touching and the
P-97   defendant by his solicitor prays an appeal from the decree rendered in this case to the next term of the supreme court at Knoxville and
the same is allowed him upon the defendant giving bond with approved security to prosecute said appeal . On or before the 15th of November next.
And then the court adjourned until court in course.

Thos. L. Williams

P-97

Monday March 1841
Be it remembered that at a chancery court opened and held for the
eighth chancery district in the fourth division of Tennessee at the Court
house in the town of Pikeville on the second Monday and eighth day   of

P-97   March in the year of our lLord one thousand eight hundred and
forty one There was present on the bench the Honorable Broomfield L.
Ridley Chancellar & C.

March 1841

P-97

George W. & C.C. Trabue)
        vs   )
Butler & Rawlings   )
)
------------------------)

Came the parties b their solici-
ors and by their consent and with
the assent of the court this case
is continued until the next term
of this court.

P-97

Thomas Sherley   )
        vs   )
Henry J. Williams   )
Edward H. Williams et al.)
)
------------------------)

Came the parties by their soliciters and by their consent and
 with the assent of the court this
case is continued until the next
term of the court.

P 98

Benjamin R. Inman   )
        vs   )
William McDaniel   )
& Eliza Kirkpatrick   )
)
------------------------)

Be it remembered that on this eighth
day of march 1841 came on the above case
for final decree before the honorable
Broomfield L. Ridley Chancellar upon
the report of the commissioners here
to fore appointed in this case - From
said report it appears said commissioners on the first of January 1841
divided the south west quarter of section twenty one in the fourth township in range second west of the basis line in the Ocea District and assigned to complainant forty acres there of by running a paralel line   .
south seventy degrees east commencing south twent degrees west   forty
poles from from the north west corner of said quarter section to a Black
Gum on the western boundry line forty poles from the north east corner of
said quarter section including his dqelling house said report being unexpe
pected to is in all things confirmed - It is there fore ordered and decreed by the court that hte legal title and right of defendants and each
of them be divested as to said forty acres and be vested in compdainant
and his heirs for ever in fee . It is further ordered that compalinant with
in cone month from this time pay into the office of the clerk and master
of this court from hundred dollars for the use of defendant McDaniel and
if not paid that an execution issue there fore and it is also ordered that
an execution issue against defendant McDaniel for the costs of this case.

March 1841

P-98

Douglass & Wood   )
        vs   )
Butler & Rawlings   ·)
)
------------------------)

Came on the parties by their soliciters and by their consent and with the
assent of the court this case is   continued until the next term of this court.

P-99

John Skillern　　　　　　　)
Anderson Skillern　　　　　)
　　　　vs　　　　　　　　　)
Joseph G. Smith　　　　　　)
　　　　&　　　　　　　　　　)
James A. Whiteside　　　　)
　　　　　　　　　　　　　　　)

Came the parties by their solicitors and by their consent and with　the assent of the court this case is continued and remanded to the rules for four months.

P-99

James Kenney &　　　　　　)
William Gardenhire　　　　)
　　　　vs　　　　　　　　　)
George W. Williams　　　　)
Nathan Shipley et al.　　)
　　　　　　　　　　　　　　　)

This day came Spencer Journajin solicitor for complainants and suggested the death of William Gardenhire one of the complainants upon the rolls and the same was not denied by the defendants.

P-99

Stephen Jones　　　　　　　)
　　　　vs　　　　　　　　　)
Luke Lea. William Agee　　)
Wiley B. McGee　　　　　　　)
　　　　&　　　　　　　　　　)
John B. Lupton　　　　　　　)
　　　　　　　　　　　　　　　)

Came the parties by their solicitors and produced in open court a written agreement between said parties authorizing the above case to be transfered to the district chancery court held at Clevland and there upon motion of said parties by their said solicitors- It is ordered by

the court that the clerk and master of this court transfer all the original papers together with afull transcript of the rules and orders had in this case in this court to the district chancery court to be held in the County of Bradley at the court house in Clevland on the second Monday of September next.

March 1841

P-99

Crutcher & Allison　　　　)
　　　　vs　　　　　　　　　)
Butler & Rawlings　　　　　)
　　　　　　　　　　　　　　　)

Came the parties by their solicitors and by their consent and with the assent of the court this case is continued.

P-100

And the court adjourned until tomorrow morning 8 oclock.

Broomfield Ridley

P-100

Court met persuant to adjournment- present on the bench the Honorable Broomfield L. Ridley Chancellar & C.

March term 1840.

P-100   March 9th, 1841

Benjamin F. Bridgman   )   Divorce
         vs   )   Be it remembered that on this 9th day
Narcissa F. Bridgman   )   of March 1841 came on this case to
)   be finally heard and determined be-
_____   )   fore the honorable Broomfield L.

Ridley Chancellar & C upon the bill taken for confessed against the defendant and the proofs in the case that the complainant and defendant
were married some time in the year 1830 and that afterward in the year
1831 the defendant wilfully deserted the bed and board of the complainant
that the defendant was guilty of Adultry with a certain Anderson Whiteside
and that she bore by said Whiteside two children one of which she called
James Bradford and the other Anderson Whiteside that said children were
the illigimate offspring of the said defendant and the said Anderson
Whiteside that the said Whiteside has since departed this life that the
complainant had chastly and properly demeande himself since the separation
where upon the court thinks fit to order adjudged and decree that the
bonds of matrimony here to fore existing between the complainant Benjamin
F. Bridgman and the defendant Narcissa F. Bridgman he and the same are here
by perpetually disolved and it is further ordered adjudged and decreed by
the court that the complainant pay the costs in the prosecution of   this
P-101   suit expended in the first istance and that he have judgment a-
gainst the defendant for the same and that execution may issue for said
costs as at law.

P-101
    David Beck   )   This day came the parties by their solici-
        vs   )   tors and it appear ing to the satisfaction
    William Brown   )   of the courtnfrom the report of the master
)   filed in this case that no account had been
    _____   )   made or taken in this case as required   by
an interloctury decree here to fore rendered in this case It is therefore
ordered by the court upon the motion of the complainant by his solicitor
that the interloctury decree rendered in this case at the March term 1840
ordering an account be remined and that the clerk and master precede to
open and state an account in said case according to the directions   of
said decree and report hereof at the next term of this court .

                        March 1841

P-101
    Nathan Sweat and others   )   Came the parties by their solicitor
            vs   )   and from reasons appearing to the sat-
    John & William Henson   )   isfaction of the court this case is
)   continued and remanded to the rules
    _____)   for four months.

P-101
    James L. Schoolfield   )   This day came the complainants by
    & James P. Spring   )   their solicitor James P. Thompson
            vs   )   and directed their bill to be dis-
    Alexander H. Montgomery   )   missed It is thereofre orderedad-
    & Joseph F. Reid_____)   judged and decreed by the court

P-101 that the bill be dismissed and that the defendant go hence there
of discharged and recover of the complainant all costs in this behalf ex-
P-102 pended for which an execution may issue as at law.

P-102
G & S. Williams) Came the parties by their solicitors and on
vs) motion of the complainants time is allowed x
John Brown) until the May rules 1841 to file a bill of
) revireor in this case.

P-102
James Rankin)
surviving partner of) Came the parties by their solicitor
Rankin & Roberson) and on motion of the complainant by
vs) his said solicitor this case is con-
John K. Tate) tinued and remanded to the rules and
&) it appearing to the satisfaction of
Littleberry Stone) of the court from the Allegatives
) in the bill that Littleberry Stone
) one of the defendants is not an
inhabitant of this state It is there fore ordered by the court that publication be made in Central Gazette a news paper published in the town
of McMinnville and state of Tennessee for six successive weeks requiring
the said defendant to appear at the next term of the court to be held at
the court house in Pikeville in the second Monday of September next and
answer the bill or the same will be taken for confessed and set for
hearing en- parte as to him.

P-102
Amy Lowe) Be it remembered that this case came on
vs) to be finally heard and determined before
James Ormes) the honorable Broomfield L. Ridley ch an-
&) cellar upon the bill and when it appeared
Andrew Lowe) to the court that the object of the bill
) had been fully attained It is there fore
) ordered adjudged and decreed by the court
P-203 that the bill be dismissed and that the defendants pay the costs
in this behalf expended for which an execution may issue as at law.

P-103
David Rankin) This day came James P. Thompson Esq.
vs) solicitor for the complainant and
Alexander W. Coulston) suggested the death of the defendant
&) William Wilson upon the rolls and the
William Wilson) same was not denied and by consent
) of the parties by their solicitors
it is agreed that this case be revi-
ved against Charles Coulston executer of William Wilson and that this
suit be prosecuted against the said Charles Coulston and Alexander W.

P-103   Caulston and that the defendant have until the next term of this
court to file their answer.

March Term 1841

P-103

        George Brown   )   This day came Spencer Journajin solicitor
             vs   )   for the defendant and suggested the death
        Mary Carnett   )   of Mary Carnett one of the defendants
        John Carnett Sr.   )   on the rolls and the same was not denied.
        John Carnett Jr.   )
             &   )
        James Russell   )
        _____   )

P-103

        This day came R.B.Roberson into open court as was duly qualified as a
practicing attorney in this court.

P-103

        Joseph F. Read &   )   This case being opened this the
        Jane Read his wife   )   9th day of March 1841 before
             vs   )   the Honorable B.L.Ridley chan-
        James Loyd &   )   cellar by consent of parties the
        Clarinda Jane Read   )   court is pleased to make an
        By her next Friend   )   P-104   interlocutory order and
        Eli Thurman,   )   does order and decree that the
             vs   ))   clerk of this court state an
        Cross bill   )   account showing the amount   of
        James Loyd and others   )   the estate of David Spring de-
)   ceased that has come to the
        _____   )   hands of said James Loyd either
as administrator on the estate of said Spring or as guardian of his
children including the rent of the real estate and hire of the slaves also
showing the amount of disbursements made for and on account of the estate
both real and personal of said David Spring up to the time of stating
said account also showing what amount said Loyd has paid for the use of
the children of said Spring and how much he has advanced to either of them
and when and said clerk further ascertain and report what would be reasonable compensation to said Loyd for trouble for trouble and expense if any
aside from the per cent usually allowed in such cases growing out of the
peculiar circumstances of thiscase that he also report the number of
slaves belonging to said estate and how many thereof designating them by
name will be the distribution share of said Claranda Jane Read the   girl
Amy and it is now ordered that said girl Amy be sold by said Loyd either
at public or private sale as he may choose he accounting for the proceeds
of such sale . It is further ordered and decreed by the court that Samuel
McReynolds Pleasant Vernon and William Foster be and are hereby appointed
commissioners to designate and lay off the share of the said Clarinda
Jane Read of the real estate of said David Spring deceased and report to
the next term of this court so that a trustee may be appointed and the

P-104   title to said land vested in such trustee for the use of the said
Clarinda Jane Read.

March   1841

P-104

Samuel B. Mead   )
        vs   )
Martin Wyrick   )
William Stone   )
Burgess Mathhews et al.   )
)
_ _ _ _ _ _ _ _ _ _ _ _ _ _ _ _ _)

Came on the defendants by the solicitors and moved the court to
dismiss the complainants bill for
want of procedure and it appearing
to the satisfaction of the court
that two terms had elapsed without
any steps having been taken in

said case It is ordered by the court that said hire be dismissed and there
upon came the complainant and for reasons appearing to the satisfaction of
the court from the affidavit of said complainant it is ordered by the
court that this case be reinstalled upon the docket and that complainant
be permitted to file his bill of revive in the case which was done.

P-105

Alexander H. Montgomery and   )
Ephraim Pl Story Administrator   )
of Samuel Story deceased   )
        vs   )
The Planters Bank of Tennessee   )
and others   )
)
_ _ _ _ _ _ _ _ _ _ _ _ _ _ _ _ _ _ _)

It is ordered in this case
that James A. Tullas be
and is appointed guardian
to answer for Mary Story,
Emily Story and Lavinia
Story and Matilda A. Story
infant children of Samuel L
Story deceased in this case

and who has filed his answer as such- It is ordered that the inquisition in
this case be disposed so as to allow Jane Story exparte at law and report
the judgments he has.

P-105

Ephriam P. Story   )
administrator of   )
Samuel L. Story   )
        vs   )
The Planters bank   )
of Tennessee James Loyd   )
and others   )
)
_ _ _ _ _ _ _ _ _ _ _ _ _ _)

Be it remembered that this case came
on to be heard before the Honorable
B. L. Ridley Chanceller and C. this
the 10th day of March 1841 when it
appeared to the satisfaction of the
court that publication had been made
as dircted by the actof assembly in
such case made and provided so as to
include the minor hairs and it further

appearing to the court that complainant Ephriam Pl Story., had not been
endowed of the lands tenements and houses of which her husband died
scurzed and possessed where upon the court thought fit to order and decree
that the clerk and master take and state an account of the assets belonging to said estate and that David F. Cook S cott Terry and Eli Thurman
be appointed to assign and set apart to said Ephraim her dower in the
real estate mentioned in said hill according to the rule and act of
assembly and make report that they have cone to the next term of this
court and also that the clerk and master report to the next term of this
court all other matters being reserved until the coming in of the report

P-105   as above directed.

March 9th 1841

P-105
    Alexander Kelly Administrator of
    David Oats deceased
    Ex partis
P-106
    B. it remembered that this case came in to be heard before the Hon-
orable B.L. Ridley chancellar counsil when it appeared to the court that
Daniel R. Rawlings appointed trustee of Elizabeth Campbell and her infant
children mentioned in a former interlectury decree had not accepted said
trust nor filed his answer It is ordered by the court that the decreable
order made in this case at the last term be revived and and continued in
order that said Rawlings may come in and accept same and file his answer.
    And the court adjourned until tomorrow morning 8 oclock.

                                                        Broomfield Ridley

P-106   Wed. 10 March 1841

    Court met pursuant to adjournment present on the bench the Honorable
B.L. Ridley Chancellar & C.

P-106
    Benjamin Cendra   )   Decree
        vs   )   This the 10th day of March 1841 came on this
    John Medley   )   case for hearing upon the bill and answers
    _ _ _ _ _ _ _ _ _ _)   before the Honorable B. L. Ridley Chance-
                             ller when it appeared to the satisfaction
                             of the court that in the year 1826 complain-
ant purchased of one Richard Medley two tracts of land one of forty acres
and one of one hundred acres and paid him and paid him the sum of   two
hundred and twenty eight dollars and executed to him three several notes
under seal dated the 2nd of December 1826 the part due and payable   the
25th of December 1828 for one hundred and sixty one dollars That complainant paid part of said notes that some time after this purchase said Richard Medley died having never had any title to the land he sold to   said
complainant That same year after the death of said Richard Medley defendant John Medley was appointed his administrator and in that character
received in the circuit court for Marion County three judgments upon said
P-107   notes, or for the balance due there on against complainant at
the November term 1839 of said circuit court One for the sum of two hundred and one dollars and seventy six cents for debt damages and costs. One
other for two hundred and seventy four dollars and fifty eight cents for
debt damages and costs and the third for the sum of thirty nine dollars
and ninety cents for debt damages and costs. The aforesaid notes appear to
have been given for said tracts of land upon the foregoing facts the court
is pleased to order and does order and decree that the aforesaid   John
Medley be and is hereby enjoined from proceeding upon said judgment

P-107   recovered by him as administrator and that the same be perpetually enjoined and that the saiddefendant pay the costs of this case and
also the costs of the suit at law to be levied of any assets in his hand
as administrator of Richard Medley deceased.

P-107
     Michael R. Allen   ) Be it remembered that on this 9th
              vs   ) day of March 1841 this came on to
     A.S. Lenior, R.A. Ramsey   ) be heard and delivered before the
     Allen Kennedy & Others   ) Honorable Broomfield L. Ridley
) Chancellor & C upon the bill ans-
     -------------------------------) wered replication and proof in the
case and because itmappears to thwsatisfaction of the court that the complainant was not an occupant with in the perview and meaning of the act to
dispose of the vacant and unappropiated lands in the Ocoee (Ocoee) district
not until the relief prayed for in the bill it is there fore ordered adjudged and decreed that the bill be dismissed and that the complainant pay
the costs of this case for which an execution may issue as at law.

P-108
     Ruth Shelton & Asa Shelton Administrator   )   Interlocutory
     of the estate of David Shelton deceased   )   Decree
              vs   )   B. it remember-
     Abner B. Robinson, Landen A. Kincannon etal.)   ed that on the
)   10th day   of
     ---)   March 1841 this
case came on to be further heard before the Honorable Broomfield L. Ridley
Chancellor & C upon exception filed to the report of the clerk and master
to this term of the court when it was divided by the court the exceptions
taken to the allowance made the complainant for the payment of $,280
P-108   Temperance Shelton the payment of $ 100. to Erasmus Alley of $35
to Isaac Hale the items marked David B. in the report for incoherent debts
which could not be collected and the allowance to administrators the complainant for insolvencies in he hands of Griffin for $ 488-61 cents and
claim stated to be collected on judgment against Griffin and his securities of $ 85.66 and claim against G.W. Rice for $ 82.00 be allowed as
exceptions properly taken and that said report with regard to said items
be recommitted to the clerk and master with instructions to take and require proof in regard to said items of payment and insolvency and not to
allow the same unless proved and not to allow the said item of $ 280
paid to Temperance Shelton unless it be proved that the same was actually
paid and that said debt was really contracted and that he shall report
what he shall have done together with the proof to the nest term of this
court and the --------- fe the report is duly confirmed.

P-108
     Joseph Martin   )
          vs   )   Be it remembered that on the 10th day of
     George W. Rice   )   March 1841 this case came on to be further
)   heard upon motion of defendants solicitor
     -----------------)   to dissolve the injunction on the face of
the complainants amended bill last filed from matters apparent on the

P-108   March 10th 1841

face of the sum where upon agreement of solicitor on both sides the court
was pleased to ordered adjudged and decrees that the said injunction   be
dissolved and that the said George W.,Rice have judgment against the
complainant Joseph Martin for the balance of the judgment heretofore rendered by a decree of this court on the 12th day of March 1840 for   five
hundred dollars and forty eight dollars and ninety cents on which has been
paid the sum of one hundred and forty three dollars and fifty six cents
with interest up to this day the amount of said balance of judgment with
said interest up to twenty nine dollars and thirty four cents & on motion
of the said George W. Rice by his solicitor It is also ordered adjudged
and decreed that said George W. Rice recover have decree and judgment of h
this court for said sum of four hundred and twenty nine dollars and thirty
five cents against the said Joseph Martin and also jointly against him
and Thompson Gardenhire, James M. Carroll and Edward B. Holloway   the
P-109   securities of the said Joseph Martin in the injunction bond and
that executed as at law issue jointly against the said Joseph Martin and
his said securities for the said sum of money upon the said Geo. W. Rice
giving bond to refund according to law.

P-109

     Elizabeth White widow and John M. Hamon   )   This the 10th day
     & his wife Jane. Elanor White, Henry Hamon   )   of March 1841
     & Ann Eliza his wife, Wm. C. White   )   This case came on
     Thomas W. White, Alexander White, Wilton   )   for final hearing
     White, Addison White, and Newton   )   upon bill answer
     White heirs at law of James White   )   replication and
     deceased   )   proofs before the
)   Honorable B. L.
              vs   )   Ridley Chancellor
)   all of which being
     Allen Kennedy, Albert S. Lenior   )   read heard and
     & Reynolds A. Ramsey   )   understood   by
)   the court and
     --- _)

agreement of counsel made it appears to the court propper? in this case
to make a reference to the clerk and master,
     It is therefore ordered and decreed that this case be referred to
the master to ascertain from the proofs on file and any others party may
produce before him what persons were in actual possession and residing up
on the south East fractional quarter of section twenty in the second
fractional township fourth range west of the basis line in the Ocoee district at the time of the survey of the lands in said district besides
Sparks & Legg mentioned in the pleadings who they were and how long they
remained there and which of them assigned and transfered their right   of
prefference to defendant Kennedy, Lenior and Ramsey upon which the entry
has been made by said defendant It is ordered by the court that the award
set up by defendants be set aside and on the coming in of the report here
directed the court will appoint commissioners to partition the   land named
in the pleadings amongst complainant and those who were joint occupants w

P-109   with their assignees at the time of the survey and who continued
upon the same and were in possission at the passage of the law to dispose
of the land in the Ocoee District whose right, and interest in the entry
P-110   and grant of defendants all other matters are reserved until
final hearing.

P-110

Patience Read by)
her next friend)
    vs   )
David Read   )
)
_ _ _ _ _ _ _ _ _)

This day came the compleinant by her at-
terney and dismiss her bill and there upon
came the defendant David Read into open court
in his own proper person and confessed judgment for all costs. It is there fore orderd
and decreed by the court that the defendant
pay the costs in this case expended for which an execution may issue.

P-110

John Horn   )
    vs   )
Joseph G. Smith)
)
_ _ _ _ _ _ _ _ _)

This day came on the compiainant exception to the defendants answer to be heard
and delivered upon an appeal from the de-
cision of the clerk and master there on a
and after argument council and delibera-
tion of the court had there on - It is considered by the court that the
said exceptions are well taken and it is further ordered by the court that
the defendant file a sufficient answer in this case with in two months.

P-110
    Be it remembered that new at the March term of Chancery Court at
Pikeville Thomas N. Frazier tendered to the court his resignation as Clerk
and Master of said Court which was accepted b y the chancellor here upon
the court thought fit to appoint and does appoint Alexander H. Montgomery
who came into court took the several oaths prescribed by law and received
of Thomas N. Frazier his predecesser all the books memoranda and papers
belonging to said office of clerk and master said Alexander Montgomery tendered to the court the here following bond which were accepted by the
P-111   chancellor and the several obligaraxxx there to i.e. A.H. Montgomery Daniel F. Cooke Jeremiah Dorsey, James A. Tullas and Bird Thomas
having severally in open court acknowledged the signature to each bond to
be their respective act and deed for the purpose there in expressed the
same was ordered to be entered of record on the minutes of the court said
bond in the words and figures following.
    i.e.

    Know all men by these presents that we A.H. Montgomery, Daniel F.
Cooke, Jeremiah Dorsey, James A. Tullas Bird Thomas are held and firmly
bound unto James K. Polk Governer of and over the state of Tennessee and
his successer in office in the sum of one thousand dollars the payment of
which will and truly be made and done and we bind ourselves our heirs and
executors and administrators jointly and severally by these presents
signed with our names sealed with our seals - This the 10th day of March
1841.

P-188

John Kelly)
vs)
Barby D. McClure)
& Nathan Shipley)
William P. Shipley)
& James Roddy)
)

On motion of by his soliditors leave
is granted to take the depositions of
the defendants Nathan Shipley and
James Roddy saving all legal exceptions and the death of defendant William
P. Shipley is suggested which is not
denied.

P-189

James Loyd)
vs)
David H. Spring & Others)
)

This day came the parties by their
solicitors and by their consent
and with the assent of the court
this case is continued and remanded
to the rules.

Court adjourned until tomorrow morning 8 oclock.

Broomfield Ridley

Court met pursuant to adjournment present on the bench the Honorable
B.L. Ridley Chancellor & C.

P-189

John P. Long)
vs)
Calvin McChandain)
Isaac Rainey)
James Park &)
William Park)
)

This day came the complainant by his
solicitor and on his motion the complainants bill is dismissed and the
court is pleased to order adjudged a
and decree that the respondent recover of the complainant the costs in
this case for which an execution may
issue at law.

P-189

Mary Bell by)
her next friend)
Wm. Gibbons)
vs))
Isaac Benson &)
Others)
)

Be it remembered that on this the 12th
day of September 1843 came on this
case before the Honorable B.L. Ridley
chancellor for an interloctury order
and distinctions- It appeared to the
satisfaction of the chancellor that
complainant claims an interest in two
notes on defendant Stephen I. Godsey

extended by him to the defendant Isaac Benson and by him transfered to
defendant Haggard Bean upon one of said notes defendant Beam recovered a
judgment on the 14th of May 1842 for the sum of one hundred and thirty
P-190 dollars sixty one and a fourth cents and execution stayed by
William Gibbons on the other note Godsey confessed a judgment on the 18th
of June 1842. for one hundred and twenty five dollars and fifty cents the
collection of said judgments had been enjoined in this case by means

Sept. 1843

P-190

where of it is apprehended as may accrue upon these facts the court is
pleased to order and decree that the amount of said judgment with the accruing interest be paid to the clerk of this court for the further order
and desposition of the court that the clerk issue to defendants Godsey
notice to pay said judgments and interest to him and after service of xx
said notice if not paid in thirty days that the clerk and master   issue
executions for the collection thereof returnable to the next term an   a-
gainst Godsey and stay on William Gibbons and the other against Godsey
alone said monies when collected to await the further order of the court.

P-190

Henry Griffith)	Be it remembered that on this the
vs)	11th day of September 1843 before
Orville Paine)	the Honorable Broomfield L. Ridley
Franklin Locke)	Chancellor & C. the above case came
Administrators of)	on to be heard upon bill answers re-
John Locke)	plication & proofs and it appearing
deceased)	to the court that in the summer or
)	fall of the year 1839 complainant
)	pledged or mortgaged to defendant

intestate a note which he held on Isaac Elsea and Charles Cox for four hundred and twenty four dollars due the 29th day of February 1842 as collat-
eral security to secure the repayment of the sum of one hundred and thirty
dollars advanced or loaned by defendants intestate to complainant- It is
ordered that the clerk & master of this court take and state an account
P-191 in this case showing the amount of money and the amount and interest collected by defendants on said note of Isaac Elsea and Charles Cox and the
time when collected also the time when defendants intestate advanced the
one hundred and thirty dollars to complainant and the amount of interest
due there on up to the time a sufficient amount to pay it was collected
on the Elsea and Cox note and also the balance collected on said note
after paying the one hundred and thirty dollars interest with interest
from the time collected up to the time of taking the account and it   is
further ordered that complainant pay the costs of this suit for which   an
execution may issue as at law.

P-191

Jacob H. Love)	Ordered by the court that the
vs)	judgment pro confesso entered in
Samuel M. Love)	this case be set aside as to all
William N. Love)	the defendants except Permroy
Wm. H. Shelton)	Carmichael and Jefferson B. Love
Margaret Shelton)	the other defendants having ans-
Samuel Frazier)	wered and complaints has leave
Robert N. Gillespie)	to file replication which is done
Thomas Bell)	
Permaray Carmichael &)	
Jefferson B. Love)	

P-191

James J. Green)
vs)
Samuel Cathey).
&)
Adam Lamb)
_ _ _ _ _ _ _ _ _ _)

For reasons appearing to the satisfaction of the court from the affidavit of
the complainant this case is continued
until the next term of this court   and
by consent this case is remanded to the
rules and leave given the parties to take
depositions generally in this case.

P-192

Samuel B. Mead)
vs)
William Stewart et-al)
)
_ _ _ _ _ _ _ _ _ _ _)

This day came the complainant
by his solicitor and the court
being satisfied that the security
given for the prosecution of this
case has left the state on his

motion this is continued on condition that the complainant give new and
additional security on or before the second rule day or this case   to
stand dismissed.

P-192

Nathaniel Langly)
vs)
Isham Hale)
&)
Henry K. Bennet)
_ _ _ _ _ _ _ _ _)

This day came the parties by their solicitors and this case is continued on
the affidavit of the respondant with
leave granted to take the depositions
of Henry K. Bennet, John Delancey and
Thomas J. Hoodenpyle and Charles Bed-
well within three months on his   own

costs and that complainant has leave to take rebutting testimony without
costs.

P-192

Almira R. Hunter)
by the guardian)
vs)
John Locke)
James H. Lock et-al)
_ _ _ _ _ _ _ _ _ _)

This the 12th day of September
1843 came on this case before the
Hon. B. L. Ridley Chancellor upon
the report of the clerk and master
and exceptions there to by defendants all of which being heard and
understood by the court it is or-

dered that the first, third and fourth, sixth and seventh exceptions be
disallowed that the second , fifth and eighth exceptions be allowed the
court is pleased to order and decree that this case be recommitted that
the master restate his account so as to charge for the hire of the slaves named in the pleadings nor interest on the hire and to charge interest onthe amount the slaves sold for only from the time the purchase
P-193   money became due said report is in all respects confirmed - It
is further ordered that the clerk show the amount yet due each distribu-
tor after deducting advancements and allowing the administrators reasonable compensation for their services as such and that he report to the
next term.

P-193

Anderson Skillern	)
John Skillern	)
Henry Miller	)
vs	)
Joseph C. Smith	)
	)

This the 12th day of September 1843 came on this case before the Hon. B. L. Ridley Chancellor for final hearing decreed upon the interloctury order made and report of the clerk and master the report being unexcepted to is in all things confirmed. It appearing from said report that the costs and charges and other incidental expenses in silling the lands named in the pleadings was two thousand five hundred and ninety six dollars and fifty three cents to one twelfth of which being two hundred and sixteen dollars and thirty eight cents defendant Smith is entitled to a credit as against complainant which being deducted from the amount for which the partnership lands were sold leaves the sum of three thousand two hundred and eighty three dollars and sixty two cents that the interest upon that sum up to the 9th of September 1843 amounts to sixteen hundred and nine dollars making in all four thousand eight hundred and ninety two dollars sixty two cents to be equally divided between complainants and defendants that each share amounts to twelve hundred and twenty three dollars and thirteen cents the court is there fore pleased to order and does order adjudged and decree that defendant Smith pay to each of said complainants the said sum of twelve hundred and twenty three dollars and thirteen cents and that an P-194 execution issue for each against said Smith for that amount.

P-194   Sept. 1843

James & William Park	)
vs	)
John C. Everett et-al	)
	)

In this case it is ordered that the interloctury order of last term be revived and that the trustee David Chandoin here to fore appointed in this case be ordered to report his proceedings in this case to the next term of this court.

P-194

Richard Hale	)
vs	)
John Hale	)
	)

It is ordered in this case that the same be docketed and the clerk and master is directed to take and state an account between the parties according to the directions contained in the decree of the supreme court all other matters reserved till the coming in of said report to this order, complainants excepts.

P-194

Azariah Shelton	)
vs	)
Henry A. Shelton et al	)
	)

In this case came the parties by their solicitors and it appearing to the satisfaction of the court that the report here to fored ordered in this case had been continued until next term by consent of the parties, It is ordered that the interloctury decree of last term be revived and the clerk and master proceed to open and state said account and report thereof to the next term of this court.

P-194

    E.M..Smith   )   Came the respondants by their solicitor
        vs   )   on motion and from sufficient reasons ap-
    John Bridgman   )   pearing to the court from respondants
    & John Warner   )   affidavit this case is continued and re-
)   manded to the (Pahe 195) rule with leave
                              granted to both parties to take deposi-
P-195   tions for five months.

P-196

    E.M. Smith   )   This cause is continued on the affidavit
        vs   )   of respondant with leave granted for both
    Samuel Rankin   )   parties to take depositions for the next f
)   five months.

P-195

    E.M.Smith   )   Came the parties by their solicitors
        vs   )   and upon the affidavit of respondant
    E.M. Evins et al   )   this cause is continued and remanded
)   to the rules with permission to both
                              parties to take testimony for the next
five months.

P-195

    Joseph G. Smith   )   Be it remembered that this case
        vs   )   came on again to be heard upon
    Anderson Skillern   )   the report of the clerk and master
        &   )   this the 12th of September 1843 e
    James V. Skillern   )   before the Honorable B. L. Ridley
)   which report being unexcepted to
                              is in all things confirmed from
which report it appeared that Anderson Skillern is indebted to complainant in the sum of $ 2338.17 where upon the court doth decree that the com-
plainant recover of the defendant Anderson Skillern the sum of two thousand three hundred and thirty eight dollars and seventeen cents together
with the costs of this suit for which execution may issue as at law.

P-195

    Samuel McReynolds and
    Valentine Spring, trustees for
    Clarinda Jane Reed and her children this day appeared in open court
P-196   to and presented their report in compliance with the order of
last term which was received by the court and ordered to be filed.

P-196

    Nathan Sweat et al   )   Be it remembered that this case came
        vs   )   on to be heard before the Honorable
    John Henson et-al   )   B.L. Ridley Chancellor 11th of Sept-
)   ember 1843 upon bill answer replica-
                              tion and proof and bill taken   for
confessed against William and others and argument of councel on both sides

P-196   it appeared to the satisfaction of the court that some time
in 1831 the defendant John Henson and William Henson became the purchaser
of the tract of land in the pleadings mentioned of Glentworth and Thompson that the said John & William continued to live on the land and possessed their respective arguing that the conditional line made by Kelly
should be the dividing line between them and that their possession was
joint that in 1834 defendant John took a deed for all of said land   to
himself and that said purchase was a partnership purchase and further
that defendant William claimed his part that John had not made a deed
down to 1840 that William be came indebted to complainant in the sum mentioned in the bill as charged that a judgment was rendered against William
and no personal property to be found by the officer to satisfy the fi fo
and it further appeared that complainants debts are unpaid but because he
the court is not satisfied as to how much of the consideration of the land
was paid by each of the defendants John and William or whether the consideration was not paid out of their partnership monies of John and William
Henson and the court is not satisfied as to the amount due complainants
both principal and interest (Page 197) that William departed this life
P-197   in 1842 leaving the defendants his heirs and that James A. Tullas
is his administrator and further that there on no assets to pay complainants debt there upon the court doth decree and order that   the clerk and
master enquire who paid the purchase money and whether it was paid equally
that how much each of the defendants John and William paid one half or
whether it was paid out of partnership effects or moniesand further state
what amount of complainants judgment judgment of $ 174 is yet   calculating interest also the other debts due the other creditors calculating interest there on and the clerk in taking said account is authorized
to hear and take additional proof so as to ascertain the truth of the
matters referred and report to the next term all the matters reserved till
the coming in of said report.

Sept. 1843

P-197
    Samuel C. Lowe)
        vs)
    Green I. Holding)
       &)
    Bird C. Kinchelow)
)

Be it remembered that on this the
12th day of September 1843 came
on this case to be finally heard
upon the bill answers replication
and proof before the honorable B.
L. Ridley & C. and it appearing t
to the satisfaction of the court
that the complainant had no equity in his bill when open court was pleased to order and decree that said bill be dismissed and that the complainant pay the cost of this cause for which execution may issue as at
law.

P-197
    Jubal Dixon)
        vs)
    Ralph Shelton)
    Asa Shelton Adm.)
    and G.H. Fryer)
)

Be it remembered that on this the 12th
day of September 1843 before the Honorable Broomfield L. Ridley Chancellor
& C the above case came on to be heard
up on defendants (Page 198) demurrer

P-198

to complainants bill and it appearing to the court that no ground for equitable relief is stated in the bill it is ordered adjudged and decreed that the demurrer there to be sustained and that said bill be dismissed. It is further ordered and decreed that the complainants pay the costs of this case for which an execution may issue as at law.

P-198

Adam Lamb)	Be it remembered that on the 12th
vs)	day of September 1843 before the
James M. Anderson)	Honorable B.L.Ridley the above case
and others)	upon the defendants motion to dis-
)	solve the injunction granted in the
)	case came on to be heard upon bill

and answers and it appearing to the court that the defendants Whiteside, Wood Gatcher Lutterell, Clift Rogers and Smith ought not to be enjoined from the collection of their judgments and debts described in the bill it is there fore ordered adjudged and decreed that the injunctions granted in this case be dissolved so far as to premit them to proceed at

law and collect their said judgments and debts further that the injunction in all other respects be continued.

P-198

John C. Everett who)	Be it remembered that on this th
sues for the use of)	the 12th day of September 1843
Elizabeth Rice Adm.)	before the Honorable Broomfield
of W. Rice deceased and)	L. Ridley Chancellor & C the ab
E. Alley)	bove case came on to he further
vs)	heard upon the exceptions taken
Samuel B. Mead)	by complainants to the report
David Rankin et al.)	of the clerk and master made and
)	stated in this case on the 10th
)	of March 1843 and after examina-

P-199   tion and argument it appearing to the court that the said exceptions are not well taken it is ordered and adjudged that they be over ruled and that the report in all things be confirmed and it further appearing from said report that there was due to I and S Hicks on the 15th of March 1843 the sum of nine hundred and eighty six dollars and ninety eight cents for which they are entitled to indemnification out of the funds in the hands of the complainant Alley who has here to fore been appointed a receiver in in 5 is case and also from the report of   said receiver made at the present term that since the last term he has collected and now has in his hands of said fund the sum of one hundred and two dollars and forty four and one half cents it is further ordered that said Alley forthwith pay over to the said I & S Hicks the amount so collected b him toward their said debt of $ 986. 98 or that he pay the same immediately to the clerk and master to be by him paid over to them and it is further ordered that said receiver as fast as he can make collection of the fund in his hand pay over to said I & S Hicks what ever he may receive until the amount paid shall with the amount received here to fore received by them pay the full amount of their debt of $ 986.98 and interest until paid and that he report to each term of this court the

P-199   amount of collections made by him and the condition of the fund
in his hands as receiver and it further appearing from said report that
the clerk and master in obedience to an interloctury dedree extended in
this case on the 22nd day of November 1842 proceed to sell the land
mentioned in said interloctury decree on the premises in the County of
Marion and George W. Campbell purchased the same for the sum of four
hundred dollars he being the highest and best bidder it is there fore
P-200   ordered and decreed that the said sale be cinfirmed and that the
right title interest and demand of the defendant Samuel B. Mead be and
the same is here by devisted out of him the said Mead and is vested in
the said George W. Campbell and his heirs forever.

P-200

    John Horn   )   Be it remembered that on this the 12th
       vs   )   day of September 1843 this case came on
    Joseph G. Smith   )   to be finally heard before the Honor-
    _ _ _ _ _ _ _ _ _ _ _ _   )   able Broomfield L. Ridley Chancellor up-
                                       on the bill answer replication and proof
all of which being read heard and understood by the court and after argument of counsel the court was pleased to order and did order adjudged and
decree that complainants bill be dismissed and that the defendant recover of the complainant all the costs of this case for which an execution
may issue as at law.

                         Sept. 1843

P-200

    Thomas W. Spicer   )   Be it remembered that on this the 12th
          vs   )   September 1843 before the Honorable B.
    Thomas Sherley   )   L. Ridley Chancellor came on this case
    _ _ _ _ _ _ _ _ _ _ _ _   )   to be finally heard upon report of the
                                       clerk and master which was unexcepted
to and which being read heard and understood by the court was in all
things confirmed and the defendant Sherley is discharged and the court
was pleased to further order adjudged and decree that the complainant
Thomas W. SPicer pay the costs of this case for which execution may issue,
as at law.

P-201

    Edwin Beaty Adm.   )   Be it remembered that this ca
    of John M. Beaty   )   case came on to be heard be-
         &   )   fore the Honorable Broomfield
    James Stephens   )   L. Ridley Chancellor & C this
       vs   )   the 11th day of September 1843
    Benjamin F. Bridgman   )   on bill answers replication
    John Tollett &   )   and proofs in presence of
    Lonzo D. Martin   )   counsel argued on both sides
)   and it appeared to the satis-
    _ _ _ _ _ _ _ _ _ _ _ _ _ _ _)   faction of the court that the
defendant Lonzo D. Martin sold to complainant intestate John M. Beaty
the Jack named in the pleadings named Judge for the sum of three hundred

P-201   dollars that the said Lorenzo D. Martin falsely and fraudently
represented said Jack to be healthy and sound and a sure foal getter when
in truth and in fact the evidence proved him to be neither a sound Jack
nor a sure foal foal getter and it further appeared that the said John
M. Beaty executed in his life time to Lonzo D. Martin his note for the
sume of three hundred dollars with James Stephens his security that after
said note fell due the defendant Martin transferred it to his codefendant
Bridgman and Tollett after said note fell due that said defendant bought
suit on said note and recovered a judgment for the sum of t hree hundred
dollars and ninety nine cents and twenty five dollars($325.99) which was
enjoined by complainant and at the last term of this court said injunction was dissolved and the defendants Bridgman and Tollett collected said
sum of three hundred and twenty five dollars and ninety nine cents   together with one years interest there on since the payment of the same and
with sheriffs commissions for the collection of the same It further appeared that John M. Beat y departed this life in the summer 1843 and it
further appeared that the complainant Edwin Beaty was appointed his administrator and it further appeared that on the 19th day of September 18 42
P-202   that the said Bridgman and executed their refunding bond with
***----- Hicks as a security covenanting to refund the sum of $ 325.99 with
interest there on amounting to nineteen dollars and fifty cents making a
total sum $ 342.49 upon the whole case the court is of opinion that the
defendant Martin committed a fraud in the sale of said Jack to complain-
anst intestate John M. Beaty where upon the court thought fit to adjudge order and decree and doth accordingly adjudge order and decree that
said sale contract was fraudent and void and is ordered to be recended
and set aside and it is further ordered adjudged and decreed that complainants recover of defendant Benjamin F. Bridgman and John Tollett the
sum of $ 345.49 and that the defendants Bridgman & Tollett recover of
the defendant Lonzo D. Martin the said sum of $ 345.49 and it is further
ordered and decreed that the defendant Bridgman and Tollett pay the costs
of this case and have judgment over against the defendant Martin for
which execution may issue as at law from which decree the defendants pay
an appeal and to them the same is granted and bond executed according to
law.

                              Sept. 1843

P-202
     Orville Paine &   )   Be it remembered that on
     his wife Elvira Paine   )   this the 12th day of Sept-
              vs   )   ember 1843 this case came
     Franklin Locke Adm.   )   on to be heard and was
         and   )   heard upon the bill ans-
     Willis H. Cunningham & wife   )   wers replication and
)   proofs and argument of co-
     ---------------------------------)   unsel on both sides when
it appeared to the satisfaction of the court that John Locke the executor
of the complainants and defendants departed this life intestate in the
County of Rhea some time in A.D. 1840 thqt he left the complainants and
defendants his only heirs at law as stated in the pleadings that he left
P-203   no relict or widow she having died some years since and   that

P-203   complainant Orville Paine and the defendant Franklin Locke and
Newton Locke administrator of the estate of John Locke deceased in the
County of Rhea some time in the year 1840 and gave their bond as required by law and took upon themselves the burden of administration of said
estate and it further appeared that John Locke left a considerable personal estate which came to the hand of said administrator and that after
the laspe of two years from the granting of said administration Franklin
Locke and Newton Locke two of said a dministrators made a settlement with
the clerk of the county court as stated in the pleadings but because it
does not appear to the court what amount of assets came to the hands of
the administrators especially nor what amount of debts have been paid by
said administratorsnor how the affairs of said estate have been administered it is there fore ordered adjudged and decreed that an account de
novo be taken the defendant arguing there to the master in taking said
account shall not regard the settlement here to fore made by the county
court for the reassurance that the defendants agree to a general account
de novo the clerk and master is tomregard all legitimate testimony already
taken as well as any additional proof either party may deem necessary to
produce in taking and stating said account the clerk and master is here
by directed to charge the said administratbrn respectively with the assets
that have come to their hand or might have been collected by ordinary
diligence the clerk and master shall further in taking said account credit
said administrator with all sums of money necessary expended in the case
of said administrator and likewise allow reasonable compensation for their
legal disbursments respectively and and trouble as administrators aforesaid should the clerk and master consider them entitled to it and that the
P-204   clerk and master in his report state what balance yet remains in
their hand if any with interest there on after the expiration of two years
after the expiration of two years from the date of the administration of
said estate that may yet be due the complainant and further the master
shall examine either party upon interrogations his advisary propounding
such interrogations under the direction of the clerk and master and report unto the next court such his proceedings all other matters reserved
until the coming in of said report.

                    Sept. 1843

P-204
    John Skillern   )   The debt in this case
    Anderson Skillern and Henry Miller   )   this day prayed and ap-
         versus   )   peal from the decree
    Joseph Smith   )   pronounced in this case
)   during the present term
---)   of this court in so
much of the decree as was pronounced against him in favor of complainant
John Skillern proposed to prosecute said appeal in forma paupies but the
Chancellor referred to allow said appeal without taking the whole case to
the court supreme the decree being joint and several and the Chancellor
having this day at the instance of debt on his bill filed made his fiat
enjoining the issuance of an execution on the dedwae in favor of Anderson
Skillern and Henry Miller as to $ 200 of his part of the amount decreed
to which refusal of the chancellor debt excepts - There being no further
business requiring the action of the court it is ordered that the   same

P-204   be adjourned to the 2nd Monday in March next .

Broomfield Ridley

March 1844

P-205   Be it remembered that at a chancery court met opened and held for the eighth chancery district in the fourth division of Tennessee at the court house in Pikeville on the second Monday and seventh day of March one thousand eight hundred and forty four was present on the bench the Honorable

Broomfield L. Ridley
Chancellor & C.

P-205

Foster & Sherter vs David Yarnell et al	Came the respondant by their attorney and suggested the death of David Yarnell one of the respondants which is not denied.

March 1844

P-205

Samuel B. Mead vs William Stone et-al	Came the parties by their solicitors and it appearing that the complainant Samuel B. Mead had failed to justify form or give new security for the prosecution of his bill it is there fore ordered by the court

that the complainants bill be dismissed and that the defendants go hence there of discharged and recover of the complainants the costs in this case for which an execution may issue as at law.

P-205

Gideon B. Thompson vs John Hardwick	Be it remembered that this case came on to be heard before the Honorable Broomfield L. Ridley presiding in chancery at Pikeville on the 11th day of March 1844 upon the bill and judgment

pro confesso and because it appears that the (Page 206) judgment pro confesso had been regularly entered in cause and because it further appeared to the satisfaction of his Honor the chancellor that the complainant and respondant had entered into contract where by the complainant bound himself to the defendant to convey to him a certain tract of land mentioned in the complainant bill when he should furnish brick, lime and do certain hauling and build certain buildings which tract of land contains two hundred and seventy acres more or less situate in the county of Rhea and in the pleasant garden Valley including the Rattle Snake spring and the defendant bound himself to build said brick buildings furnish brick lime and dirt and do certain hauling and because it further appeared to the satisfaction of his honor that the defendant furnished

March 1844

P-205   brick and done all the balance except the part here to fore mentioned towit To furnish brick and build the brick office to make the pavements to laynthe hearths to pencil the buildings to plaster the arches over the windowsand doors inside of the building he failed to underpin the porch to lay the brick floor in the smoke house to furnish lime and dirt and do the hauling and because it further appeared to the satisfaction of his honor that the complainant was ready to convey the title when the respondant would have completed said works and building(Page 206) and   because it further appears to the satisfaction of his honor that the complainant has recovered a judgment for cash that was due from respondant to the complainant for the sum of $ 26147 1/2 ¢ debt and the costs of suit making in all $ 1268.89 and that the respondant is a nonresident and has no effects to satisfy the same except his equity to the land in the complainants said bill mentioned. His honor is there fore pleased to order adjudged and decree and does order adjudge and decree that said two hundred and seventy acres of land (P-207) more or less be sold to satisfy

P-207   the complainants said judgment together with the residue of the consideration undertook by the respobdant to be given to complainant andh and that the clerk and master take and state an account between the complainant and respondant in which he shall state or show the amount due up on complainants judgment and in which he shall state and in which he shall ascertain if there is ten dollars due from respondant to complainant for money paid to Henry   Price for the purpose of promoting obtaining brick as per the use of a brick yard to make said brick upon per said building and in which account he shall ascertain and state and show how much it woulf have been worth to furnish brick and build the brick office, what it would have been worth to make said pavements what it would have been worth to have laid said hearths. What it would have been worth to have plastered the arches over the doors and windows inside of said buildings what it would have been worth to underpin said porch what it would have been worth to have laid a brick floor in the smoke house, what it would have been worth to have penciled said buildings, what it would have been worth to furnish lime and dirt and do all the hauling and reterm of this court and that all other matters and things be reserved until the coming in of the clerk and masters report.

March 1844

P-207
    Elizabeth White et al-   )   Came the parties by their solic-
              vs   )   itors by their solicitors and
    Thompson Gardenhire   )   from sufficient reasons appearing
    and others   )   to the court this case is continued
    _____C_____)   on the affidavit of respondant
                                       Thompson Gardenhire and is remand-
ed to the rules (P-208) This day came John C. Everett in open court and
P-208   was duly qualified as a practicing attorney of this court.

March term 1844

P-208

    Jackson Pryor   )
    Adm. of   )
      Thomas Burnett   )
    deceased   )
           vs   )
    Erasmus Alley &   )
    William A. Harris   )

Came the parties by their solicitor and on motion of the defendant time is allowed them until the first rule day to file their answers and the same is not to delay the hearing of the case.

P-208

    Eliza Campbell by her   )
    attorney Peter May A   )
    citizen of the Cherokee Nation)
           vs   )
    Alexander Kelly defendant of)
    David Oats deceased.   )

Eliza Campbell is the guardian of her children and that she duly empowered and authorized Peter May to rece ceive sue for and take into his possession all the negroes held by the

by the late (PP-209) David Oats deceased as trustee for Campbell and which
P-209   came to the possession of defendant Kelly as administrator tere slaves towit Dick and Dinah and their c hildren Lettie, Feilding, Richard Caroline and her child and three others and it further appeared that said Peter May wa s fully authorized to settle with said Kelly before he said Kelly delivers over said slaves or kim that may be due and in his hands on settlement the power of attorney the court doth consider sufficient authority for the delivery over of said slaves and settlement with said Kelly and settlement with said Kelly Cherokee Nation.

    Know all men by these presents that I Eliza Campbell guardian for Mary, Sarah, William, John, Hugh and Margaret heirs of Eliza Campbell (formerly Holt) by these presents do appoint and constitute Peter May of the said nation my true and lawful attorney for me and in my name as guardian afor esaid to transact settle collect and recover and use all lawful means in recovering certain negroes towit Dick and Dinah and their children Letty Fielding Fielding Richard & C and now in the state of Tennessee lately the property of Elishas Holt deceased and his last wil and testament bequeath to the heirs of his daughter Eliza the said negroes as above named here b satisfying and can firmly who so ever my said attorney may lawfully do and perform in the premises for the final settlement and recovery of said negroes and to give such acquaintance and discharges to all and every person having the said negroes in charge or to any other person having charge as aforesaid and to do all other things relating to the premises as if I was personally present to do, and perform
P-210   the same . Given under my hand and seal at Le C.C. Queen? Cherokee Nation this the 18th day of November in the year of our Lord 1843.

Witness

W.S. Adair
William Holt
Cherokee Nation

P-210

    Personally appeared before me Jesse Bushyhead Cheif Justice of the supreme court of the Nation aforesaid William L. Holt one of   the subscribing witness to the within power of attorney and makes oath in due form saith that he saw Eliza Campbell sign the within power for the purpose there in set forth amd that W.S. Adair was a subscribing witness to the same with himself , Sworn to and subscribed before me this 18th day of November 1843.

                                      Jesse Bushyhead
                                      Cheif Justice

                         William L. Holt

P-210

    I am satisfied of the correctnerr of the above signatures and of the intentions of the power of attorney

Cherokee Agency
Fort Gibson

                                    Peter M. Britten
                                    Cherokee Agent

19th Nov. 1843   )   To all of whom this may concern know you
Cherokee Nation   ))   that I Riley Keys judge of the district
Taklequah District)   aforesaid do here bt the power in now wet

vested appoint Eliza Campbell wife of John Campbell both of the Cherokee Nation and district aforesaid Guardian to Mary, Sarah, William ,John , Hugh and Margaret children of the aforesaid Eliza & John Campbell she having com-
P-211   plied with the law made and provided for in such cases. Given under my hand and private seal there being no seal of office this the 17th of November 1843.

                                      Riley Keys (Seal)
                                      I.D.C.

P-211

    This is to certify that Riley Keys whose signature is here in attached to the letter of guardianship is an acting Judge of the District court in Takklequah District and all faith and credit is due to all his official acts as such . In testimony whereof I have here unto subscribed my name and affixed my private seal (There being no seal of office) at Taklequah This the 23rd day of November.

                                      John Ross Principal
                                of the Cherokee Nation

P-211

    Where upon the court doth order and decree that the said Kelly de- liver over the said slaves to said Peter May after setling up all   the matters of costs his expenses and compensation are adjusted taking his receipt there fore and this court doth order that the costs of this suit be paid out of the funds in his hands.

P-211

Hopkins Heirs	)
vs	)
Locke Heirs	)
	)

It is ordered in this case by reason of the incompetency of the Hon. B.L. Ridley Chancellor & C that the same be transfered to the Circuit Court for Bledsoe County to be then heard before the Ho. Circuit Judge at the july term of said court 1844 and that said case be and remain at the rules to take proof on both sides till the setting of said court and the same to be set down for hearing at the setting P-212 of said court and the clerk will send all the papers in P-212 case to the said court with a transcript of the rules transfer taken in this court.

P-212

Henry Griffith	)
vs	)
Orville Paine	)
Franklin Locke	)
Administrators of	)
John Locke deceased	)
	)

Be it remembered that on this the 11th day of March 1844 this case came on to be finally heard and determined before the Honorable B.L. Ridley Chancellor & C upon the coming in of the report of the clerk and master in this case said report being unexcepted to is in all things confirmed from which it appears that the defendant collected of Elsea and Cox the sum of $ 431.91 on the 28th of July 1844 for principal and interest on the date mentioned in the pleadings that out of said sum there was due the defendant the sum of $ 145.60 leaving a blaance due the complainant of the sum of $ 300.91 it is therefore ordered adjudged and decreed by the court that the defendants out of the assets of their intestate John Locke deceased pay the complainant the said sum so found due him by the report.

P-212

Scott Terry	)
vs	)
Bird Henson	)
&	)
John Thomas	)
	)

Be it remembered that this case came on to be heard this the 11th March 1844 befo re the Honorable B.L. Ridley upon bill answer and bill taken for confessed against Thomas and replication and proof when it appeared to the satisfaction of the court that on the 2nd March 1839 the defendant Thomas received of his co-defendant Henson the sum of $ 275 and complainant and defendant gave their obligation to pay the said sum to Henson in twelve months after the date there of that complainant was security to said note and it further appeared that after said note fell due Thomas gave P-213 the defendant Henson thirty dollars to adjudge him twelve months longer and that Henson refused to do so with out the assent of the complianant which complainant assented to upon the whole case the court is of opinion that defendant did not delay being or indulged Thomas in any w way prejudiced with out consent of complainant, where upon the court doth order and decree that complainant bill be dismissed and tha t compalinant pay the costs of this suit for which execution may issue as at law.

March 1844

P-213

Amy Lowe &)
William B. Lowe)
& James S. Lowe by)
their next friend)
Amy Lowe)
     vs)
Henry Sherrell & his wife)
Rebecca A. Sherrell)

Be it remembered that on this the 11th day of March 1844 this case came on to be finally heard and determined before the Honorable B. L. Ridley Chancellor and C upon the bill answers replication and proofs in the cause and because it appears to the court that Andrew R. Lowe in the year 1824 entered a tract of land in the county of Bledsoe in the name of Rebecca A. Lowe since Rebecca A. Sherrell one of the respondents bounded and described as follows towith beginning at on elm in the valley near a spring corner to Rebecca Lowes tract thence with her line 23o East 26 polex to an elm Sherrels corner thence with Rebecca Lowes line the case continued south 36o East 56 poles to a black oak on the tip of a ridge thence along said ridge south 67o East 116 poles to a red oak on a rodky point of said ridge thence north 65o west 84 poles to a white oak on a line of a 26 acre tract of A. R. Lowe thence with his line due north 28 poles to a hickory also corner of said tract thence East 54 pols to a black oak thence north 84o East 92 poles to the beginning and it

P-214   further appearing to the court that afterward and before the marriage of the said Rebecca A. Lowe to the defendant Henry Sherrell she executed a bond to said Andrew R. Lowe for title to said land and that complainant Amy Lowe is the widow of the said Andrew R. Lowe when upon the court is of the opinion that the said defendants held said land in trust for the benefit of said Andrew R. Lowe and his heirs and that the said complainant Amy Lowe is entitled to dower in the aforesaid tract of land and also another tract mentioned in the pleadings containing 40 acres adjoining the land above described of which her husband the said Andrew R. Lowe died seized and possessed - It is there fore ordered adjudged and decreed by the court that the said grant to the defendant Rebecca be delivered up and cancelled that the injunction here to fore granted in this case to stay the proceedings on an action of ejectment founded on siad grant be made perpetual and that Peter Hoodenpyle , William Brown and James L. Schoolfield be appointed commissioners to allot and ste apapt dower according to the acts of assembly in relation to dower and make report there of to the next term of this court . It is further ordered and that the defendant pay the costs in this suit expended and also the costs of the action of ejectment in the suit at law all other matters reserved until the coming in of the report of the commissioners.

P-214

James and William Park)
     vs)
Benjamin R. King et-al)

Came the parties by their solicitors and in motion of respondant leave is given defendant King to file a cross bill in this case on condition that he give bond and security according-

P-215   ing to law.

    Court adjourned until tomorrow morning half past 8 oclock.

               Broomfield Ridley.

P-215   March 1844

Court met pursuant to adjournment present on the bench the Hon. B.
L. Ridley Chancellor & C.

P-215
This day came Charles F. Keith into open court and was duly qualified
as a practicing attorney of this court.

P-215

Samuel & O.R. Bean)	Came the parties by their solicitors on

Samuel & O.R. Bean) Came the parties by their solicitors on
         vs   ) motion of respondent time is allowed h
Samuel B. Mead   ) him until the first rule day to file
_____) h is answers and the same is not to de-
                      lay the hearing of the case.

P-215
Erasmus Alley   ) In this case it is argued by the par-
         vs   ) ties the defendant Samuel B. Mead
Samuel B. Mead   ) allowed until the first rule day to
_____) file his answer which is not to delay
                      the hearing of the case.

P-215
Jacob H. Love   ) Came the parties by their soli
         vs   ) icitor and on motion of com-
Jefferson B. Love et-al) plainant it is ordered that the
_____) bill be taken for confessed
                          against Joseph N. Love and the
complainant is allowed the time of four months to take depositions of
Jefferson B. Love who is a citizen of the state of Missouri and one of
the defendants in this case.

P-216
John Hankins   ) Came the parties by their solicitor
         vs   ) and on affidavit of respondant Pomly
Aladin Pomly et-al) this case is continued and the time
_____) of four months is allowed respondant
                      to take the deposition of Jacob
Travil with leave for complainants to take rebutting proof.

P-216
Isaac Benson   ) Came the parties by their solicitor
         vs   ) and on the affidavits of Hazard
Samuel Worthington) Bean and the respondants solicitor
_____) Samuel Frazier this case is contin-
                      ued and remanded to the rules and the
time of four months is allowed complainant to take the depositions of
James L. Moorhead a citizen of the state of Virginia with leave for defendants to take depositions generally and it is further ordered adjudged
and decreed by the court that the complainant pay half the costs of this
case for which execution may issue as at law.

P-216   Court then adjourned until tomorrow morning half past 8 oclock.

Broomfield Ridley

P-217

Court met pursuant to adjournment present on the bench the Hon. B. L. Ridley Chancellor .

P-217

Thomas H. Thompson)	In this case it is ordered by the
and others)	court that the complainants have
vs)	leave to make full proof that said
Ann Thompson)	complainants are the lawful heirs
)	of William Thompson deceased late

of Marion County and state   of
Tennessee and that said order here to fore made in sadd case ordering
the clerk and master of this court to make and state an account in this
case be revived and it is ordered that the clerk and master report   to
the next term of this court the acct by him taken.

P-217

Nathan Sweat et-al   )   Be it remembered that this case came
          vs   )   on to be heard this 12th of March
John Henson et-al   )   1844 before the Hon. B. L. Ridley up-
)   on the report of the clerk and master
                              here to fore ordered in this case and
which is unexcepted to in all things confirmed that William Henson paid
the sum of 423.62 1/2 in part consideration of the tract of land purchased
of Glentworth and Thompson and that William and John divided said thact
of land adopted the conditional line of division here to fore agreed upon
by the Kellys and that William had his part and John his share and it
further appeared that John paid the sum of $ 1576. 37 1/2 in part of said
purchase and that John over paid one half the sum of $ 576.37 the orig-
inal amount (Page 218) money being $ 200.00 and it further appeared that
P-218   complainants debt that is the amount due Nathan Sweate $ 219.19
that William is indebted otherwise to McReynolds & Stranahan the sum of
$ 113.40 where upon the court doth order and decree that the clerk and
master proceed to sell the tract of land owned by William and divided by
the Kellys after advertising the day at three places in the county and at
the court house door in Pikeville upon credit of six months taking bond
and security for the purchase money and retain loin upon the land till
the purchase money is paid and it is further ordered and decreed that the
proceeds of said sale be first applied to the payment of complainants debts
and interest there on till paid it is further ordered that the balance
of the proceeds if any be applied to the payment of John Hensons advance
say $ 576.37 1/2 with interest on the same from Feb. 1830 It is further
ordered that the claim of complainants interest first be paid before Johns
debt is to be paid and that defendant John pay the costs of this suit all
other matters are reserved till the coming in of the masters report   to
be made to the next court and that said sale is to be made on the premises and notice be given in the neighbourhood of the land in Marion
County from which decree defendants pray an appeal which is granted to

P-218   him and bound executed according to law.

P-28

The President and   )   Be it remembered that on this the
Directors of the   )   11th day of March 1344 came on
Bank of Tennessee   )   for hearing before the Hon. B. L
    vs   )   Ridley Chancellor upon the bill
Joseph McDonald   )   answer proofs and grants procon-
James McDonald   )   fesso and it appearing to the
Robert N. Gillespie   )   P-219   satisfaction of the
Bryant R. McDonald   )   court that respondent Joseph
and Charles McDonald   )   McDonald had sold and conveyed his
)   property to Bryant R. and James
                                    L. McDonald and for the same the
said Joseph McDonald held a note on the said James L. McDonald for the
sum of six hundred and thirty three dollars in current bank notes of the
state of Tennessee due the 25th day of December 1842 which note is credited on the 29th day of October 1841 with the sum of twenty two dollars and
eighty three cents and that said note had been transferred to Charles
McDonald only   ?   for the purpose of cancelling the
debts of complainant and it further appeared that in obedience to an
order of this court Bryant R. McDonald had paid into the office of clerk
and master the sum of two hundred and thirteen dollars the full amount of
his said note and that James M. McDonald had paid into the office of the
clerk and master of this court the sum of three hundred and twelve dollars
and ninety five cents in part of his said note and that said note have also
been filed by Robert N. Gillespie on the office of the clerk and master
of this court It is ther fore ordered adjudged and decreed by the court
that respondent Joseph McDonalad pay over to complainant the sum of four
hundred and sixty two dollars and fifty cents the amount of the judgments
at law together with the further sum of sixty five dollars and forty two
cents interest there on from from the 2nd day of November 1841 the time
of the rendition of said judgment at law up to this time making in all
P-220   the sum of five hundred and twenty seven dollars and ninety two
cents and the costs of this suit and that the clerk and master pay over
to the complainants the afore said sum of $527.92 out of the nomies depos-
ited in his office and that the said clerk and master retain the costs
of this case out of the money so deposited in his offece and it is further
ordered by the court that the said James L. McDonald pay into the office
of the clerk and master the balance of the amount of his said note It is
further ordered by the court that the cle k and master after retaini g
the afore said sum of five hundred and twenty seven dollars and ninety two
cents and the costs of this suit when the same is by him received shall
pay over the balance of said two notes so deposited in his office to
Robert N. Gillespie to secure him in his demand and that he may pay the
same over in discharge of his receipt and that this case remain in this
case for the purpose of executing this decree.

P220

George W. Rice agt   )   Be it remembered that on this 11th day
John W. Solomon and   )   of March A. D. 1844 this case came on
John P. Cunningham   )   to be heard before the Honorable Broom-

P-220   field L. Ridley Chancellor &nC upon bill answer replication and proofs as to Cunningham and John W. Solomon pro confesso and it appearing to the satisfaction of the court that respondant Solomon in 1840 & 41 became indebted to the complainant Rice for goods wares and merchandise b to the sum of two hundred and eighteen dollars and twenty six cents by the movements of interest there on after twelve months and it further appears to the satisfaction of the Chancellor that the complainant Rice paid for the respondant Solomons on the 13th day of December A.D. 1842 a judgment of one hundred and thirty six dollars and forty three cents with the further sum of nine dollars and fifty two cents interest accruing there on since the payment of the same .

    It is there fore ordered, adjudged and decreed by the chancellor that complainant Rice recover of the respondant (Page 221) Solomon the
P-221   aforesaid sums amounting to three hundred and sixty four dollars and twenty cents . It further appeared to the satisfaction of the Chancellor that the respondant purchased of his co-defendant Cunningham the four several tracts of land mentioned in the pleadings and paid the purchase money there fore whthh the title out standing in his co defendent Cunningham it is there fore ordered adjudged and decreed by the Chancellor that the clerk and master sell the aforesaid several tracts of land after advertising forty days at the court house door in Jasper and three other public places in the county of Marion on a credit of twelve months recovering a lein on the land until the purchase money be paid and the title be vested from Cunningham and Solomon in the purchase and that the proceeds arising from such sale be applied to the payment of the costs and the complainants judgt of $ 304.20 ¢ and report to the next term of this court.

I.C. Roberson Sol.

P-221
    John Skillern et-al   )   It being suggested that a writ
         vs   )   or error and supersedias has been
    Joseph G. Smith et-al   )   granted in the case of Skillern
)   and Miller against Smith determi-
    _ _ _ _ _ _ _ _ _ _ _ _ _ _)   ned at the last term of this court
the present bill having been filed upon the fe fas   from the decree
supened as above the court doth order that this case be continued over till the next term and not required to file their answer till the further order of this court.

P-221
    Almira R. Hunter
    by her guardian
    I.W. Hunter   )   Be it remembered that on
    John Locke, James H. Locke Adm.)   this 11th day of March
    and others   )   1844 came this case for
)   P-222   hearing before
    _ _ _ _ _ _ _ _ _ _ _ _ _ _ _ _ _)   the Honorable B. L.
                                          Ridley Chancellor upon
the report of the clerk and master made in this case at the present term of this court and said report being unexcepted to is in all things confirmed and it appearing to the satisfaction of the court from said report that there is due to complainant Guardian of Almira Rebecca Hunter   the

P-222 sum of three hundred and thirty eight dollars and forty four and one half cents her distribution share as an heir of the estate of Robert Locke deceased it is there fore ordered adjudged and decreed by the court that respondant John Locke and James H. Locke Adm. of Robert Locke decd. apy over to complainant the sum of three hundred and thirty eight dollars and forty four and one half cents and that execution issue as at law it is further ordered and decreed that complainant pay one half the costs and that respondant pay the other half.

P-222

| Weatherston S. Greer Administrator of John Kimmer Deceased vs Ambrose Shroak et-al |))))))) | Be it remembered that on the 13th day of March 1844 the above case came on to be heard before the Hon. B.L. Ridley Chancellor & C. upon the will of complainants taken for confessed and be- cause it does not appear to the court what amount the defendant |

are indebted to complainant it is ordered adjudged and decreed that the clerk and master of this court take an account of the amount due from the defendant to complainant calculating interest up to the time fo taking the account and that he report to the next term of this court.

P-223

| Nathaniel Langley vs Isham Hale et al |)))) | Be it remembered that this case came on to be heard before the Honorable B. L. Ridley chancellor upon bill answers replication and proof this the 13th day of March 1844 when it a peared to the |

satisfaction of the court from the proofs in this case that defendant was indebted to complainant and in order to secure the payment of the same the defendant conveyed absolutely to complainant the one hundred acres of land mentioned in the pleadings and it further appeared that com- plainant by parole agreed that defendant might redeem said land in twelve months by paying up his debt which in the opinion of the court is a morgage but the court is not informed as to the amount due complainant it is order d that the clerk take and state an account showing what balance is due complainant and report there of.

P-223

| N. Langley vs Isham Hale et al & |)))) | Be it remembered that this case came on agin to be heard upon the report of the clerk and master which is unexcepted to and is in all things confirmed from which report it appears that defendaent Hale |

is indebted to complainant in the sum of three hundred and five dollars and fifty cents ehrer upon the court doth order adjudge and decree that said morgage be fore closed by a sale of the land to be made by the clerk and master on the premises after advertising said sale at three of the m most public places in Marion County on a credit of one year taking bond and security (P-224)for the purchase money and the proceeds be applied to the payment of complainants devt and retain a lien on the same till the purchase money is paid and it is further ordered that should defendant

P-224   pay to the clerk and master said sum of $ 305.50 interest and the costs of this suit in ninety days from this date then the clerk will not sell said land and it is further ordered that the costs of this case be first paid out of the proceeds of the sale of said land.

P-224

John Billingsley)
vs)
William Brown et-al)
)
- - - - - - - - - - - - - - - -

leave to take rebutting testimony.

Came the parties by their solicitor and on affidavit of respondent this case is continued with leave to take the deposition of Scott Terry within three months and the complainant has

P-224

George W. Rice)
vs)
Bank of Tennessee)
)
- - - - - - - - - - - - - - - -

This case is continued and remanded to the rules and the defendants an allowed until the second rule day to file answers so as not to delay the hearing of this case.

Be it remembered that now at the present term of the chancery court at Pikeville James Kelly tendered his resignation as clerk and master of said court which was accepted by the chancellor where upon the court thought fit to appoint and does appoint Thomas N. Frazier clerk and master of said chancery court who came into the court and took the several oaths prescribed by law and received of James Kelly predecessor all the books memorandas and papers belonging to said office of clerk and master said Thomas N. Frazier tendered to the court here the following bonds which
P-225   was accepted by the chancellor and the several obligations there to towit Thomas N. Frazier, Benjamin F. Bridgman Samuel McReynolds & James Schoolfield having severally in open court acknowledged their signatures to each bond to be their respective acts and deeds for the purpose there in stated the same were ordered to be entered on record on the minutes of this court said bonds are in the words and figures following.

March 1844

P-225

Know all men by these presents that we Thomas N. Frazier, Benjamin F. Bridgman Samuel McReynolds and James L. Schoolfield are held and firmly bound unto James C. Ivers Governor in and over the state of Tennessee and his successors in office in the sum of five hundred dollars to the payment of which well and truly be made we bind ourselves   our heirs, executors and administrators jointly and severally firmly by these presents signed with our names and sealed with our seals the 13th day of March A.D. 1844.

The condition of the above obligation is such that where as the above bound Thomas N. Frazier has been appointed clerk and master of the Chancery Court at Pikeville for the eighth chancery district in fourth division of Tennessee.

Now if the said Thomas N. Frazier shall duly collect and pay into the public treasury all such tax and suits as may arise in said court of

P-225   chancery at such time and in such manner as is or may be prescribed by law during his continuance in office then the above obligation
to be void otherwise to remain in full force and virtue given under our
names the day and date above written.

                                        Thomas N. Frazier (Seal)
                                         Benjamin F. Bridgman (Seal)
                                          Samuel McReynolds (Seal)
                                        James L. Schoolfield (Seal)

        The execution of this bond was this day acknowledged (Page 226)   in
P-226   open court by the respective obligators there to and accepted
and accepted by me this 13th day of March 1844.

                                        Broomfield Ridley
                                        Chancellor

P-226
        The second bond is as follows:

        Know all men by these presents that we Thomas N. Frazier Benjamin F
Bridgman Samuel McReynolds and James L. Schoolfield held and firmly bound
unto James C. Ivers Governor in and over the state of Tennessee and his
successor in office in the sum of ten thousand dollars to which payment
well and truly be made and done we bind ourselves our and each of our
heirs executors and administrators jointly and severally firmly by the
presents signed with our names and sealed with our seals with our seals
this 13th day of March A.D. 1844 The condition of the above obligation
is such that where as the above named Thomas N. Frazier hath been appointed clerk and master of the chancery court held at Pikeville in the eighth
chancery district in fourth chancery division of the state of Tennessee
now if the said Thomas N. Frazier shall truly and honestly keep the records
of said court and discharge the duties of said office according to law
then the above obligation to be void otherwise to remain in full force
and virtue. Given under our hands the day and date above written.

                            (Thomas N. Frazier (Seal)
                                     Benjamin F. Bridgman (Seal)
                                      Samuel McReynolds (Seal)
                                     James L. Schoolfield (Seal)

P-226
        The execution of this bond was this day acknolwedged in open court
by the respective obligators and accepted by me 13th March 1844.

                                        Broomfield Ridley
                                        Chancellor
P-226
        The third bond is as follows.
        Know all men by these presents that we Thomas N. Frazier, Benjamin
F. Bridgman Samuel (Page 227) McReynolds and James L. Schoolfield   are

P-227   firmly bound unto James C. Ivers Governor in and over the state
of Tennessee and his successors in office in the sum of one thousand
dollars to which payment well and truly to be made wo bind ourselves
and each of our heirs executors and administrators jointly and severally
and by these presents signed with our names and sealed with our seals
This 13th day of March A.D. 1844 the condition of the above obligation
is such that where as the above bound Thomas N. Frazier hath been appointed clerk and master of the chancery court held at Pikeville in the
eighth chancery district and fourth chancery division of the state of
Tehnessee now if the said Thomas N. Frazier faithfully collect and pay in
the manner required by law as in the manner that shall here after   be
required by law the fines and forfietures that may arise in said court
during his continuance in office . Then the above obligations be void oth
otherwise to remain in full force and virtue- Given under our hand this
day and date above written.

                              Thomas N. Frazier (Seal)
                              Benjamin F. Bridgman
                                        (Seal)
                              Samuel McReynolds (Seal)
                              James L. Schoolfield (Seal)

P-227
    The execution of this bond by the respective obligators there to was
t is day acknowledged in open court and accepted by me.

                              Broomfield Ridley
                              Chancellor

P-227
    John Kelly   )   Came on bthis case to be heard
        vs   )   upon the exceptions to respondant
    Darby D. McClean et-al   )   answer where upon it was ordered
)   by the court that the exceptions
    ------------------------   )   be sustained and the defendant is
allowed until the third (Page 228)   rule day to file his amended answer
so as not to delay the hearing of this case and it is further ordered that
the motion to dishonor the injunction in this case be over ruled and the
order of last term to take depositions be revived.

P-228
    Thomas J. Kelly   )   Be it remembered that on this 13th
        vs   )   day of March 1844 this case came on
    Nancy Ann Kelly   )   to be heard finally and determined
        &   )   before the Honorable B.L. Ridley
    William W. Pile   )   Chancellor upon the bill and answer
)   of Nancy Ann Kelly and judgment pro
    ------------------------   )   confesso against William W. Pile tohe
other responda t because it appears to the court that at the July term

P-228   1837 of the circuit court of Rhea County the defendant William
W. Pile recovered a judgment against Abraham Can for the sum of $ 1.58
that executions issued there on upon which a garnishment was issued and
severed upon the complainant as well as the defendant Nancy Ann Kelly
and they failed to appear and answer there to that proceedings were ~~held~~
had there as and a final judgment was rendered against them for the amount
of said debt and it further appearing to the court that there were sufficient reasons why they did not attend and answer said garnishment and that
they had no money or effects of the said Abraham Can in their hands at
the time of the services of said garnishment as any other time where upon
the court is of ppinion the judgment is inequetous and ought not to be
enforced at law it is there fore ordered adjudged and decreed by the
court that the collection of said judgment a t law so recovered by the
said William W. Pile against the complainant and the defendant Nancy Ann
Kelly be perpetually enjoined and that the defendant William W. Pile pay
the costs of this case for which execution mau issue as at law.

P-229

        James I. Green   )
             vs   )
        Samuel Cathey   )
            &   )
        Adam Lamb   )
        _ _ _ _ _ _ _ _ _ _ _ _)

Be it remembered that on this the 13th
day on March 1844 came this case on to
be finally heard and determined beforet
the Honorable B.L.Ridley Chancellor &
C upon the bill answer of respondant
replication and proof in the case and
because it appears to the satisfaction
of the court that the complainant is not

entitled to the relief prayed for in the bill for the reasons amongst
others that the note on Green was to assigned to Lamb before the purchas-
ing of Cathey note from Bridgman decreed by the court that the complainants
bill be dismissed and that he pay all costs in this behalf expended for
which execution may issue as at law.

P-229

        Evander M. Smith   )
             vs   )
        Samuel Rankin   )
)
        _ _ _ _ _ _ _ _ _ _ _ _)

Be it remembered that on this the 13th
day of March 1844 this case came on to
be heard and was heard before the Honorable B. L. Ridley chancellor and D. up
on bill answer replication and proof and
it appeared to the court that on the
loth day of August 1839 the defendant

purchased from complainant the two slaves Dice and child Easter and paid
him for them the sum of eight hundred dollars and that complainant executed to him his bill of sale of that date and at which time defendant received possession of them which he still holds and it apparing like wise
that the consideration paid by defendant was a fair price for them and
that and that complainant received and appropriated the same to his own
use and benefit and it also further appears that at the ti e of the sale
the complainant wasa minor under the age of twenty one years. It is
there fore ordered djudged and decreed that complainant be permitted to
disaffirm and avoid his said contract for the sale of the slaves Dice and
Easter upon restori g to the defendant the said sum of eight hundred dollard and the interest arising there on from the time complainant received
it until paid and it is further ordered adjudged and decreed that upon

P-229
complainants refunding to defendant the consideration paid for said slaves
as aforesaid the defendants deliver over to complainant the said slaves
together with reasonable hire for them (P-229)   since the time they
P-239   first came to his posession and to ascertain the interest on
the money paid by defendant and the hire of said slaves. It is further
ordered and decreed that the clerk and master of this court take an account of the same and report to the next term and that the complainant and
defendant each pay one half the cost, from which decree the complainant
prays an appeal to the next term of the supreme court of the state of
Tennessee to be held at Knoxville on the second Monday of September next
which the chancellor is pleased on complainants motion to order shall be
granted Before the account ordered in this case be taken upon complainants
giving bond and security as required by law and the rules of this court
and that the complainant have until July rules to give security or prosecute his appeal as a pauper.

P-230

| Mary Bell by her next friend William Gibbons vs Isaac Benson James T. Moorehead Stephen J. Godsey and Haggard Bean |))))))))) | Be it remembered that on this the 13th day of March 1844 this case came on to be heard before the Honorable B. L. Ridley chancellor and C upon a motion to disolve the injunction in this case upon bill and answers and it appearing to the satisfaction of the court from the inspection of the bill and answers that said injunction ought to be dissolved. It is |

therefore ordered by the court that said unjunction be dissolved and it
appearing to the court that the amount of the two judgments that were
enjoined have been paid into the office of the clerk and master of the
court pay over to Haggard Bean one of the respondents the sum of two
hundred and thirty seven dollars twelve and one half cents the amount of
the judgments tohether with the interest up to this time upon the said
Haggard Bean executing his bond with good and sufficient security to refund the amount of so decreed upon the final hearing of this case.

P-231

| Evander M. Smith vs John Bridgman and Ephriam M. Evans and others |))))))) | Be it remembered that on this the 15th day of March 1844 this case came on to be heard before the Honorable Broomfield L. Ridley chan- cellor and C. upon bill answer rep- lication and proof and it appering to the court that on the first day of October 1836 the defendant Evans |

purchased from complainant with the consent and approbation of his guardian and from his co-defendants John Smith and William Smith the land described in complainants bill and took the joint deed of complainants
defendants John and William Smith for the same execution of which was
duly acknowledged by complainants on the 14th day of March 1839 exeept

P-231

forty seven acres which were in like manner purchased and conveyed by
deed dated March 3rd 1838 and acknowledged by complainant on the 14th of
March 1839 on consideration for which defendant Evins paid the sum of
two thousand and forty dollars of which complainant received and appropriated to his own use and benefit or his guardian did for him one third
being six hundred and eighty dollars and it further appearing that defendant Evins sold and conveyed the same to defendant Bridgman by deed
dated 19th of October 1841 who now has possession there of and it also
further appearing that at the time of the sale by complainant the defendant Evins he was a minor under the age of twenty one years. It is there
fore ordered adjudged and decreed that complainant be permitted to disaffirm and avoid his said contract of bargain and sale for his interest
in the land described in his bill upon his restoring or refunding to the
defendant Bridgman the assinee of Evins the s id sum of six hundred and
eighty dollars with interest from the time of the purchase until paid
over by complainant under this decree and it is further ordered adjudged and decreed that upon complainants refunding to defendant Bridgman
the consideration paid to complainant for said land with the interest
there on the defendant Bridgman shall recover to complainant one conditional interest of one third in the land described in complainant bill
and that defendant Evins pay to complainant one third of the rents and
P-232   profits arising from said land from the time he obtained posession under his purchase up to the time when he sold the land to
Bridgmand and that Bridgman account and pay to complainant one third of
such rents and profits as may have arisen from that time to the time
when complainant shall refund the purchase money under his decree and to
ascertain the interest on the money paid by Evins to complainant and the
value of the assets and profits of one third of said land. It is further
ordered and decreed that the clerk and master of this court take an account of the same and that the complainant and defendant each pay one half
of the costs and report to the next term from which decree the complainant prays on appeal to the next term of the superem court of the state
of Tennessee to be held at Knoxville on the second Monday of September
and which the chancellor is pleased on complainants motion to order shall
be granted before the account ordered in this case be taken upon complainant giving bond and security as required by law and the rules of the
court and that the complainant have until June rules to give security or
prosecute his appeal as a pauper.

P-232

Evander M. Smith vs John Bridgman and John Warran	Be it remembered that on this the 13th March 1844 this case came on to be heard and washeard before th- Honorable B. L. Ridley and it ap- peared to the court that on the 14th day of October 1839 the def- endant Bridgmand procured from

complainant the two girls slaves Sarah and Emily and paid him for them
the sum of seven hundred and fifteen dollars and that complainant executed to him his bill of sale for said girls of that date at which time the
defendant Bridgman received the possession of them and it further appearing

P-233

that defendant Bridgman now has the posession of the girl Sarah and that the defendant warren now has in his posession the girl Emily holding her by purchase from said Bridgman or his assignee and it appearing likewise that the consideration paid by defendant Bridgman was a full and fair price for them and that and that complainant received and appropriated the same to his own benefit and it also further appearing that at the time of the sale the complainant was a minor under the age of twenty one years It is there fore ordered adjudged and decreed that complainant be permitted to disaffirm and avoid his said dontract for the sale of the firls Sarah and Emily upon restoring to defendant Bridgman the consideration paid for said slaves aforesaid that the defendants deliver over to the complainant the said slaves together with reason able hire for their service the time they first came to Bridgman pasoession and to ascertain the interest on the money paid by Bridgman and the hire of said ls aves It is further ordered and decreed that the clerk and master of this court take an account of the same and report to the next term and that the complainant and defendant each pay one half t he costs in this suti from which decree the complainant prays an appeal to the next term of the supreme court of the state of Tennessee to be helf at Knoxville on the second Monday of September next which the chancellor is pleased on complainants motion to order shall be granted P- 234   before the account ordered in this case be taken upon P-234   complainants giving bond and security as required by laaw and the rules of the court and the complainants have until June r le to give security and prosecute his appeal as a pasuper.

P-2 34

Azariah Shelton et al)
vs)
Henry A. Shelton et al.)

Be it remembered that this case came on again to be heard upon the report of the clerk and master here to f ore ordered and which report being accepted to It appeared to the court that said exceptions were well taken by the complainants except as to the amount reported to be due from defendant Johnson where upon the cort doth order that defendant Johnson pay in to the office of clerk and master said sum of one hundred and thirty dollars with in thirty days form this date and in default an execution may issue as at law against defendatn Johnson and that the clerk and master taken and state an account demono as to the administation of said estate desregarding the settlement made by the clerk of the county court of Rhea county and report there of to the next term.

Marion M. Randolph)
vs)
Joseph G. Smith and)
Henderson Pope)

Be it remembered that this case came on to be heard before the Honorable B. L. Ridley chancellor and C. On this the 13th day of March 1844 upon the bill answer replication proof and by consent of parties where it appeared to the court that the defendant Pope and

P-234   and complainant were partners in the house joining business
that said partnership commenced in 1840 that said parties doing said
partnership did various jobs that among others it appears they built   a
house for the defendant Smith and Smith and said parties have never set-
tledup and accounted for said work and that said partners were to have
an equal portion of their (Page 235) earnings of all the work done as well
for Smith as others and that said partnership extended to all the various
P-235   branches of house joining where upon the court doth order that
an account be taken and stated of the value of the job done for Smith
and also for all other work by said partners and that the clerk and master
take and state an account and report the amount due from Smith also   of
what each is entitled to out of the proceeds of said partnership work
from the beginning to the end of said partnership and report there of to
the next term of the court.

P-235

James Loyd Guardian   )
         vs   )
Nicholas Spring   )
Margaret Ann Spring   )
         &   )
David M. Spring by   )
their guardian and c.   )
)
- - - - - - - - - - - - - - - - -)

Be it remembered that this case
came on to be heard before the
Honorable B. L. Ridley Chancellor
& C. on this the 13th day of
March 1844 upon the bill and answer of defendants when it appeared
to the satisdaction of the court
that complainant was appointed
guardian of defendants some four

years ago that Nicholas & David are now in the state of Alabama with their
mother the said Nicholas became headstrong and unmanageable and refused
to remain with complainant that complainant is becoming old and infirm
and is desirous to settle and pay his accounts and be   of his trusts
so that defendants be made wards of this court and that he be premitted
annually to pay his accounts and it further appeared that complainants
and defendants guardian Schoolfield have audited and settled the said
account and have reported the result from which report it appears   that
said complainant has in his hands the sum of two thousand one hu dred and
thirteen dollars and eighty five cents assets after making all allowances
for compensation and expenses incidental to the discharge of his duty of
guardian, and it further appears that no person (Page 236) can be found
P-236   to take said trust and the above balance and it further appears
from said report that the aggregate sum when divided amongst defendants
will show that a balance of six hundred thirty nine dollars and twenty
cents to be due Nicholas, Margaret the sum of five hundred and twenty
six dollars and three cents and David M. Spring the sum of nine hundred
forty eight dollars and fifty seven cents where upon the court doth order
and decree that said report being unexcepted to is in all things confirmed and that this case remain on the docket for the purpose of paying
said accounts annually and that the costs of these proceedings be paid
out of the trust fund.

P-236

Ephraim M. Evans   )
         vs   )
A. H. Montgomery &   )
E.P. STORY Administrators   )

Be it remembered that this
case came on to be heard before the Honorable B.L.
Ridley Chancellor & C. upon

P-236   the coming in of the report of the master here to fore ordered
in this case and by the agreement of the parties and with the assent of
the court said report is set aside and the case is referred to Stephen
Hicks who is hereby appointed commissioner with the paower of master in
chancery to state an account and that the same be stated according to the
directions in the first decretal order made in this case and that   he
report at the next coming in of said report.

P-236

George W. Rice	)	Be it remembered that upon exceptions
vs	)	being taken defendants answer the court
South Western	)	is of opinion that they are well taken
Rail Road Bank	)	and allows them where upon the court
	)	doth order that the (Page 237) defend-
	)	ants put in a sugficient answer on or

P-237   before June rules so as not to delay the hearing and further the
motion to dissolve the injunction be overruled and defendants have leave
to take the answer from the agreement of the counsel that Miller Francis
is in precarious health on motion of complainant allowed to take his depositions to be read in this case upon giving the defendant twenty days
notice.

March 1844

P-237

William B. Cozby	)	Be it remembered
David Ragsdale &	)	that on motion of
William McDonald	)	the defendant to dis-
Administrator of John Cozby	)	solve the injunction
deceased	)	in this case the
	)	court is of opinion
vs	)	that the answer of
Samuel Worthington & Isaac Benson	)	defendant meets and
	)	answers the equity

in complainants bill where upon the court doth order and decree thatbthe
injunction be dissolved and that the defendant Samuel Worthington recover
of complainants and Alexander H. Montgomery their security the sum of
$ 210 . with interest from the date of the rendition of the judgment at
law and that execution issue upon the defendant Worthington givingnbond
and security to refund.

P-237

Thomas H. Thompson et-al	)	It is ordered that Ralph
vs	)	Shelton and James Rankin or
George W. Rice Ann Thompson	)	either of them who now holds
et-al	)	in their hands the hire
	)	monies for the slaves of
	)	Ann Thompson as reciver is

here by directed to pay the same into the hands of the defendant Ann
Thompson whose receipt for the same shall be a discharge said payment to
be made in thirty days from this 13th of March 1844.

P-238

Thomas Smith	)
vs	)
Aron Brannon et al	)
_ _ _ _ _ _ _ _ _ _ _ _ _ _ _ _ _	)

Be it remembered that this case came
on to be heard this the 12th of
March 1844 upon bill and answers
replication and proof and bill taken
pro confesso against Marcum and
wife when it appeared to the court
that some time in 1839 Ephriam Brannon then a citizen of Marion County departed this life leaving the defendants his heirs, ten in number posessed
of the lands mentioned some four or five hundred acres that on the 21st
January 1841 the defendant conveyed to complainant four tenths of said land
for which he received from complainant the sum of six hundred dollars which
was paid in a family of negroes at one thousand dollars leaving four hundred dollars due complainant and it further appeared that complainant took
a lien upon the boy as payment of two hundred and twenty dollars which
defendant owed him and it further appeared that defendant Brannon and
Benjamin R. King agreed to pay said sum which is now due and that they
are insistent that Brannon fraudently refuses to perform his contract and
has sued complainant for said one hundred and eighty dollars and it further appears that defendant has only two shares in said land leaving a
balance of the consideration of the land traded unpaid of three hundred
dollars but because the court is not satisfied as to the propriety of selling or dividing said land the clerk is to inquire whether it would be to
inquire whether it would be to the interest of the heirs to sell or divide
said land and report in   it further appeared that
Widows dower had been assigned her   Be it remembered that this case came
on again to be heard upon the report of the clerk and master which is
unexcepted to and up on bill there on confirmed and it appeared to the
court that it would be manifestly to the interest of said (P-239) heirs
P-239   to sell said land where upon the court doth order and decree
that the clerk and master proceed to sell said land on a credit of one
and two years taking taking nond and security which sale is to be made on
the premises and subject to the widows dower after advertising the same
according to law and it is further decreed that he sell the negro boy mentioned in the pleadings to be applied to the payment of the two last claims
and defendant Brannon is perpetually enjoined from prosecuting his action
at law against complainant and that the costs of this suit be paid by
complainant and judgment over against Brannon for the same.

P-239

Adam Lamb	)
vs	)
Daniel I. Rawlings et al	)
_ _ _ _ _ _ _ _ _ _ _ _ _ _ _ _	)

Be it remembered that this
case came on to be heard upon
bill answers replication and
proof before the Honorable B.
L. Ridley this the 12th of M
March 1844 when it appeared to the satisfaction of the court that complainant and defendant James M. Anderson, John Anderson and David I. Rawlings purchased of the defendants as commissioners in the town of Harriman
and executed their notes jointly for the purchase money all being principal obligars in said purchase and it further appeared that defendant
Rawlings took lots No. 20 and 22 designated in the plan of said town and
it further appeared that complainant paid on the 13th of February 1844
to the commissioners the sum of two hundred and eighty three dollars and

P-239   eighty three dollars and eighty four cents and also the sum of
$ 276.40 said two sums making the to tal amount paid by complainant the
sum of 559.00 and it further appeared that said sum was the purchase money
of lot 22 on Market Street and lot no. 20 on Broadway in said town   of
Harriman upon the whole case the court of opinion that complainant is entitled to have his money (Page 240) so where upon the court doth order
adjudge and decree that unless the defendant Rawlings do,pay into the office of the clerk and master of this court within ninety days from this
the said sum of $. 559. with interest from the 13th of February 1844 and
the costs of this suit there upon failure to do so the clerk and master
will proceed to sell said lot No. 20 and 22 for cash after advertising 40
days at the court house in the town of Harrimen and the defendant pays
the cost of this suit and report to the next court all other matters reserved until the final hearing of this case.

P-240
    Scott Terry   )   In this case complainant prays
        vs   )   an appeal to the next term
    Bird Henson and John Henson   )   of the supreme court of the
)   state of Tennessee to be held
)   at Knoxville on the second

Monday of September next which is granted to him condition that he enter
into bond and security according to law on or before the first rule day.

March 1844

P-240
    Alexander H. Montgomery   )   Be it remembered that this
    From Clerk and Master   )   case came in t be heard be-
        vs   )   fore the Honorable B.   L.
    James M. Anderson Sheriff   )   Ridley on this the 13th day
    of Hamilton   )   of March 1844 upon the motion
)   here to fore entered in this
                                     case and the proofs there on

and because it appears to the court that a decree was pronounced in this
court against Thomas Sherley in favor of Thomas W. Spicer at the September
term 1840 for the sum of $ 1308.42 debt and further sum of $ 391.13 costs
of suit that an execution had issued there on which said execution came to
the hands of the defendant Anderson sheriff of Hamilton County on the
P-241   second day of September 1841 and the same had been levied upon a
large amount of real and personal property and said execution was returned to the September term 1841 of the court with an indorsement there on
that there was not time to advertise and sell said property and it further appearing that a rendition exponas issued to the defendant directing
the sale of said property and the same came to the hands of the defendant
as sheriff as aforesaid on the 18th of September 1841 and that the defendant had failed to execute and return said writ according to law and it
further appearing from a certified copy of defendants bond that Joseph
G. Smith Daniel J. Rawlings, Sheldrake McCombs, Benjamin B. Cannon John
Anderson and A.G.W.Puckett were the securities of the defendant as Sheriff
of Hamilton County and it further appearing to the court that the aforesaid sum of three hundred and ninety one dollars and thirteen cents of the

P-241   of the aforesaid suit is still due and unpaid the court is
pleased to order adjudged and decree that the said James M. Anderson
Sheriff as aforesaid and his securities the said Joseph G. Smith, Daniel
J. Rawlings, Sheldrake McComb, Benjamin B. Cannon, John Anderson and
Andrew G. W. Puckett pay into the office of the Clerk and Master of this
court the aforesaid sum of $ 891.17 and the costs of this motion for all
of which an execution may issue as at law.

March 1844

P-242

Orville Paine and   )
Elvira Paine his   )
Wife   )
        vs   )
Franklin Locke and   )
Newton Locke two of   )
th   the administrators of)
John Locke deceased   )
    and Wyly H. Cunningham)
    and Elivira his wife   )

- - - - - - - - - - - - - - - -)

Be it remembered that on this
the 13th of March 1844 this
case came on to be finally
heard and determined before
the Honorable Broomfield L.
Ridley Chancellor & C. upon
the bill answers replication
proofs interloctury decree report of the clerk and master
and the complainants exceptions
to said report and because it
appears to the court that the

complainant exceptions to said report of the clerk were not well taken
it is ordered and decreed by the court that said exceptions be over ruled
and that said report of the clerk and master be in all things confirmed
from which said report it appears that a full and correct administration
of the estate of John Locke deceased mentioned in the pleadings has been
made that on a final settlement there of was for distribution the sum of
$ 8271.98 of which sum the complainant as distributees have received
$ 2063.41 the defendant Cunningham and wife the sum of $ 2060.97 the defendant Newton Locke the sum of $ 1500.00 and the defendant Franklin
Locke the sum of $ 1250.00 and it further appears from said report that
the share of each distributee amounts to the sum of $ 2067.99 and   it
further appearing from said report that there is due to complainant the s
sum of $ 4558 that there is in the hands of defendant Cunningham over
and above his distributive share of said estate the sum of $ 9298 ½ where
upon the court thinks fit to order adjudge and decree and it is here by
ordered adjudged and decreed that the defendant Franklin and Newton
P-243   Locke pay to the said complainant the said sum of $ 4.88 and
that the defendant Cunningham refund and pay over to the defendants Franklin Locke and Newton Locke the said sum of $ 92.98 found in his hands as
aforesaid and it is further ordered and decreed by the court that complainant pay one half the costs of this case and that and that the respondant pay the other half of said costs for all of which execution may
issue as at law.

P-243

On motion of Chaltin F. Pollard by his solicitor and on his affidavit
said Pollard is premitted to file a cross bill in the case of W. S. Greer
Adm. of John Kemmer deceased against Ambrose S. Shreak and John Shreak on
giving bond as the law directs and one month allowed him to file the same.

March 1844

P-243

Joseph G. Smith vs Anderson Skillern & James V. Skillern	In this case Anderson Skillern for reasons satisfactory to the court is permitted to file his bill of review on or before the first rule day subject to all legal objections to the same by demurrer or therwise.

Court adjourned until court in course.

Broomfield Ridley

September 1844

P-243
State of Tennessee   )
Bledsoe County   )
)

July term of the circuit court holden? at the court house in the town ———— of Pikeville on this the 12th of July 1844 th e Honorable Ebnezer Alexander

presiding.

P-243

Be it remembered that at the March term 1844 of the district Chancery Court held at Pikeville the Honorable B. L. Ridley Chancellor then presiding certified upon the records that he was incompetent to hear   and determine a case there in pending where in James H. Roades and the other heirs at law of Thomas Hopkins deceased are complainant and Franklin Locke and the other heirs of John Locke deceased and others are defendants where upon the said Chancellor ordered said case to be transferred to the circuit court of Bledsoe County to be heard and determined by the
P-244   Judge of said court under the provisions of an act of assembly passed for such purposes and now because it appears to said circuit judge that said case is not in a condition to be heard abd detefmined it is therefore ordered by the court that said case be remanded to the rule and remain open for taking testimony on both sides until the next term   of this court and by the agreement of the parties it is further ordered that notice to take depositions served on James H. Roads one of the complainants and Franklin Locke one of the defendant shall be sufficient notice to all of the parties complainants and defendants and it is further ordered that the depositions of Ralph B. Locke and Rovert N. Gillespie here to fore taken in this case be set aside and suppressed.

Court then adjourned until court in course .

E. Alexander

P-244
State of Tennessee   )
Bledsoe County   )
)

Be it remembered that at a chancery Court opened and held for the eighth chancery district in the fourth division of Tennessee at the court house in the town   of

September 1844

P-244

Pikeville on the second Monday and the 9th day of September one thousand
eight hundred and forty four there was present on the bench the Honorable
Broomfield.L. Ridley Chancellro &C.

P-245

Able A. Pearson)
vs)
Robert M. Swan)
John S. Coffee)
John Shugart &)
William M. Maddy)
)
————————————————)

Be it remembered that on this 9th day
of September 1844 came on for argument
the demurrer filed by respondant to
complainants bill the Honorable Broomfield L Ridley Chancello r and after
argument of council and because it
appears to the satisfaction of the
court from the obligations in com-

plainants bill that complainant has no equity in his case because he had
a fair adequate and complete remidy at law he has therefore no right to
come into this court to be relieved . The court is therefore pleased to
order adjudge and decree that complainants bill be dismissed and the injunction be dissolved and that the defendant Robert M. Swan have   execution against the complainant and David M. Gill his security in the
injunction bond. The sum of eighty four dollars the amount of the judgment
before Thomas W. Spicer a justice of Hamilton County Tennessee together
with the further sum of fourteen dollars and twenty six cents the interes
est accrued there on up to the time and the costs of this suit at law
and that the respondant recover of the complainant and his said security
David M. Gill all the costs of this suit for which an execution may
issue as at law.

P-245

Gideon B. Thompson)
vs)
John Hardwick)
)
————————————————)

Be it remembered that on this
9th day of September 1844 This
case came on to be finally heard
before the Honorable B. L.
Ridley Chancellor upon the re-

port of the clerk and master here to fore ordered in this case which
report is unexcepted to and is in all things confirmed and because it
appears to the satisfaction of the court from said report that there is
yet due to the complainant upon the respondant the sum of five hundred
and thirty eight dollars and ninety seven cents of the consideration and
purchase money for the land sold by the complainant to (Page 246)   the
respondant on the 19th day of April 1841 it being and lyingnin the
P-246   County of Rhea and state of Tennessee containing two hundred and
seventy four acres more or less lying in pleasant garden valley including
the rattle snake spring and bounded as follows beginning on an old marked
post oak on David Caldwells line then south 40 o westbwith a line   of
Daniel Regan Rawlings 356 poles to a small black oak on a line of the
pleasant garden 5000 acre tract thence south with a line of the same 290
poles to a branch thence down the same as it meanders crossing an old
marked post oak at 70 poles in all 190 poles David Caldwells line thence
with his line which call for north 45 o East 170 poles to the beginningn
where upon the court is pleased to order adjudged and decree and does

P-246   order adjudge and decree that said tract of land be sold by the
clerk and master of this court to the highest bidder at the court house
in said county of Rhea upon a twelve months credit after first having advertised the same thirty days in the Chattanooga Gazette a newspaper published in Chattanooga Hamilton County Tennessee taking bond and security
for the same bill if any over and above the said amount yet due the complainant and that the costs of this suit be paid out of the proceeds of
sale and that thirty dollars be paid down for that purpose all other matters reserved until the coming in of the report of the master in this
case.

September 1844

P-246

George W. Rice   )
     vs   )
The Southwestern   )
Rail Road Bank   )
)
_____   )

Be it remembered that on this the 9th
day of September came the respondant
by counsel and from sufficient rea
son s appearing to the court the
judgment pro confesso here to fore
entered in this case is set aside

P-247   and the respondant is permitted to file an answer and there fore
said case came on to be heard upon a motion to dissolve the injunction
here to fore granted and because it appears to the satisfaction of the
court that the complainant equity is fully denied by the answer It   is
there fore ordered adjudged and decreed by the court that the injunction
be dissolved that the said Southwestern Rail Road Bank recover of the
complainant George W. Rice and John Haley and William S. Griffith his
securities in the injunction bond the sum of two thousand three hundred
and twenty three dollars and nineteen cents being the amount of the judgment at law with interest there on to this day for which an execution may
issue upon the respondant giving bond with security to refund the same
in case the final decree of this court, shall be against the respondant
and it is agreed that no execution issue for 30 days.

September 1844

P-247

Elizabeth Lowe   )
     vs   )
Samuel C. Lowe   )
)
_____   )

Be it remembered that this case came on
to be heard this the 9th day of September
1844 Before the Honorable B. L. Ridley
chancellor upon the bill taken for confessed and that the proof in the case and

because it appears to the satisfaction of the court that the respondant
has been guilty of horse stealing and there by rendered infamous, It is
there fore ordered adjudged and decreed by the court that the bonds of
Matrimony here to fore existing between complainant and respondant be
dissolved and that complainant be restored to all the rights and privil-
eges of a feme solo and complainant pay the costs inthis behalf expended.

September 1844

P-247

Joseph Hixon	)
Administrator of	)
Margaret Hughes	)
deceased	)
Petition Exparte	)
	)

This case came on to be heard this the 9th day of September 1844 before the Hon. B. L. Ridley Chancellor upon the petition of the administration verified by oath and it appearing to the court that the petitioners intestate adparted this life on the 9th of April 1844 possessed of eleven slaves towit Jim a man aged about thirty two years Sally a woman aged about thirty five years and her nine children towit Mariah, Jenny , Solomon, Reuben, Rebecca, Berthey, Jacob, Alfred and an infant child and it further appearing to the court that distribution of said slaves cannot well be made amongst distributees of said estate and that a sale of said slaves would be for the interest of said distributees . It is therefore ordered and decreed that the said Joseph Hixon administrator sell said slaves on a credit of twelve months after giving forty days public notice in the Chattanooga Gazette of the time and place of said sale taking bond or notes with good and sufficient secubity for the pyrchase money and that the said administrator report hare of at the next term of this court.

September 1844

P-248

Amy Lowe et-al	)
vs	)
Henry Sherrell &	)
Rebecca Sherrell	)
&	)

Be it remembered that this case came on to be finally heard and determined the Honorable B. L. Ridley Chancellor on this the 9th day of September 1844 upon the report of the commissioners here to fore appointed by the court to allot and set apart dower to the complainant which report being unexcepted to is in all things confirmed- From which it appears that the said commissioners had assigned tothe complainant as dower out of the lands mentioned in the pleadings a tract of land lying in the County of Bledsoe and State of Tennessee on the waters of Sequatchie Creek beginning at a cherry tree in a line of Charles K. Sherrell s tract thence south seventy degrees west one hundred and eight poles to a stake in a line of that portion of dower here to fore alloted to the said Amy Lowe thence northwardly to Holdings line thence with a line of the said Holding to the aforesaid Charles K. Sherrell line and thence with his line to the beginning it is there fore ordered and decreed by the court P-248 that a life estate in the above described land be vested in the said Amy Lowe and that the said Amy Lowe pay the costs of the commiss-, ioners for assigning said dower.

P-249

Willis Huddleston &	)
Creed Huddleston	)
vs	)
R. Drane, James Drane	)
Johnson G. Page & Samuel B. Mead	)
	)

It appearing to the satisfaction of the court that no steps have been taken for the prosecution of th this case for two

Sept. 1844

P-249   terms It is there fore ordered by the court that the same be
stricken from the docket for the wont of prosecution and that the compl
lainants pay the cost of this suit for which an execution may issue as
at law.

P-249

Audley H. Martin   )   Came the parties by their   sol-
        vs   )   icitor and from sufficient rea-
Thompson Gardenhire   )   sons appearing to the satisfaction
& William L. Gardenhire   )   of the court this case is   con-
)   tinued and remanded to the rules
)   and the defendant William L.
Gardenhire is allowed until the second rule day to file his answer and
the same is not to delay the hearing of this case.

P-249
    Nathaniel Langley   )   Be it remembered that on this the 9th
        vs   )   day of September 1844 this case came
    Isham Hail &   )   on to be heard on the report of the
    Henry Bennet   )   Clerk and Master here to fore ordered
)   in this case at the last term of this
)   court before the Honorable B. L. Ridley
Chancellor which report being unexcepted to is in all things confirmed
from which it appears to the satisfaction of the court that the clerk and
master after advertising the tim and place of sale proceeded to sell the
tract of land mentioned in the pleadings on the premises on the 20th day
of July 1844 on a credit of twelve months to the highest and best bidder
The same was struck off to Nathaniel Langley the complainant & being the
highest and best bidder at the sum of three h undred and thirty dollars
and it further appeared that no part of the purchase money was paid down
where upon the court thinks fit to order adjudge and decree that the
P-250   legal title the one hundred acres of land mentioned in the pleadings be divided out of the defendant Hail and vested in the complainant
and his heirs forever, Said tract of land being situated in District No.
2 in Marion County Tennessee on the north west side of sequatchie river
adjoining the lands of Ephraim Thomas and John Lewis being the same on
which the said Isham Hail now lives. Beginning on an ash above the head
of the spring thence running down the branch the corner of the same being
the line south 81o E 18 poles thence south 20 East 17 poles thence south
East 84 poles to a stake thence north 80 poles to a post oak thence whest
a direct line to a fifty acre survey made by James Elloge thence south
46o West 160 poles to a stake thence East 125 poles to the beginning and
a reference to Hales deed for more certainty and it is further ordered and
decreed that the complainant pay the costs of this suit out of the three
hundred and thirty dollars and that complainant have a writ of posession
directing the sheriff of Marion County to put him in posession of the said
free hold

September 1844

P-250

Thomas Smith)
vs)
Aaron Brannon &)
to other heirs of)
Ephraim Brannon)
deceased)
)
— — — — — — — — —)

Be it remembered that on this the 9th day of September 1844 came on this case again to be heard before the Honorable B. L. Ridley Chancellor upon the report of the clerk and master here to fore ordered in this case which said report being unexcepted to is in all things confirmed from which report it appears that said clerk and master after having advertised the time and place of sale according to law and the directions in the decretal order here to f fore made in this case proceeded to expose to sale to the highest bidder the lands and negro boy mentioned in the pleadings on a credit of one and two years when on the 31st day of August 1844 on the premises the said negro boy Fideleo was struck off to Thomas Smith he being the highest and best bidder at the sum of three huhdred and seventy five dollars and also at the same time the place the whole tract of land mentioneed in the pleadings was struck off to the said Thomas Smith he being the highest and best

P-251 bidder at the sum of one thousand dollars and the said Thomas Smith executed hisbond with security for the payment of the sa e where upon the court thinks fit to order adjudge and decree that the three hundred and seventy five dollars bid for the negro boy Fideleo be first applied to the extinguishement of the lein which the complainant Smith had on said boy for the payment of the sum of two hundred and twenty dollars and the residue of said sum being one hundred and fifty five dollars and that the residue of said sum being one hundred dollars the value of the two shares in the land sold by the defendant Aron to Smith to which he failed to make title leaving still due to complainant Smith the sum o f one hundred and forty five dollars with interest there on from the date of the contract and that the complainant Smtth have execution against the defendant Aaron Brannon for the costs of this suit in the first instance and that he have execution over against Aaron Brannon for the same except the costs of the sale of the land and negro which the said complainant is permitted to deduct equally from the price of each share of the land and it is further ordered and decreed that the cast stand over and remain in court until the purchase money be credited with two hundred dollars being his proportion for the two shares here to fore decreed to him and also with any other shares he may legally acquire and that a writ of posession issue to the sheriff of Marion County commanding him to put the complainant into the posession of said land mentioned in the pleadings.

And then court adjourned until eight o'clock.

Broomfield Ridley

Tuesday
September 10, 1844

P-251

Court met pursuant to adjournment present on the bench the Honorable Broomfield L. Ridley Chancellor and C.

P-252

George W. Rice   )
   vs   )
John W. Salmon   )
John Cunningham   )
)

Be it remembered that on this the 9th day of September 1844 came on this case to be again heard before the Honorable B. L. Ridley Chancellor upon the clerk and master report in all things confirmed from which it appears that the four several tracts of land mentioned in pleadings wereon the 18th day of July 1844 at the court house door in the to n of Jasper Marion County Tennessee sold on a credit of twelve months for the sum of three hundred and fifty dollars to the complainant George W. Rice where upon it is ordered adjudged and decreed by the court that the legal title to the above four several tracts of land mentioned in the pleadings be divested out of the defendant Salmon and Cunningham and vested in the complainant George W. Rice and his heirs forever - That the complainant have execution against the defendant John W. Soloman for residue of the decree against him in this case and the costs of this suit are paid and that execution may issue against the complainant Rice for said costs and that a writ of possession issue to the sheriff of Marion County directing him to put the complainant in possession of said several tracts of land.

March 1844

P-252

Noble Ladd   )
   vs   )
Evans James   )
)

Be it remembered that on the 10th day of September 1844 this case came on to be heard before the Hon. B. L. Ridley Chancellor upon the bill taken for confessed and it appearing to the satisfaction of the court that the respondent became indebted to the complainant in the sum of forty four dollars and seventeen cents by judgment the 18th July 1842 and the responda and gave complaint a mortgage on the three several tracts of land there in specified first tract containing twenty acres the second fifteen acres and the third twenty five acres. It is therefore ordered adjudged and decreed by the court thaththe defendant shall have until the first duke day to pay said sum of forty four dollars and (Page 252) seventeen cents and P-252 six dollars and ninety six cents interest in all fifty one dollars and thirteen cents in to the office of the clerk and master of this court on a credit of twelve months except the sum of twenty dollars to be applied to the payment of the costs of this suit which is required to be paid at the time of the sale all other matters reserved until the coming in of the report of the clerk and master.

P-252

Henry Stoddard &   )
John Wood   )
   vs   )
Jackson Pryor   )
George W. Bennett   )
Berry Bennett   )
Green H. Pryor et-al   )
)

Came the complainant by their counsel and prove reasons appearing to the satisfaction of the court from the affidavit of Samuel B. Mead that the defendant George W. Bennett and Berry Bennett arse minors under the age of twenty one years It

Sept. 10, 1844

P-252

is there foreordered that R.B. Roberson Esq. be as is hereby appointed
guardian Ad litem for said minor heirs and that process issue to him as
such.

P-253

John Dame	)	This day came the complainants by his
vs	)	solicitor and asked the court for pre-
William Griffihh	)	mission to dismiss his bill and prose-
Charles B. Rains	)	cuted to the court a written agreement
David Rankin &	)	signed by the defendant Joseph P. Kelly
James P. Kelly	)	agreeing to and authorising a decree
	)	to be rendered against him for the
	)	costs of this suit where upon the court

is pleased to order adjudged and decree that said bill be dismissed and h
that the complainant recover of the defendant Joseph P. Kelly the costs
of this suit according to the terms of said adjournment and that   an
execution issue for the same as at law.

Tuesday Sept. 10th 1844

P-254

James Loyd guardian	)	Be it remembered that on this the
of	)	10th day of September 1844 before
Nicholas A. Spring	)	the Honorable Broomfield L. Ridley
Margaret A. Spring	)	Chancellor came on this case to
and	)	be heard upon the petition of the
David H. Spring	)	guardian verified by oath and the
Petition Exparte	)	report of the clerk and master
	)	and it appearing to the satisfac-
	)	tion of the court that Nichalos A

Spring Margaret Ann Spring and David H. Spring are minors and under the
age of twenty one years and that James Loyd is their guardian and further
that they own by devise from their deceased farther David Spring a tract
of land lying in Bledsoe County Tennessee in lot No. 7 on the west side
of sequatchee river , containing two hundred and sixty four acres more or
less, and being a part of a tract of four hundred acres conveyed by George
W. Campbell by his attorney in fact John McIver to David Spring by deed
bearing date the 24th of March 1824 and adjoining and bounded by the lands
of Elisha Kirklin, Samuel McReynolds and Benjamin F. Bridgma n and being
the portion of said four hundred acre tract of land remaining after allot-
ing and setting off to the other devices of David Spring their part of
the same -- and it further appearing to the satisfaction of the Court from
the allegation in the petition. And from the report of the clerk and
master that the same is not preceptible of an advantageous devision between
the said Nicholas A., Margaret Ann, and David H. and that it would be manifestly for their interest that the same be sold- It is therefore ordered
adjudged and decreed by the court that after having first given forty
days notice at the court house door in Pikeville and at four other public
places in Bledsoe County of the time and place of sale, the Clerk and

P-254   Master of the court do proceed to sell the said tract of land
of two hundred and sixty four acres, at public auction, at the court
house door in the town of Pikeville to the highest bidder upon a credit
of one and two years in equal installments, taking notes under seal to
himself with good and sufficient security for the payment of the purchase
money, and that he also retain a lean on the land for the same until paid
and that he report thereof to the next term of court-

Tuesday September 10th 1844

P-255

    Hazeltine Haddock &   )   This day came the complainants
            vs   )   by their counsel and from suffi-
    Ephraim M. Evans et-al   )   cient reasons appearing to the
)   court the complainants are premi-
    ─────────────────────────   )   tted to file an amendment to their
original bill in this cause making new parties thereto-

P-255

    George W. Rice   )   On Motion of complainant is order-
            vs   )   ed that he have leave to partake
    The S.W. Rail Road Bank   )   the depositions on file in this
)   cause and any other testimony he
    ─────────────────────────   )   may think necessary or may wish
to do and it is further ordered that the Decretal order heretofore made
desolving the injunction in this cause be suspended for the space of
thirty days and after that time subject to the furt er order of the
chancellor should it be necessary to reinstate the said injunction , the
aplication? being filed in said cause.

P-255

    Mahala Walling by   )   Be it remembered that this cause are
    her next friend   )   to be heard and was heard on the 10th
    Hiram Walling   )   day of September 1844, before   the
            vs   )   honorable Broomfield L. Ridley Chanc-
    Jacob Whittenberg   )   ellor upon the bill taken for con-
)   fessed, and the testimony in the cause
    ─────────────────────────   )   when it appeared to the satisfaction
of the court; that the complainant Mahala Walling was a minor of tender
age, that she was residing with her father , and that she Mahala had
been given to one Underwood to be married by the consent of the said
Mahala and her father David Walling, and it further appeared to the court
that on the 20th of February 1843, the complainants sister and brother in
law mentioned in the pleadings decoyed and ordered Mahala to go to their
residence, and that they constrained the complainants by menaces and
threats to accompany them to the town of Pikeville on the night of the
20th of February 1843, for the purpose of having complainant married to
the defendant Jacob; and it further appeared that said marriage was pronounced on the night Tuesday September 10th 1844 without the consent of
P-256   the said Mahala and that she was a stranger and had no friend
to relieve her from her deplorable condition upon the whole case the
court is of opinion that said marriage was pronounced by force, menace,
threat, and fraud of the defendant and his associates, and that the same

P-256

is utterly void as having been obtained without the consent of complainant or her father. Whereupon the court thinks fit to order adjudge and decree that the bonds of matrimony pronounce on the 20th of February 1843 be disolve and decreed null and void and that the complainant Mahala be restored to all the rights of a single woman and that the denfendant Jacob Whittenberg pay the costs of this suit, for which an execution may issue as at law—

And then the court adjourned until tomorrow morning 8 o'clk A. M.

Broomfield Ridley

P-256

Wednesday September 11th 1844

John Hankins vs Aladden Parmley et al) This day came the parties by their solicitors and from sufficient reasons appearing to the satisfaction of the court. it is ordered that this cause be continued and remanded to the rules for four months to take testimony generally—

Isaac Benson vs Samuel Worthington) Be it remembered that this cause came on and to be heard and was heard this 10th day of September 1844. before the Honorable B. L. Ridley Chancellor upon the bill answer reprication? and proof.
when it appeared to the satisfaction of the court that on the 10th day of January 1840 the said Samuel Worthington loaned to Isaac Benson the sum of $800. and to secure the payment thereof the said Isaac Benson together with John Corby executed their joint note of that date for $1000. due 12 months after date to James T. Morehead who endorsed the same to Samuel Worthington. and the court is of opinion that the said contract was asurious? but it being executed.

Wednesday 11th September 1844 what sum was originally enacted by the said Worthington. It is therefore ordered by that court that that Clerk & Master take and state an account showing the amount of money actually loaned by the said Worthington together with the legal interest thereon until paid that he also state and show the amount of money asuriously enacted by the said Worthington. That he also ascertain and show the amount of money that has been paid to the said Worthington on said contract. and whether the same or any part there of was paid in Bank notes and if so show the amount and at what discount the same was received by Worthington and report to the next term.

P-257

Thomas W. Thompson vs George W. Rice Ann Thompson et al) Be it remembered that on this 11th day of September 1844, this cause came on to be heard upon the report of the Clerk and master here to fore ordered in the cause and which report by the

P-257

consent of parties is not expected to from which report is appear that
there are in the hands of Geo. W. Rice one hundred and seventy ning dollars. And that complainants have received five hundred and forty five
dollars and eighty cents. and that the defendent Ann Thompson, has
received eighteen hundred and three dollars, and five cents. and it
further appears that there is about the sum of one thousand dollars of
interest and suspended debts and it is further agreed by the parties in
the cause, that all the ensolvent debts be handed over to Thompson W.
Thompson, one of the complainants as reported by the Clerk and Master,
and that said Rice deliver over to complainant Thomas W. Thompson upon
the application all the personal effects of said estate in discharge of all
claims against respondent Rice and Ann Thompson but it is expressly
agreed between the said complainants and Ann Thompson, that this decree
is in no wise to effect any claim that complainant may here to fore set
up to the accepancy, that William Thompson, decd. in possession of in
the Ocoo district and that Ann Thomspn is hereby discharged from all
liability to refund any sums of money she may have received from personal
P-258   estate from the Administration Rice. and it is further agreed
that the said Thomas W. hompson is authorized to use the name of George
W. Rice the Administrator upon his indemnifying him against the costs of
all suits and that the cost of this suit be paid out of the effects in the
hands of the administrator George W. Rice, and that execution issue for
honestly administered of said estate.

P-258

John Kelly	)	Be it remembered that on the 11th day
vs	)	of September 1844 this cause came on
Darby D. McClure	)	to be heard before the Honorable B. L.
Park Shipley	)	Ridley Chancellor upon the bill answer
Nathan Shipley and	)	of McClure replication and proof when
James Roddy	)	it appeared to the satisfaction of the
	)	court that one William Shipley was in-
	)	debted to the defendant Darby D. McClue
		in the sum of twenty five hundred and
		fifty dollars. and that complainant

and Nathan Shipley and Thomas Stipp? excuted their obligation under seal
with Willaim Shipley their principal for said sum of twenty five hundred
and fifty dollars in two notes bonds or obligations for twelve hundred
and seventy five dollars both of said bonds dated the 3rd December 1838.
The first of said notes fell due the first of January 1839 and the second
due the 1st of March 1839 and it further appeared that the co securitiesto
said notes made a contract with William Shipley. and it further appeared
to the satisfaction of the court that D. D. McClure entered into an agreement with Nathan Shipley and James Roddy agreeing to extend the time fo the
payments of said two notes to which complainants was surety and that said
defendant McClure did in pursuance of said second agreement receive from
Roddy and Shipley Co. securety of complainant was made on the second day
of April 1840. and which since said agreement was made without the knowledge or consent of Kelly and in his absence upon the whole case the court
P-259   is of the opinion that the said agreement, extending the time of
the payment of said two notes operated as a full discharge and release

P-259   of complainant from all liability by reason of said securtyship
whereup on the court doth order adjudge and decree that complainant be d
discharged and released from the payment of said two notes or any partof
and that the defendant Darby D. McClure be perpetually enjoined from the
collection of said notes on complainant Kelly and that the defendant Mc-
Clure pay the costs of this suit for which an execution may issue as at
law, from which judgment the defendant McClure prays an appeal to the next
term of the supreme Court to be held at Knoxville on the second Monday
of September 1845. And that he have until the second rule? day to give
securety.

P-259

    Adam Lamb   )   Be it remembered that this cause
        vs   )   came on to be heard on the 11th
    Daniel J. Rawlings et al   )   day of September 1844. Before
)   the Honorable B. L. Ridley Chan-
                                  cellor upon the report of the
Clerk and Master here to fore ordered in this cause which is unexcepted
to and in all things confirmed, from which report it appears that   the
defendant Daniel J. Rawlings has paid to complainant Lamb the sum of
three hundred dollars in satisfaction of his line upon lot No. 20 on
broadway in the town of Harrison Hamilton County Tennessee and that complainant relinquishes his line upon lot No. 20. It is further ordered
that the interlocury? decree at the March term 1844 be receivedand that h
that the Clerk and Master proceed to execute the same by selling the other Lot therein named unless the defen dant Rawlings shall pay unto the
office of the Clerk and Master of the court the balance of a complainant
judgment and all the costs of this suit within ninety days from this
date, and that the Clerk and Master report hereof at the next term.

P-259

    Elisha Kirklin   )   Be it remembered that on this 11th
        vs   )   day of September 1844 this cause
    John Anderson &   )   came on to be heard before the Hon-
    Eswell D. Luttrell   )   orable B. L. Ridley Chancellor up-
)   on the agreement of the parties and
                                with the asserts? of (Page 260) the
court the following decree is rendered. The defendant John Anderson comes
and confesses himself indebted to the complainant in the sum of two thou-
P-260   sand dollars as the amount agreed by himself to be due the complainant on settlement of all the affairs of the partnership charged in
the bill and the defendant further by his attorney James A. Whiteside
agrees that the land mentioned in the bill shall be considered as purchased with partnership fundsand granted to defendant said tract of land
being known and designated by the description of the North west quarter
of section 19 township 2 and range 2 west and the second tract designated
as the North quarter of section 24 . fractional township 3 north and range 3 west of the base? line in the Ocoe district, the first tract containing one hundred and sixty acres, and the second tract containing one hundred and sixty acres being the same on which the defendant now resides
in Hamilton County Tennessee. And the defendant further agrees that the
court may devest the title to the said two tracts of land, out of   the

P-260   defendants, and vest the same in the complainant and discharge
of said two thousand dollars. Therefore it is ordered adjudged and decreed by the court that the legal and equitable title to said two tracts
of land above described be devested out of the defendants , and be vested
in the complainant and his heirs forever. And it is further decreed that
said two tracts so vested in the complainant is in full discharge of said
two thousand dollars. And it is further decreed that the complainant pay
the costs of this suit, in the first instance. And that he have execution
over against the defendants for one halfe of the same, for all of which
execution may issue as at law.

P-260
    John Billingsley   )
         vs   )
    William Brown   )
         &   )
    Stephen G. Hankins   )
)

Be it remembered that on this 11th
day of September 1844, this cause
on to be heard before the Honorable
B. L. Ridley Chancellor upon the b
bill answer replication and proof
and the bill taken for confessed
against Robert Cravens (Page 261)

P-261   when it appeared to the court that about the 30th of September
1840. The defendant Cravens executed his note payable to the Bank of
Tennessee at Sparta for the sum of $ 175 , due in six months after date
and was indorsed first by John Prestlet, second by respondent William Brown
thirdly by complainant fourth by Scott Terry and fifth by Stephen G. Hankins and sixth by Cravin Sherrill, and all of said endorsers liabilities
seised by protest and notice that judgment was rendered there on in the
circuit Court of Bledsoe County for the sum of$191.75 debt besides costs
of suit in all the sum of $ 203.65 which judgment was rendered on the 17hh
March 1842. And it further appeared that Brown by his plea of nonestfac-
tion was discharged from all the further liabilities and it further appeared that the complainant paid all of said debt to the Bank to wit the
sum of $ 203.65 and interest thereon up to this date, and it further appea-
red that the defendant Cravens abscond ent? and left the state to parts
unknows that before he left he placed property in the possession of said
Brown to pay said note of various kinds set forth in the bill but because
the court is not satisfied as to the value of the prope ty desposited with
Brown for the purpose of indemnifying sold Brown, it is ordered by the
court that the Clerk and Master take and stake an account of the value of
all of said property left with defendant Brown and that he state additional
proof if deemed necessary and report hereof at the next term of this court.

P-261
    Jacob H. Love   )
         vs   )
    Jefferson B. Love   )
    Samuel M. Love   )
    Thomas Bell   )
    Turnuroy# Carnichael   )
    William N. Love   )
    Margaret Shelton   )
    Samuel Frazier   )
    Robert N. Gillespie   )
    and others   )

Be it remembered that this case
came on to be heard on this 11th
day of September 1844 before the
honorable Broomfield L. Ridley
Chancellor, upon the compromise
and agreement of the parties.
When it appeared to the court
that the parties had made and
entered into the following agreement to wit, I Jacob Love having
compromised a suit pending in the

P-262

Chancery Court at Pikeville Bledsoe County and state of Tennessee wherein
I am complainant and Samuel Frazier Robert N. Gillespie adms. of Mary E.
Love decd. and Jefferson B. Samuel M. Williams Joseph N. Love and Margaret
Shelton and her husband Wm. H. Shelton heirs at law and distributies of
Mary E. Love deceased and others are repondent now I do hereby agree on
my part to dismiss said suit and pay all the costs which have accruied ?
since the origination of said suit or that may hereafter acrue in the
dismissal of the same and that they and each of said respondents shall
not be liable for any costs that has accrued or that may accrue until
the final dismission of said suit. I have also received of the said
Samuel Frazier and Robert N. Gillespie administrators of Mary E. Love deceased two hundred and sixty five dollars in full of all my interest
claim and demand of in and against the estate of Joseph Love deceased
or of in and against the estate of Mary E. Love deceased I do also
pledge and bind myself my heirs administraors and assigns to hold harm-
less the said administraors, heirs at law and others against any claim
or claim that I the said Jacob H. Love either as heirs at law or other
wise have or may have against either of said estates, either presecuted
by myself or any person for me or through me. Wherein said administratos
or heirs may be made liable either in law or equity. Given under my hand
and seal this 9th day of 1844

Jacob H. Love   (Seal)

Attest.
Jacob T. Berch
Charles Wood
State of Illinois
Wayne County-----------

This day appeared before me Jefferson L. Womack notary public in and
for the county of Wayne and state of Illinois the within named Jacob N.
Love with whom I am personally acquainted, and then and there acknowledged
to be his act and deed for the intents and purpose therein mentioned.

Given under my hand and seal of offce at Springfield
this 9th day of August 1844

Jefferson L. Womack
Notary public--

P-263

Whereupon the court thinks fit to order and decree that said bill
be dismissed and that the complainant Jacob H. Love pay all the costs
of this suit for which an execution may issue as at law.

Stoddard Thood? agt?   )
Jackson Pryor, admr. of   )
Thomas Burnette, decd.   )
)
-----------------------------)

Be it remembered that on the 10the
day of September 1844. This cause
came on to be heard and was heard,
before the Honorable Broomfield L.
Ridley Chancellor and C. upon other

bill answers, and C. when it appeared to the satisfaction of the court
that Thomas Burnete, departed this life some time in the year 1843--That

P-263

Jackson Pryor was appointed his administrator.--That interstate? left a
widow Eliza, with ten infant children George Westley, and Berry Burnete,
and that proof has been secured upon others and K. B. Roberson appointedt
their guardian That at his death he was the owner of three negro slaves
one of whom have since died, and it further appeared that intestate was
the owner of some town lots in Jasper and a tract of land on the Tennessee river, refference being had to the pleadings will more fully appear;-
that the widow of deceased is entitled to dower therein, and that the said
Eliza is also entitled to her own years maintenance:--It is therefore ord-
ereda adjudged and decreed that the said two slaves Becky aged about six
years, and Delphia aged about 35 years to sold on a credit of six months
The Clerk and Master taking bond and approved security thereon, enough h
however of said purchase money to be paid down or may be sufficient to
be paid down or may be sufficient to pay the widow Eliza her years support, provided it shall appear to the clerk and Master that the same
shall still be unpaid said sale to be at Jasper, after giving 40 days
notice;-It is further ordered that said Rankin, W. L. Griffith W. A
Sorrele, Geo. W. Rice, and Samuel Mitchell other surveyor, be appointed
Commissioner to lay off the widow her dower in said town lots, and land
on the Tennessee river, and report at the next term of this court;- That
the Clerk and Master give notice in the Chattanooga Gazette and all the
creditors of said interstate? to come in and prove other claims against
said estate, and that he report to the next term of this court all proceedings in said cause all other matters decreed? until the sumering?
of said reports.

P-264

Wednesday September 11th 1844

Geo. W. Rice agt?   )   In this cause by the consent of
The Bank of Tennessee   )   the parties it is ordered by the
at Athens.   )   court, that the judgment pro?
)   conffesso? entered in this cause
------------------------------------)   is recorded? to the rules, and th
that a copy of the bill, be taken and considered as the orginal bill,
with the Inscription attached thereto, and that the defendant have until
the second rule day to file other answer, so as not to delay the trial,
and in the meantime the complainant is permitted to go on and take his
proof.

James P. Thompson agt?   )   Be it remembered that on this
John Stone.   )   11th day of September 1844,
&   --------------------------------)   this cause came on to be heard
                                        before the Honorable B. L.
Ridley Chancellor and C. upon the bill taken for confessed when it appeared to the satisfaction of the court that the respondent became indebted
to the co plainant a mortgage on two hundred acres of land partionary?
mentioned in the pleadings, in order to secure said debt.n It is therefore
ordered adjudged and decreed that unless the respondent pay into the
office of the Clerk and Master said sum of two hundred dollars principal
and interest Eighteen? dollars interest, and all the costs ofhhis cause,
on or before the 2nd rule day Then the Clerk and Mastes shall proceed
after giving 40 days publec notice to sale at the court house in Pikevill
said land on a credit of twelve months, selling however said premises for

P-264

so much ready money as may be sufficient to pay all the costs of the suit
and report to the next term of this court.

Erasmus Alley agt.   )   Be it remembered that upon motion of defendat
Samuel B. Mead.   )   and the court being satisfied with the reason
)   why his answer was not filed in time, and the
- - - - - - - - - - - -)   court seeing that the defendant has now
answer ready to file, doth order that the judgment pro? confesso against
the defendant to set aside, and he be permitted to file his answer,
which is accordingly done.

P-265   Wednesday September 11th 1844

    Azariah Shelton, and others   )   Be it remembered that on h
    Henry A. Shelton, and others.   )   this 11th day of September
)   1844 came on this cause to
- - - - - - - - - - - - - - - - - -)   be heard before the Honorable B. L. Ridley, Chancellor and C. upon the report of the Clerk and
Master hereupon the report of the Clerk and Master heretofore ordered in
this cause, and other exceptions thereto filed by the defendants Johnson
when the court having considered of said exceptions, thinks fit to dis
allow the first, the deed sustained, and the balance of said report
confirmed, and that as far as the actual amount of said estate received
by each of the distributers? is concerned the Clerk is directed to
enquire, how much each distributer has received of said estate exclusive
of the price of the negro boy Campbell, which has heretofore been diso
tributed, and is no to be taken into his accoun :- and report to the
next term of this court.

    Jackson Pryor, admr. of   )   Be it remembered that this
    Thomas Burnette, decd, agt:)   cause came on to be heard
    William A. Harriss and others.)   before the Honorable B. L.
)   Ridley, Chancellor and C.
- - - - - - - - - - - - - - - - - -)   on this 11th day of September
1844, upon a motion to disalow? the Inspiration? heretofore granted in
this cause against the defendant Harriss, and because it appears to the
court that the equity of complainant bill has been fully met and desired
by the answer of the defendant Harriss:-

It is therefore ordered adjudged and decreed by the court that said
Injunction dissolved so far as reports the claims is Ressie? Robersons
hands, and all the books and accounts, notes and other evidences of
debts belonging to the alledged firm of Burnett and Harriss, hereto
fore placed in the hands of receiver Roberson, be delivered over to the
said Harriss But alone on this condition that the said William A. Harriss
on or before the 2nd rule day, give bond with good and sufficient security to be taken and approved of the Clerk and Master of this couet, in
the sum of three thousand dollars, conditioned that the said Harriss
Shale faithfullyand apply to the payments of the debt of the said form
of Burnett and Harriss, or to them intitled to the same all such debts
due said firm, or can be collected, and render a just account of the
effect of said firm which may come to his hands; But this order is not

P-265

to effect in any way the claims in Alleys hands: It is further ordered
that said Harriss be authorized to compromise and adjust said bad and
doubtful debts, of said firm in his hands in such a manner as he may
deem best and that the same authority be allowed to the receiver Alley,
That they report at the first term of the court afte all such compro-
mises may have been made, in what maner they shale have done the same.

P-266

        Samuel and O? R. Duns.   )   Be it remembered that this cause
        Samuel B. Mead.   )   came on to be heard on this 11th
)   day of September 1844 before the
        ──────────────────────   )   Honorable B. L. Ridley, Chancellor
and C. upon a motion to dissolve? the insparation? heretofore ordered in
this cause, and because it appeared to the court that the defendant answer heretofore filed fully must and denies the equity in the complainant
bill, and because it further appears to the court that Jeremiah Maxwelle
is security for the complainants in the insertion? bond in this cause for
the sum of ninety seven dollars and twenty four cents and interest thereon from the 17th July 1843 It is therefore ordered adjudged and decreed
by the court that said Insertion be dissolved, and that the complainants
and Jeremiah Maxwelle other security afoesaid the said sum of ninety
seven dollars and twent four cents, with the interest thereon from the
date aforesaid; But that no excertion? issue thereon until the defend-
and Mead shale give bond and security to refund said money if upon the
final hearing of the cause the same shall be so decreed against him.

P-266

        J. C. Everett, for the   )   Be it remembered that by
        use of E. Alley and others.   )   the consent of all the
        apt. Samuel B. Mead,   )   parties the following dec-
        and David Rankin   )   ree is ordered That is
)   Isaac Hicks, appears?
        ──────────────────────   )   that he has received the
money for which receiver Alley has his receipt and the claims mentioned
in Exhibit A, to Alleys report made to this court, amounting to $842.75
which claim he will endeavor to collect and whatever amount in cash he
may realise on them shall together with (P-267) the money received
by him from Alley and others on this account be a credit on his debt
against Mead stated in the former decrees of the court, and said Hicks
further agrees to pursue no further the assets in Alleys hands for the
balance which may be due him. he also agrees to report to this court
from time to time the condition of the said debts included in exhibit
A. so that the correct amount of Meads credithwith him may be known,
and he further agrees that so far as he is concerned the court may make a
order in relation to balance of the apts of Mead in Alleys hands Alley
and Mead agree that Alleys judgments against Mead be credited for four
hundred dollars for money collected off of Wesley Glazier as stated in
the bill and with the further sum of four hundred and twenty eight dollars and fifty two cents being claims selected out of Meads apets in

P-266   Alleys hand as receiver, and described in Exhibit B. to said receivers report mad e to the present term. It is further agreed that receiver Alley deliver over to Mead the balance of all books notes and accounts remaining in his hands and be fully discharged as receiver   and make no further report to this court as such. It is further ordered adjudged and decreed by the court that Erasmus Alley and Isaac Hicks pay each pay each one half of the costs out of the apets in their hands mentioned in the foregoing part of this decree.

P-267

   Elizabeth White Administratrix of James White decd. who sues for herself and on behalf of William Y.C. White Admr. of the said James White

vs

Samuel B. Mead, Thompson Gardenhire, John Rogers Edward Holloway & James M. Carroll

   Be it remembered that on this 11th day of September 1844 this cause came on to be heard before)Page 268)   the Honorable B. L. Ridley Chancellor upon the bill supplemental bill answer replication and proof in the

P-268   cause, when it appeared to the court that the defendants Mead, Rogers and Gardenhire became indeb'ed to the complainants interstate James White in the sum of $ 1080.86, that sometime in 1838 the said James White departed this life interstate in the State of Virginia and the said Elizabeth White was appointed his Administratrix who bought suit on said debts, and on the 25 July 1840 The said William Y. C. White having been joined as administrator by the county court of Blount recovered two judgments against the defendants Mead Rogers and Gardenhire amounting in all to the sum of $ 1394.95. it further appears that respondants Mead and Rogers are exsolvent and that execution have been issued on such judgments nulle? bono? and it further appeared to the court that respondant Gardenhire was largely indebted prior to 1838. perhaps in the sum of $ 3800 aside from the complainants enterstate doth and that down to the 1st of June 1839, respondant Gardenhire was considered solvent and good for his debts In having in his possession down to that time the lands and negroes mentioned in the pleadings of considerable value. It further appeared that the respondant Holloway and Carrol intermarried? whth the daughter of respondant Gardenhire in the year 1839 that they were poor at the time they married and possessed but title property it further appeared that about the first of June 1839. Gardenhire conveyed to his son in law James M. Carrol one hundred and sixty acres of land for the pretended sum of $ 500 , and that on the same day he conveyed to his other son in law Edward Holoway a negro man named Lige for the pretended sum of $ 800, and it further appeared that defendant Gardenhire was the reputed owner of a valuable ferry on the Tennessee river that Edward Holoway had entered sixty four acres of land with the money of respondant Gardenhire and obtained a g ant in the name of said Holoway, by grant No. 307 mentioned in

P-269   the pleadings that Gardenhire obtained a grant for one hundred a acres more or lessand from the one hundred and sixty acres f audulently conveyed to respondant Carroll by grant No. 791 mentioned in the pleadings the second for one hundred and sixty acres by grant No. 299 the last conveyed fraudulenty to Carroll, and it further ap- to the court that respondant Carroll and Holoway were too poor at the time of the purchase to pay the amount of the consideration of so large amount property contained in said conveyance or that Holoway was too poor to have furnished   the

P-269   money to have entered the 64 acres of land contained in his grant
and that a resulting trust is created for the benefit of defendant
Gardenhires creditors and that the same ought to be subjected to the
payment of his debts before the whole cause the court is of opinion that
said two deeds made to Carroll and the one to Holoway was made by respondant Gardenhire for the intend and design? to hinder and delay the
collection of the debts due from the defendant Gardenhire to his creditors as well as complainant and that the grant obtained for the 64 acres
was obtained for the purpose of sheilding and protecting the same from
the creditors of respondant Gardenhire where upon the court doth order
adjudged and decree that the said conveyance madeon the first of June
1839. to respondant Carroll and Holoway for the two negroes and 160
acres of land mentioned in pleadings having been obtained fraudulenty to
defect creditors in the collection of their debts and that the same one
fraudulent and void, and it is further ordered and decreed that the Clerk
and Master proceed to sell 100 acres tract of land after giving forty days
notice of the time and place of said sale at the court house door in the
town of Jasper Marion County Tennessee on a credit of twelve months
taking bond and security for the payment of the purchase money and retain
a lein on the land for the same and that the defendants Edward Holoway and
James M. Carroll each pay one half of the costs of this suit, hereof at
the next term , and that the clerk report)(Page270) after the foregoing
P-270   decree was pronounced the respondant Gardenhire came into court
by his counsel Benjamin Rush Montgomery and presented the affidavits of
respondant Gardenhire and George W. Rice praying the court to rehear said
cause or to Edward Holoway which said petition was considered by the court
and there upon it was ordered that the same might be reheard or to Holoways
interest and hat the respondant Holloway and complainants have come to
state testimony generally touching Holloway's interest in the 64 acres
of land upon his paying one half the costs of this and thereupon the respondant James M. Carroll , by his attorney prayed an appeal to the next
term of the supreme court to be held at Knoxville, Tennessee, on the 2nd
Monday of September mext- Which is granted upon his giving bond and security as required by law, or prosecuting his appeal in former possession
on or before the first rule day.

P-270

Samuel N Johnson apt?   )   On motion of defendant the
  Cross Bile   )   court thinks fit to order t
)   that the injunction hereto-
Azariah Shelton and others) fore granted in this case ,
)   be so modified as to premit
)   the clerk and Master, to
                              distribute to each 63 the
distributer mentioned in the pleadings except Henry Shelton and Sarah
Shelton an equal portion on their respective shears money arrising from
the sale of the slaves heretofore ordered, and the sum of the same upon
such distribution giving bond and security to refund the same if upon the
hearing of this case it shall be so decreed.

September 1844

P-270

W. S Greer Admr. of)
John Kimmer , deceased, Apts?)
John Shreck, and)
Ambrose S. Shreck ------)
--------------------------)

This day came the parties
by their counsel and on this
motion, and it appearing to
the court, that the report
ordered at the last term
of this court , has not been
made it is therefore ordered that the order desiding? the master   to
make a report at the last term ne required and that he procede to take
said account or desided in said order, and report to the next term of this
court(Page 271)

P-271

Wednesday September 1844

Mary Bell by her next)
friend William Gibbins)
vs)
Isaac Benson James T)
Morehead, Stephen J. Godsey)
& Hazzard Bean)
--------------------------)

Be it remembered that on this
11th day of September 1844
came on this case to be heard
before the Honorable B . L.
Ridley Chancellor upon the
bill answers replication and
proofs in the cause when it
appeared to the court, that
Robert Bell by his last will and testaments, had bequeathed to the defendant Benson a tract of land described in the pleadings in trust that the
proceeds there of should go to the use and benefit of the complainant Mary
Bell out of the rents and profits of which the said trustee was to radsexs
and maintain complainant, and keep her decently clothed and to eduuate her
in English literature or should be preordered? by his execution, that said
trust was to terminate on the first day of January 1850, and the land to
vest in fee in complainant and it further appeared that in the fall of
1834, Benson took possession of the land and of the custody of the complainant or his word and took upon himself the execution of said trust that on
the 13th day of March 1837 Benson sold the land to defendant Morehead for
the sum of one thousand dollars, for the whole term of his trust being
untill the first January 1841. The defendant Morehead sold said land to
said Godsey for nine hundred dollars , for the terms and untill the first
of January 1850, that for the purchase money of said land the said Godsey
executed to Morehead his several notes after paying $ 175 in hand, one
note for $ 175, Due the 1st March 1842, which was by Morehead transfered
to Bensonrand by Benson to Hazzard Bean with a credit of $ 88.50 paid to
Benson, also one note for $ 300 Due the 1st March 1842, which was also by
Morehead transfered to Benson, and it further appeared that $ 122.50 a
part of the $ 300 note passed into the hands of Bean he having full know-
ledge that the same was a portion of the purchase money for the complain-
P-272   ants land and also $ 114.62 with interest thereon making in all
$ 237.12 which said Bean received from the Clerk and Master on the 11th
day of March 1844, it having been paid into the office under a former
order of this court, and being a part of the proceeds of the sale of said
lands together with $ 42.50 which the said Godsey paid to Bean himself
and it further appeared that the said Godsey executed another note to
Morehead for $ 250, d e the first of March 1843, which was also for the

P-272   purchase money for said land and which is outstanding and unpaid
and it further appeared that the balance of the $300 note is in the hands
of Benson and unpaid and it further appeared to the court that the defendant Benson used and appropriated the funds and proceeds of said sale   to
his own use and speculate on the same and that Benson is inslovent , that
defendant Godsey is in possession of the land under his purchase , upon
the whole case the court is of opinion that the sale and transfer of the
land made by Benson to Morehead is a violation of duty as trustee and guardian , and in law is a fraud on the trust fund, and is void , and that it
wa s a breach of trust as guardian that the sale made by Morehead to Godsey
is a continuation of the fraud on the trust fund created by deceased will
and that both of said sales were unauthorized by the power confered upon
Benson by the will that Benson ought to be removed from said guardianship
and that the complainant should be made a ward of this court where upon
t e Court thinks fit to order adjudge and decree that the sale and transfer
of the land by Benson to Morehead be declared fraudlent and void and likewise the sale and transfer from Morehead to Godsey that Thomas N. Frazier
Clerk and Master of this court take into his possession said tract of land
and receive the rent and profits and appropriate the same according to th
directions contained in the will and that the said Thomas N. Frazier take
charge of Mary the complainant , and see that she be clothed maintained
and educated as directed in said will (Page 273) and it is further order-
P-273 ed and decreed that the defendant Hazzard Bean pay into the office of the
Clerk and Master the sum of two hundred and seventy nine and 62 cents the
amount he has in his hands of the purchase money for said land in thirty
days from the adjournment of this Court and in default there of that execution issue for the same , as at law, and it is further ordered and decreed that the defendant Godsey recover over against the defendant Benson
the amount paid him and Bean deducting the rent and occupation ? of the
land during the time the said Godsey has had the same in possession and th
that the defendant Morehead recover against Benson the amount he has paid
deducting the v lue of the rents of said land for thetime the said Morehead had the same in possession and it is further ordered and decreed that
P-273   Godsey deliver the possission of said land to Thomas N. Frazier
on the first day of January 1845.

And that Godsey recover over against Morehead the sum of $ 175, with
interest thereon untill paid and that execution issue for the same as at
law, and it is further ordered and decreed that the outstanding note for
$ 250 , and a part of the $ 300 mote in the hands of Benson be delivered
up and canceled , that Hazzard Bean recover over against the defendant
Benson the sum of $ 279.62 and that execution issue for the same as at law
and because the Court is not satisfied as to how the defendant Benson has
discharged his trust as guardian toward his ward It is ordered by the Court
that the Clerk and Master take and state an account , of the rents and
profits of said land from January 1834 to January 1845, receive annually
or the value of said land annually charging said Benson therewith and crediting him with all sum he may have necessarily paid out and expended in
the education and maintainance of his ward, and ascertain of the value of
the rents annually are suf ficient to effecuate the trust created by said
will and that the Clerk and Master call before him) Page 274) the   com-
P-274   plainant Mary , and ascertain if she is satisfied with her former Guardian and the Clerk and Master is directed to take and state an
account between Godsey and Benson as to the rents received by Godsey while

P-273   In possession of the land mentioned the money paid by Godsey to
Benson and also an account between Moorehead and Benson as to the rents
received by Morehead and money paid by him to Bensön, and report to the
next term of this court and it is further ordered and decreed by the
court that the defendant Morehead Bean and Godsey pay each one third of
the costs of this suit for which execution may issue respectively issue,
and that the said Morehead, Bean and Godsey have execution over against
the defendant Benson for their respective properties of said Cost. Provided however the defendant Benson by the next rule day give bond and
security to be approved of by the master in the sum of $ 1000. Condition-
ed to support maintain and educate the girl Mary Bell as provided for and
directed in the will of Robert Bell and deliver to her the peaceable possession of the aforesaid tract of land at the time directed by the will
and further that he will pay all the cost in this cause then this decree
shall be cancelled and estimated null and of no effect.

P-274
    Joseph G. Smith   )   Bill of Review
        vs   )
    Anderson Skillern)   Came the parties by their solicitors
)   and by their counsel and the opent?
                      of the court , time is allowed Joseph
                      G. Smith untill the fourth Monday of
November next to file his answer to the bill of review filed in this cause and the same is not to delay the hearing of this cause.

P-275
Wednesday 11th September 1844

    Ephraim M. Evins   )   Be it remembered that this cause
        vs   )   came on to be heard upon the report
    A. H. Montgomery &)   of the commissioner heretofore ap-
    E. P. Story   )   pointed in this cause, and exception
)   thereto and from sufficient reasons
                      appearing to the satisfaction of the
court this cause is continued untill the next term of this court.

P-275
    Keng & Gardenhire Heirs)   Came the parties by their attor-
        vs   )   nies and it appearing to the
    Samuel Williams et al   )   satisfaction of the court that
                        Pharoh Williams and Calvin
                      Williams two of the defendants
in the complainants bill of revevor? filed in this cause are infants under the age of twenty one years , it is therefore orderedby the court t
that Samuel Williams be appointed their guardian and that procep issue
to him as such.

And their being no further business mentioned for the section of
this court , it is ordered that the same be adjourned to the 2nd Monday

in March next.

                                                        Broomfield Ridley

P-276
State of Tennessee   )   November term of the Circuit Court holden
Bledsoe County   )   at the court house in the town of Pikeville
)   on the second monday of November 1844.
_ _ _ _ _ _ _ _ _ _ _ _ _ _   The honorable John O. Cannon presiding.

        Be it remembered that at the March term 1844 of the Chancery Court
held at Pikeville Bledsoe County Tennessee the honorable Broomfield
L. Ridley Chancellor presiding certified upon the record that he was in-
compitent to hear and determine (Page 276) a cause therein pending where-
P-276   in James H. Roads and the other heirs of Thomas Hopkins deceased
are complainants and Franklin Locke deceased and others were defendants;
Whereupon the said Chancellor ordered said cause to be transfered to the
circuit court of Bledsoe County to be heard and determined by the judges
of said court, under the act of assembly in such case. And now said cause
coming on to be heard on the 13th day of November 1844 before the honar-
able John O. Cannon judge of the said Circuit Court as aforesaid because
it appears to the satisfaction of the said Judge from the affidavit of
Thomas Hopkins one of the complainants in said cause that the same is not
in a condition to be heard at this term. It is therefore ordered that said
cause be continued until the next term of the circuit court for Bledsoe
County , and remanded to the rules and remain open for both parties to
take testimony generally.

        And then the court adjourned untill court in course.

                                                        John O. Cannon

P-276
        George W. Hopkins and Others   )   Be it remembered that this
                vs   )   cause came on to be heard
        Franklin Locke and Others   )   before the honorable John
)   O. Cannon one of the judges
_   of law in the state of
Tennessee, setting at a circuit court opened and held for the County of
Bledsoe, at the court house in Pikeville, on the second Monday of March
1845. and on tuesday of said term upon the certificate of the incompetency of the honorable B. L. Ridley the chancellor assigned to hold the
Chancery Court at Pikeville, and for reasons appearing to the satisfaction of said Judge , from the affidavit of Thomas Hopkins one of the
complainants , this cause is continued until the next term of the circuit
court for said County, and remanded to therules, so far as to permit the
complainants to take the deposition of W. B. Lewis subject to all legal
exceptions, upon the complainants paying all costs occuring since the
transfer of said case from said chancery court , to the said circuit
court , and that the respondents have cause to take further proof as they
may deem? necessary and than the court adjourns until said court in
course.

                                                        John O. Cannon

P-277   Monday March Term 1845

State of Tennessee)
Bledsoe County)

Be it remembered that at a Chancery Court opened and held in the fourth Chancery division at the court house in the town of Pikeville on the second Monday and 10th day of March 1845. There was present on the bench the honorable Broomfield L. Ridley & C.

P-277

Gideon B. Thompson
vs
John Hardwick)

Be it remembered that on this 11th day of March 1845 this cause came on again to be heard finally and determined before the honorable Broomfield L. Ridley Chancellor & C upon the report of the Clerk and Master made under the decreetal order rendered at the last term of the court, which report being unexcepted to is in all things confirmed, from which it appears that the master had sold the land mentioned in the pleadings after giving due notice, on the 4th day of November 1844 at the Court house in the town of Washington in the county of Rhea and state of Tennessee to Gideon B. Thompson the complainant he being the highest bidder for the sum of five hundred and seventy dollars, that being the amount of said complainants debt heretofore decreed and the cost of this suit which said tract of land containing two hundred and seventy four acres more or less lying in the pleasant garden valley including the rattlesnake springs in the County of Rhea and state of Tennessee, is described as follows Beginning on an old Marked Post oak on David Caldwells line then north 40 East with the line of Daniel and Rezier? Rawlings three hundred and fifty six poles to a small black oak on a line of the pleasant garden $5000 acre tract, then south with the line of the same two hundred and ninety poles to a branch thence down the same as it meanders passing an old marked post oak at 70 poles in all 190 poles to David Caldwells line. Thence with his line which calls for north 45 o East 170 poles to the Beginning. Therefore it is ordered adjudged and decreed by the court that the title to the above described tract of land be devested out of the defendant John Hardwick and vested in the complainant Gideon B. Thompson and his heirs forever and that a writ of possession Issue--- And it is further ordered adjudged and decreed that the complainant pay the costs of this suit for which an execution may issue as at law.

P-278

Tuesday March 11th 1845

Eucled Waterhouse & Others
vs
John Condley, Jas A. Darwin & Others)

On motion of James A. Darwin by his solicitors time is given him untill the first Monday in May next to file his answer in this cause so as not to delay the hearing.

P-278

E. M. Evans)
vs)
A. H. Montgomery &)
E. P. Story adms.)
)

Be it remembered that the described
order containing said cause on exceptions be ordered and continued for
argument at the next court.

Samuel McReynolds and Valentine Spring
Trustees for Clarenda M. Read

      On motion of complainant it is ordered
by the court that the Clerk and Master take and state an account of the
administration of the estate of the said Clarenda I, . of trust funds
in their hands and in taking said account the clerk is directed to make
a fair allowance to the said complainants for their services in the course
of their duties and in carying out the object of their trust and also
allow them for solicitors fees and all monies ? necessarily expended
in the execution of said trust and report to the next term of this court
All other matters reserved untill the coming in of said report.

P-278

Madison H. Randolph)
vs)
Henderson P. Pope &)
Joseph G. Smith)
)

Be it remembered that this cause
came on tobe heard upon the report
of the clerk and master, heretofore
ordered in this cause which report
being unexcepted to is in all things
confirmed- from which report it ap-

pears that complainant is indebted to Pope and Smith whereupon the court
doth order that complainants suit be dismissed and that he pay the costs
of this suit for which an execution may issue.

P-278

Isaac Benson)
vs)
Samuel Worthington)

Be it remembered tat this cause came on
to be heard upon the report of the
Clerk and Master heretofore ordered and
which being excepted to by complainant,
the court doth overrule the same and
decree that said report be in all things

confirmed-- From which report it appears that complanant has now in his
hands the sum of $ 267-82 usuriously obtained from (Page 279) Complainant
P-279   Whereupon the court doth order and decree that the complainant
offers? of the defendant the sum of $ 267.82 and the costs of this suit
for which an execution may issue as at law.
    From which decree defendant prayed an appeal to the next supreme
court to be held at Knoxville on the 2nd Monday of September 1845 and to
him it is granted upon his giving bond and security according to law on
or before the 1st Monday in April next--.

The South Western Rail Road Bank at Knoxville)
vs)
George Rice)

On motion and
by consent of
the parties

P-279   this cause is continued untill the next term of this court and
that the testimony on file is to be read as evidence on the hearing of
 this cause and that defendant Rice have leave to take the deposition
of Miller Frances and James Rankin and that complainant only have leave
to take rebutting testiomny and said cause is to be heard at the next t
term.

P-279
    James Loyd Guardian & C   )   Be it remembered that this
            vs   )   cause came on to be heard
    Nicholas Spring David H.   )   upon the report of the
    Spring and Margaret Spring   )   clerk and master, hereto-
)   fore ordered in this cause
    ----------------------------)   which said report being

unexcepted to is in all things confirmed-- From which report it appears
that complainant as guardian has in his hands the sum of $ 2066.94 and
that Nicholas is entitled to the sum of $ 641.16 ¢ exclusive of charges
and disbursments since the last settlement and it further appears that
divers persons mentioned in said report are indebted to said defendants
amounting in all to the sum of $ 157.75 it being for the hire of the
negroes for the year 1844. Thereupon it is ordered that this cause be retained on the dockett for the purpose of the complainants anually passing
his accounts in this court.

P-279
    Adam Lamb
            vs
    Daniel Rawlings James M. Anderson   )   Be it remembered
    John Anderson, James A. Whiteside   )   that this cause
    John G. Wood (Page 280) Henry Gotcher   )   came on to be
    George Lutterel William Clift Alfred M.)   heard upon the
    Rogers and Joseph G. Smith   )   report of the
)   Clerk   and
    -------------------------------------)   Master of the
)   Chancery Court

at Pikeville which being unexcepted to is in all things confirmed. From
which report it appears to the satisfaction of the court that defendant
Rawlings failed to pay the complainants debt in the time given him that
the clerk and master proceeded to sell aot No..22 on broad Street in the
town of Harrison Hamilton County Tennessee after advertising the time
and place of sale for the space of forty days to the highest bidder
when the complainant became the purchaser at the sum of $ 351.83 being
the amount of his debt and the costs of this suit--
    Whereupon the court doth order adjudged and decree that the legal
title to said lot No. 22 be divested out of the defendants and vested in
the complainant and his heirs forever, that a writ of possession issue
commanding the sheriff of Hamilton to put the complainant in the possession of the same-- And the complainant paythe cost of this suit for which
an execution may issue as at law.

P-280
    Elizabeth White Administratrix   )   Be it remembered that this

of James White Deceased)
vs)
Thompson Gardenhire Edward)
Holloway and others)

cause came on to be heard
upon the petition of the
defendant Edward Holloway
before the honorable B. L.
Ridley Chancellor, this
11th of March 1845, and
upon the additional test-

imony which had been read at the hearing . And the court being satisfied that the sixty four acre tract of land mentioned in the pleadings
was entered with the money of the defendant Thompson Gardenhire, and
that said tract of land was the property of the defendant Gardenhire
subject to the satisfaction of the complainants claim-- Whereupon it is
ordered adjudged and decreed by the court that the petition of the defendant Edward Holloway for a rehearing as to the sioty four acres of
land be dismissed, that the decree rendered at the last term in said cause
be confirmed that clerk and master proceed to sell said rtract of land
on the premises after advertising the time and place of sale 40 days in
the Chattanooga Gazette on a credit of six and twelve months. The purchaser giving bond and security for the purchase money retaining a lein
P-281   upon the land untill the purchase money is paid , And it is further ordered and decreed that the grant No. 501 for said 64 acres of
land is declared void the court being of opinion that said title was obtained by defendant Holloway with the intend and design of hindering and
delayi ng the complainent and other creditors in the collection of their
debt and that the defendant Edward Holloway pay the costs of the petition
for a rehearing.

P-281

Frey Carpenter)
vs)
George A. B. Hardin James)
Griffith Alfred Standifer)
Greene H. Priort and James Hendrix)

Be cause it a ppears
to the satisfaction of
the court that the mat-
ters in controversy be-
tween the parties as
well as the costs of
this suit, have been

fully settled and adjusted. It is ordered by the court that complainants
bill be dismissed and the defendants hence discharged--

And the court then adjourned till tomorrow morning 8 oclock

                                                        Broomfield Ridley

P-281

                    Wednesday March 12th 1845

Court met per uant to adjournment present on the bench the honorable
Broomfield L. Ridley Chancellor & C.

    James Loyd Guardian & C
                    Petition Expartee---

P-281   Be it remembered that on this 12th day of March 1845 before
the honorable B. L. Ridley Chancellor & C. the above cause came on for
further hearing upon the report of the clerk and master and the same
being unexcepted to it is ordered and decreed by the court that the same
being in all things be confirmed and further that when the notes for the
purchase money of the land become due and payable that the clerk and
master proceed to collect and hold the money collected subject to further order of this court.

        Joseph Hixson Administrator of
        Margaret Hughes
                    Petition to sell slaves Expartes
        P-282
                    Wednesday March 12th 1845

        Joseph Hixson Administrator & C reports to the court that in per-
suance of the introductry decree rendered in this cause at the last term
after giving forty days notice by advertisment in the Chattanooga Gazette
he proceeded on the 21st day of Novr. 1844 to sell at public auction to
the highest bidder the slaves mentioned in the decree-- and that at such
sale William Hixon purchased the woman sally and her child at the price
of $ 322.00
James Hixson the boy Jerr at   350.00
William Hixson the boy Alfred at   200.00
Frances Hughs the girl Miriah and child born since decree   558.00
Burwell Bennett the boy Solomon at   463.00
John Hughs the boy Reuben at   377.00
Hardy Lasseter the girl Rebecca at   400.00
Cornelious Lamb the boy Barley at   350.00
Frances Hughs the boy Jacob at   241.00
John Hughs the boy John at   406.00
                                                            $ 3767.00

        All of which were sold on a credit of twelve months.
And to secure the purchase money notes with good security were taken from
the purchasers respectively, whereupon it is considered by the court that
the foregoing report being unexcepted to be in all hings confirmed.

        P-282
        The State of Tennessee by   )   Be it remembered
        Samuel G. Frazier Att. General   )   that the demurror
                    vs   )   of the above named
        George W. Thompson Wm. S. Mooney   )   defendants came on
        Alex E. Pallow? Geo. W. Rice & Others   )   to be argued and
        David Rankin   )   was argued by coun-
)   sel on both sides
        --)   and the matters of
        the demurror was considered by the court-- that because the court was of
opinion that the law was in favor of the complainant it is ordered that
said demurror be overruled. Nevertheless the court doth permit the defendant to insist upon the demurror at the hearing by way of answer or as it
was a part of their? answers and it is further ordered that defendants

P-282   have two months from the 13th March 1845 to file this answer
in this cause-- andit is further ordered that John Kelly and Daniel R.
Rawlings two of the other defendants have 2 months to file their answers.

P-283

Wednesday March 12th 1845

John B. Seaman   )
        vs   )
William I. ? Standefer)
)
- - - - - - - - - - - - -

Be it remembered that on the 12th
day of March 1845 before the Honorable Broomfield L. Ridley Chancellor
& C the above came on to be heard
upon the bill of complaint taken
for confessed and upon the exhibits
and it appearing to the court that the complainant ohn B. Seaman and
a certian Samuel Ward were merchants of Ney York partners under the
style and firm of Seaman and Ward and that the defendant became indebted
to the there in the sum of one thousand seven hundred and sicty three
dollars for which he executed to them his note under seal bearing date
the 29th day of May 1839 and payable on day after the date thereof to
secure the payment the defendant on the 1st day of May 1840 executed to
them a mortgage deed of that date by which he conveyed to them all the
right title claim interest and demand of the said William I. Standifer
in and to a certain tract of land in the county of Bledsoe and state of
Tennessee of which the late C. I James Standifer decd. seised and possessed Known as the Mount Airy place supposed to contain about seventeen
acres more or less the part of said tract of land intended to be conveyed being one undivided fifth thereof subject however to dower of the widow of the said James Standefer deceased but to be void & of no effect
in case the defendant should pay the said debt by the 12th day of July
1845 and it further appearing to the court that Samuel Ward departed
this life abouth the ---- day of ------ 184- leaving complainant as
surviving partner of the said firm of Seaman and Ward and as such entitled to the said debt and all benefits arising from the deed aforesaid
made to secure its payment and it further appearing that the said debt
was due and unpaid on the 13th of July 1841 and that the same with all
accruing? interest thereon is still due and unpaid-- and further that
said tract of land has since the execution of the mortgage deed been par-
tioned and devided and that in said division the several parts were also
respectively designated as lots No. 1,2,3,4, & 5 and that Lot No. 1 was
assigned alloted and conveyed in severalty to the defendant to which complainant agrees his mortage shall attach and which or portion set off
in seevralty to defendant, is described as follows towit-- Lot No.   1
Beginning at a stake near the foot of the mountain on the north west
line of James Standifers old tract the last corner of the Widows dower
Thence with her line south 59 5/6 o East 158 poles crossing the public
road to a walnut stump thence with another line of the same S. 88 o   E
71 1/4 poles to a sasafrass Thence with (Page 284) another line of the
P-284   same S 8 o E. 39 poles to a dogwood thence N. 50 o W. 250 poles
crossing the publick road at 180 poles to a stake near a white oak , the
beginning corner of a 432 acre tract sold by John Bridgman to James
Standefer thence 40 o W. to the beginning contain Thwwee hundred and
thirty nine acres more or less and further that the defendat is entitled
to one fifth part in fee of that portion of the entire tract which was

P-283   assigned to the widow, to James Standefer, as dower which is
taken and considered as held by said mortgage deed. It is therefore ordered adjudged and decreed that the mortgage aforesaid be foreclosed
and that the tract of three hundred and thirty acres of land as herein
before described together with the defendants interest of one fifth of
P-284   that protion of the entire tract alloted to James Standefer
widow as dower be sold and the proceeds of the sale be applied in the
first place to the payment of the costs of this suit including such as
may hereafter accrue? therein , secondly to the payment of complainants
said debt of seventeen hundred and sixty three dollard with the interest
hhereon at the rate of six percent per anum from the 30th day of May 1839
untill paid and the balance if any be paid over to the defendant-- It is
further ordered that the clerk and master , of this court after giving
30 days written notice at three or more places in Bledsoe County one of
which shall be at the court housein Pikeville shall on the said tract
of land sell the same at public sale to the highest bidder, on a credit
of six months taking bondand good security for the purchase money and retain a lein upon the land untill the same be paid. And that he report
this court how he shall have performed the duties assigned him under
this decree.

P-284
        Samuel M. Johnson   )   Demurror
              vs   )
        Sarah Shelton & others   )   Be it remembered that this cause
)   came on to be argued upon the
    ---------------------------   )   defendants demurror to the comp-
                                          lainants cross bill and because
it appears to the satisfaction of the court that the complainants bill w
was filed to late and that the causes in said demurror were well taken .
It is therefore ordered and decreed by the court that said demurror be
sustained and the said cross bill be dismissed that the injunction heret-
tofore granted be dissolved and that the clerk and master pay over to
P-285   the defendants the funds in his hands as required by the decree
numbered upon the original bill filed by the defendants ahd that complainant SamuelM. Johnson pay the costs of the cross bill for which an execution may issue as at law.

P-285
        Joel B. Arondal   )   Came the defendant
              vs   )   Alfred Satndifer by his
        Alfred Satndifer Green H. Pryor)   Counsel and moved the
        and James H. Hendrix   )   court to withdraw his
)   answer and be permit-
    ---------------------------   )   ted to file a demurror
in this cause and it appearing to the satisfaction of the court that
said answer had been filed by the clerk through a mistake . It is ordered
that the same be withdrawn and the defendant be permitted to file a demurror . Thereupon came on this cause to be heard upon said demurror to
complainants bill and after argument of Counsils and mature deliberation
 of the court because it appears to the satiffection of the court that
the complainants ranidy? on his alledged warranty the contract having

P-285   been fully executed, is as law. and because the complainant he
has no debt upon which an attachment could lawfully issued and that complainant is entitled to no adjustice? this court. It is therefore ordered
adjudged and decreed by the court that the complainants bill be dismissed
the injunction heretofore granted dissolved and the attachment discharged
nand that complainant pay the costs of this suit for which execution may
issue as at law. From which said decree the complainant by his counsel
prayed an appeal to the next term of the supreme court to be holden at
Knoxville on the 2nd Monday of September next and the same is allowed him
upon his giving bond and security according to law on or before the first
Monday in ***---------- next.

P-285

John Hankins   )   Be it remembered that on
          vs   )   this 12th day of March 1845
Aladin Parmley Jas. M. Johnson   )   this cause came on to be
and John Henson   )   finally heard and determi-
)   ned before the honorable
---)   Broomfield L. Ridley Chancellor & C. upon the bill answers replication and proof in the cause
and because it appears to the satisfaction of the court that the complainant was informed of all the incumbrances complained of upon the land
mentioned in the bill and the complainant took from defendant Parmley a
warrentie deed of conveyance and that (-Page 286) Complainant has never
been erided therefrom upon the whole case the court is not entitled to t
the relief prayed for in his bill it is therefore ordered adjudged and
decreed by the court that the complainants bill be dismissed the injunction dissolved and the complainant pay the cost of this suit for which
an execution may issue as at law.

P-286

Weatherston S. Greer Administrator   )   Be it remembered
of John Humes deceased   )   that on this 18th
          vs   ORIGINAL Bill   )   day of March 1845
John Sheriek   )   before the honorable
Chatten F. Pollard   )   B. L. Ridley Chan-
          vs   Cross Bill   )   cellor the original
Weatherston S. Greer John Shreik   )   cause came on to be
and Ambrose L. Shweik   )   further heard upon
)   the report of the
---)   Clerk and Master ,
                                                 heretofere ordered
in this cause . And the cross bill taken for confessed. And the said report being unexcepted to is in all things confirmed. from which it appears that there was due on the 10th of March 1845 from the defendants
Shreiks to the complainant Greer is administrator of principal and interest the sum of $ 479.80 ¢ which there is due as consideration or pur-
chase money for the tract of land attended inthis cause the sum of
$ 310.48 which land is described as lying in the County of Bledsoe in
the second civil destrict in the Grassy Cove containing about one hundred

P-286   acres being the tract of land, purchased by the defendant
Shreik from Pleasant R. Gibson and is in whole or in part bounded by the
lands of W. S. Greer John Ford and William Gibson . And is suitated on
    the west side of Cove creek and it further appears from the alligations
contained in the cross bill that there is due from the defendant Shreik
to complainant Pollard the sum of $ 250 by note due on or before the 25th
day of December 1838 and that the same is also consideration or purchase
money for said land --- It is therefore ordered adjudged and decreed that
the said tract of land be sold and the proceeds applied in the first place
to the payment of all the costs in the original and cross bill and secondly
the payment of $ 310.40 ⍧ with interest from the loth of March 1845 bill
paid due to complainant Greer as purchased money on said land, and that
the balance of the proceeds remain subject to the further order of the
court (page 287) as to its appliancation . It is further ordered that the
Clerk and Master after giving forty days notice of the time and place of
sale at the court house in Pikeville and at three other places in Bledse
County two of which shall be in the 2nd civil destrict shall sell the
said land at public auction to the highest bidder at the courthouse door
in the town of Pikeville on a credit of six and twelve months taking
bond and security retaining a lein on said land and that he make report
hereof to the next term of the court.

P-287

Jackson Pryor Administrator
of Thomas Burnett deceased
          vs
Wm. A. Hargiss & Erasmus Alley

                           Be it remembered that on
                           this 12th day of March 1845
                           befor the honorable B.L.
                           Ridley Chancellor & C
                           the above cause came on to
                           further be heard upon this
bill answers and proofs; And it appearing to the court that Wm. A. Harris
has given bond and security as required in a former decretal order made
in this cause it is ordered and decreed that all the assets of the merchantile concern mentioned in the pleadings except whathare in defendant Alleys hands be placed under the control direction and management of
said Hargiss the proceeds of which he in the first plawe apply to the
payment of the merchantile debts of Thomas Burnett decd other that those
for which defendant Alley is bound as strictly and that Jesse C. Robinson
former reciever in this cause hand over to him all such books and effects of said concern as may remain in his hands and that the clerk and
master deliver over to him such as may have been filed in his office by
said Robinson taking his receipt therefor or requiring him to leave a
copy in the office-- It is further ordered that the Clerk and Master
credit and settle the account of the said Jessse C. Robinson and make
report thereof to the next term of this court allowing him just and reasonable compensation for his services--- It is further ordered that the
clerk and master take and state an account showing w hat of the effects
of the said merchantile concern were placed in defendants Alleys hands
to indemify him as Burnett herly how much said Alley is or was security
for, to whom and when due also what amount of such debts is paid, to
whom and at what time--- It is forther ordered that he take and state
an account showing of what the whole merchantile stock of Thomas (P-288)

P-288 Burnett at the time of his death consisted , including money, goods notes bonds , accounts property and e fects of were descriptive and also the amounts of the indebtedness of said Burnett on account of said concern and to whom--that he ascertain and show what portion of said effects were placed in alleys hands what portion in received Roberson and what portion remained in the hands of the defendant Hargis and in what manner such as remain ed in Hargis 's hands were disposed of by him-- That he also ascertain and report what amount of Capitol if any said Burnett advanced or put into said Mercantile consern, and what amount Hargis advanced if any-- It is further ordered that defendant Hargis and Alley each report to the next term of this court showing the amount and condition of the fund in their hands what amount they may have collected ed and how disposed of and that ach succeeding court they make a similar report at the begining of the term untill the business is closed--or untill the further order of the court.

P-288

Mary Bell by her next
f   Friend Wm. Gibbon
         vs
Isaac Benson and others

Be it remembered that this cause came on to be heard upon the report of the clerk and master, which report being unexpected to is in all t hings confirmed from which report it

appears that defendant Benson hath executied his bond with appropriate covenants with good security to faithfully perform his trust or guardianship But because the court doth think proper to make complainant a word of this court It is orderd and decreed that defendant continue his guardianship of complainant and that the further execution of said decree be suspended untill the further order of this court and that this cause continue on the dockett of this court in order to take such orders and steps from time to time as the interest and welfare of said Mary requires to effect the object of the trust confided to the defendant Benson--

P-288

Audley M. Martin
         vs
Thompson Gardenhire and
Wm. L. Gardenhire

On motion of complainant counsil this cause is remanded (P-289) to the rules and b consent of parties and the assent of the court John Kelley and Samuel Mitchell of Marion County are hereby appointed to survey the

land in controversy in the pleadings and to examine the same and report the fact as to the mistake alledged in the complainants bill and report on all the facts raised in the pleadings so as to inform the court whether complainant entered through mistake on an quarter section where it did not embrace his mill site and show whether the corners and lines of the adjoining fractions are marked and designated as required by law and whether there is such mistake as charged in the bill and to report the situation of the quarter section actually entered by complainant supposing he was ente4ing his mill site and also the one sat? in? court and also the land clamed by the defenadant.

P-289

| John Billingsley |
| vs |
| William Brown |

Be it remembered that this cause on to be heard upon the report of the clerk and master and the exceptions of the complainant thereto which exceptions having been considered of the court is of opinion that saidexceptions were well taken -- Whereupon it is ordered by the court that said exceptions be sustained and report be corrected and that defendant be charged with sixty dollars with interest thereon from Janry 1842 to h this time being ten dollars and eighty cents whereupon it is ordered and decreed that complainant receive of the defendant the sum of seventy dollars and eighty cents and the cost of this suit that execution issue for the same as at law.

P-289

| George W. Rice |
| vs |
| The Bank of Tennessee |

It is ordered in this cause that the defendants have leave to file their answer in two months with corporale seal thereto that is answer they now present, but complainant, may not withstanding go on and take the deposition of N. B. Baird, J. F. Bradford and James O. White upon the usual notice and as if replication had been filed to the answer so as to try said cause at the next term of this court and that the evidence now on file be read as evidence on the hearing.

P-290

Wednesday 12th March 1845

| Jesse W. Turley |
| vs |
| Thomas Sutherland & |
| Berden Wheeler |

Be it remembered that this cause came on to be heard on this 12th day of March before the honorable B. L. Ridley Chancellor upon the bill, answer replication and proof in the cause when by the consent of the court it is agreed that the defendant Thomas Sutherland pay to the complainant the sum of $ 115.00 and that the defendant Berden Wheeler the sum of $ 85.00 ¢ and that the defendant pay the cost of this sail whereupon it adjudged and decreed by the court that the compl. receiver of the defendant Thos. Sutherland the sum of $ 115. and of the said Berden Wheeler the said sum of $ 85.00 and that said defendant pay the cost of this suit for all of which execution may Issue as at law.

P-290

| James J ? Thompson |
| vs |
| John Horn |

Be it remembered that this cause came on to be heard upon the report of the clerk and master heretofore ordered in this cause and which being unexcepted to is in all things confirmed from

P-290   which it appears that the clerk and master sold the tract   of
land mentioned in the pleadings after advertising the same 40 days   in
the town of Pikeville on the 6th day of January 1845 to Benjim F. Bridgman for the sum of $ 121.00 he being the assignee under a contract of
complainants interest in said sale and purchased the same to perfect
his title and which sum the complainant admits he has received by virtue of the sale made to Bridgman whereupon the court doth order and decree that said tract of land by meats and bounds as herein described
tract beginning on a Black Walnut tree marked J ?H thence south 40   o
East 112 poles to a post oak saplin in a hollow thence north 50 o   252
poles to a stake hickory and two black oaks pointers Thence north 40 o
West 126 poles to a Spanish oak on the side of a ridge thence south 50 o
252 poles to a hickory   hence south 40 o E 14 poles to the beginning
containing two hundred acres the legal title be decreed out of John Horn
and be vested in the said Benjm F. Bridgman and his heirs forever in
ful compliance with complainants warranty contained in his deed-- and t
the costs of theis suit to be paid by the complainant in the first instance & said complainant have execution bwwr against the said John Horn
for the same, for which an execution may issue as at law.

P-291

Wednesday 12th March 1845

Joseph G. Smith   )   Scin? Fa
    vs   )
Daniel Qualls   )   Came the complainant by his solicitor
)   and on motion and it appearing to the
)   satisfaction of the court that a Scion?
        Faceas has been duly made known to the
defendant Daniel Qualls and that he does not appear and plead to the
same but make default . It is therefore ordered and decreed by the court
that the complainant have execution against the defendant for the sum of
Thirty four dollars and ninety & one half cents the costs on the scerie?
Faceas mentioned together with the costs of the scerie Faceas for which
an execution may Issue.

P-291
Noble Ladd   )   Be it remembered that on this 12th day of
    vs   )   March 1845 this cause came on to be heard
Evans James   )   before the Honorable B. L. Ridley Chance-
)   llor and C upon the report of the clerk and
        master heretofore ordered which said report
        being unexcepted to is in all things confirm-
ed, from which it appears that the clerk and master after giving 40 days
notice in writing at the court house door in the town of Jasper, and
three other places in the county of Marion, on the 15th day of February
1845 sold the several tracts of land mentioned in the pleadings on a
credit of twelve months to Noble Ladd he being the highest and best bidder
at the sum of $ 18.92 it being only the amount of the costs. It is there-
fore ordered adjudged and decreed by the court that the title to the several tracts of land particularly mentioned in the pleadings be devested

P-291   out of Evan James and vested in the compl Noble Ladd forever subject however to the lein for the purchase money and the costs being
unpaid it is ordered that execution issue against the complainant for
the same

      H. Stoddard and Wood   )   Be ir remembered that on this 12
              vs   )   day of March 1845 this cause
  Wm. A. Hargis and others   )   came on to be heard beore the
)   honorable B. L. Ridley chancelor
                                  and C. Upon the report of the

Clerk and Master heretofore ordered in this cause which being unexcepted
to is in all things confirmed. And it appearing from said report that
the rwo negroes Delphia and Rocky mentioned thereon were sold at the
courthouse door inthe town of Jasper on the 15th day of February1845 when
Green H. Pryor became the purchaser at the sum of $515.00 In paying down
for which the said Green H. (P-292) is liable and is to give his note,
but the clerk and master is instructed not to collect said sum of $365.
untill the question of Pryor previous lien has been settled and it
further appeared that the commissioners appointed to lay off the widows years provision allowed her $150. on which said sum was decreted
by the drecreetal order to be paid by the Clerk and Master and was paid
accordingly and it further appeared that the clerk had ordered a publication in the Chattanooga gazette a paper prented in Hamilton County
Tennessee derecting all the creditors to file their claims preparatory
to a final distrubution of said estate. But because the administrator
has made no report of the assets in his hands belonging to said estate
and the court being of opinion that it is necessary for said administrator to make such report in order to a distribution of the same
whereupon the court doth order adjudge and decree that the title to
said slaves Delphia andBetty be devasteed out of the administrator Jackson Pryor and vested in Green H. Pryor and his heirs forever subject nee
nevertheless to a lein upon said slaves for the $365.00 untill the same
be paid or untill he execute his note with security to the clerk and
master for the purchase money and it is further ordered that the sum of
$700. paid to the widow as her allowance shall not be estemated as a
portion of said estate that the clerk and master order the administrator
Jackson Pryor to come before him to render an account of all the
assets belonging to said estate and the clerk and master is hereby ordered to take and state an account of all the assets in the hands of said
administrator to be administered or which might have come to his hands
by ordinary diligence and that he further audit and settle all egal
claims or demand against said estate and report what he has done to the
next term of this court all other matters received untill the coming on
of said report.

P- 292
    Stoddard and Wood et al   )   Be it remembered that this cause
            vs   )   come on to be heard before the
    Eliza Burnett et al   )   Honorable B. L. Ridley chancelor
)   and C. upon the report of George
                                  W. Rice David Rankin Samuel B.
Mitchell, Wm. F. Griffith and William A. Sorrels commissoners appointed
to law off the widow her dower in the lands of her deceased husband

Thomas Burnett, which report being unexcepted to is inall things confir-
P-293   med from which it appears that lot No 66 in the town of
Jasper with all the improvements and evictions thereon were as signed
to said widow for her dower whereupon it is ordered adjudged and decreed
by the court that the heirs at l w be devested of their possessory
title and that the said Elizabeth Burnett be seised of a life estate in
said lot and improvements, and that she pay all costs for the assigning
of the same. And that the commissioners be allowed the sum of one
dollar each for their services as such.

P-293
   Ann Thompson   )   Be it remembered that on this 12th
       vs   )   day of March 1845 This cause came on to
   Jesse C. Robinson   )   be heard before the honorable B. L.
)   Ridley Chancelor and C. upon the bill

and answer of respondent and motion to disolve the injunction and it appear-
int to the satisfaction of the chancelork that all the equities in the
complainents bill are fully met. It is therefore ordered adjudged and
decreed by the court that the injunction heretofore ordered in this
cause be disolved--and it further appearing that Cyrus P? Clayton was
the security of the complaimnt in the injunction bond and that there
was due to the defendant on the 17th of Nov. 1844 the time for the
rendition? of the judgmnt of the justice the sum of $105.50¢ It is
therefore ordered adjudged and decreed by the court that the defend-
and Robinson recover of the compoainant and her said security Cyrus P.
Clayton the said sum of $105.50 ¢ and the interest thereon but that
no execution issue for the same untill the defendant give bond and
security to refund the same with the interest thereon if upon the
final hearing of this cause it shall be so decreed.

*293
   Azariah Shelton nnd others   )   Came the parties by their
         vs   )   solicitors and it appearing
   Sarah Shelton and others   )   that no report has been filed
)   it is ordered that the order

requiring an additional report
at the last term be revised. and it further appearing that the funds
for the sale of the negroes heretofore sold by order of this court had
not been paid in to the office, it is further ordered that the Clerk
and Master procede to collect the same and apply them as required by
the (P-294) former decree in this cause

And then the court adjourned untill court in course.

                    Broomfield Ridley

P-294   Monday,Sept. 8th 1845

State of Tennessee Bledsoe county--
   Be it remembered that at a chancery oppened and held in the

fourthe chancery division a t the courthouse in the town of Pikeville
on the second Monday and Eighth day of September 1845. there was present
on the bench the Honorable Broomfield L. Ridlery Chancellor and C.

Samuel McReynolds and Valentine Spring) Be it remembered that
      vs) as it appears to the court
J. F. Read and wife.) that the clerk and master
) was presented from taking
) and stating the accounts
between the parties it is ordered that the decreetal order made at the
last term of this court revised and that the clerk and master report to
the next term of the court.

P-294
  Azeriah Shelton and others) Be it remembered that this
     vs) cause came on again to be
  Sarah Shelton and others) heard upon report of the
) clerk and master heretofore
) ordered from which report it
appears that the defendant Henry A. Shelton the administrator failed
and refused to appear and have the account taken as directed in the
introcutory decree rendered in this cause at the last term of this court
whereupon on motion of the complainant by his counsil It is ordered by
the court that an attachment issue requiring the defendant Henry A. to
appear at the next term of this court and show cause why an attachment
presentory shall not issue against him. and it is further ordered that
the decreetal order made at the last term of this court directing an
account to be taken in this cause be revised that the clerk and master
report upon the matte s therein refered to the next term of this
court.

Monday Sept. 8th 1845

P-295
  Jackson Pryor Administrator) This day came the parties by
     vs) their Solicitors and because
  William A. Hargess and) it appears from the report
  Erasmus Alley) of the clerk and master that
) he was by sickness prevented
) from taking and stating an
account as directed in the decreetal order made at the last term of this
court--It is further ordered by the court that said decretal order be
revised and that the clerk and master report upon the matters therein
refered to the next term of this court.

P-295
  James Kenney? and the heirs of) By consent of the parties This
  Wm. Gardenhire) cause is remanded to the
     vs) rules and the parties are
  Samuel Williams and others) allowed to take depositions
) of any of the defendants

subject to all legal exceptions and on motion It is further ordered
by the court that an attachment will issue requiring the guardian adopt-
ion? of the infant to show cause why he has not answered said bill

P 295

Henry Stoddard and John Wood)
)
vs)
)
Jackson Pryor admr. and)
Green H. PryoR)
Eliza Burnett George W. Burnett)
Wm. A. Hargiss)
)
-----------------------------------)

This day came the parties y
by their Solicitors and
because it appeared from
the report of the Clerk
and master, that he was
prevented by sickness
from taking and stating
the account directed in the
introductory decree rendered in this cause at the

last term of this court. It is ordere d by the court that said intod-
uctory decree be retised and that the clerk and master report upon the
matte s therein refered at the next term of this court.

P-295

John Hazeltine Daniel Haddock)
and Wade B. Hazeltine)
vs)
Jesse H. Standifer E. M. Evans)
Arthur T. Crozier and Arthur Crozier)
)
-----------------------------------)

This day came James
A. Whiteside Esq. and
suggested to the court
that Arthur T. Crozier
departed this life since
the last continueance
of This cause.

P-296

Monday Sept 8th 1845

George W. Rice)
Vs.)
The South Western Rail)
Road Bank at Knoxville)
)
-----------------------------------)

Be it remembered that on this 8th
day of September 1845 this cause
came on to be heard before the
honorable B. L. Ridley Chancellor
and C. upon the bill answer replication and proof on the cause

because it appeared to the court that the testimony of James Rankin would
be material for respondents on the final hearing of this caus It is
ordered by the court that respondent have leave to take said Rankins
deposition and on motion of respondents co nsil it is further ordered by
the court that the respondent be permitted to file such documentory evidence as may be in possession of respondent on or before the second rule
day and that complainant Rice be allowed to take dibutting? testimorny
and further that this cause stand for hearing at the next term.

P-296

G. W. White, Elizabeth Minton)
M. G. Smith, Nancy Walker)
Martha Smith and Susa L. Smith)

Be it remembered that on
this 8the day of Sept. 1845
this application came on to

heirs at law of David Smith decd.   )   To be heard before the
    Expatie   )   honorable B. L. Ridley
application for partition of   )   Chancelor and C. upon
   Real Estat   )   the petition filed--
)   from which it appears
               that petitioners are
               the heirs at law of

David Smith decd. and that he the said David Smith decd. seised and
possessed of the lands mentioned in the petition and it further appearing from said petition that the interest of all said heirs require a
division of said lands and that the samd may be held in severally and
the names of Phillip Woods A. B. Outon Wm.L. Rogers Jacob Newman and
Jonathan Pope being sugested in said petition as commissioners to to
partition and divide said lands   It is ordered adjudged and decreed
by the court that Philip Woods, A. B. Outon Wm. L. Rogers Jacob Newman
and Jonathan Pope be appointed commissioners whos duth it shall be
to divide and set apart to each of the artitioners in severally their
respective shars of the lands and premises described in such case made
and provided and make report to the next term of this court.

        Monday 8th Septr. 1845

P-297

  Thomas Brown and   )   Be it remembered that the master
  William F. Brown   )   motion of the defendants to di v-
     vs   )   ide the injunction heretofore
  Mary A. E. McCull and   )   granted in this cause came on to
  David McCull   )) be heard and determined and be-
)   cause it appears to the court
              that the defendants answer fully

meets and deems? the equity in complainants bill It is ordered adjudged
and decreed by the court that said injunction be divided and that the
respondent proceed at law to judgment in all the causes now pending in
the circuit court of Rhea co unty, but before respondent Mary A. E.
take out execution on said judgemnts she is required to execute bond
with sufficient security to refund at the final hearing of this cause
said bond to be executed and delivered to the clerk and master of this
court--and on motion of the complainants by their Solicitors and for
reasons appearing to the satisfaction of the court leave is given them to
annul? their bill filed in this cause on or before the second rule day
upon the payment of the costs of the amendment--

The court then adjourned untill Tomorrow morning 8 o'clock

             Broomfield Ridley

P297   Tuesday Septr 9th 1845

  Court met persuant to adjournment present on the bendh the honorable
B. L. Ridley Chancelor and C.

P-297

Bird Thomas) Be it remembered that on this 8th day
vs) of September 1845 this cause came on
Austin M. Hamner?) to be heard before the Hon. B. L.
) Ridley Chancellor and C on the bill
and the demurrer? rents by the Defendant Hamner? and because it appears to
the satisfaction of the chancellor that the is no equity in the bill
which entitles the complainant to any relief ? in this court It has therefore pleased the chancellor to order adjudged and decree that the bill be
P-298   dismissed that the said Austin M. Hanmer have leave to proceed
to the collection of his judgment at law and that the complainant pay the
costs of this court for which an execution may issue as at law from which
Judgment of the court the complt appeal to the next term of the Supreme
Court at Knoxville which is granted on his giving security by 2nd rule
day.

P-298

John B. Seamon) Be it remembered that on this 9th
vs) day of Sept. 1845 before the Hon-
William I? Standifer) orable B. L. Ridley Chancellor &
) C The above cause came on to be
further heard upon the report of
the clerk and master which   is
unexcepted to and it appearing from said report of the clerk and master
that he had in the comformity ? with the decree rendered in this cause
at the last term sold the land and premises mentioned in the said decree
to James Loyd for the sum of eight hundred and seventy five dollars and
fifty cents and that he had paid the consideration in full therefore to
the satisfaction of complainant and that the complainant had paid the cost
of this suit. It is therefore by the court ordered adjudged and decreed
that the said sale and report be in all things confirmed and that the title of the defendant in and to the land named and described in the decree
be divested out of the said William I. Standifer and vested in the said
James Loyd his heirs and assigns forever and that a writ issue from this
court commanding the sheriff of Bledsoe County to place him in possession
of the same.

P-298

Hazeltine Haddock & Co.) The complainants by their soli-
vs) citor came and require proof of
E. M. Evans and Others) the death of the defendant
) Arthur T. Crozier which was yes-
terday sugested of record whereupon it is ordered by the court
that the matter be referred to the clerk and master and that he report to
the next term of this court whether the said Arthur T. Crozier be de ad
or not.

Samuel & O. R. Bean) Be it remembered that on this 9th
vs) day of September 1845 before the
Samuel B. Mead) Honorable B. L. Ridley Chancellor

P-299   & C the above cause
Tuesday Sept. 9th 1845

came on to be heard upon bill answer replication exhibits and proof and it appearing to the court that Obediah Bean complainants testator about the year ------- became bound as Meads security for the sum of $ 364 for which Judgment was rendered against them jointly in the Circuit Court of Marion County and that Mead to endemify said Obediah Bean against loss placed in his hands sundry notes and accounts amounting to the sum of six or seven hundred dollars of which the said joint judgment and something over and that he paid a portion of said collection to Mead and it further appearing that Obediah Bean departed this life about the year ------ leaving the matters unadjusted between him and Mead and that after his death a settlement took place between complainants as Obediah Bean executors and Mead in which a mistake occured in an omition to charge Mead with $ 108.50 the amount mentioned in his receipt of 7th Dec. 1838 to Obediah Bean and it further appearing that the parties agreed at the time of the settlement that any mistake thereon should be rectified--- But as it does not appear to the court how much Obediah Bean collected and paid over to the satis-faction of the joint judgment and costs and to Mead nor what amount   of the uncollected notes and accounts placed in his hands by Mead were retur-ned to him by the complainant or their testator. It is ordered and decreed that the clerk and master of this court upon the proof on file in this cause and such others as may be brought before hom to take and state   an account of the same showing the amount in notes and accounts received from Mead by Bean the amount by him clooected thereon-- what depo sition he made of the same- for what amount the complainants accounted to Mead after Obediah s death -, The amount of notes and accounts returned to him the amount for which they gave Mead their notes and date thereof & time due and the payment thereon & that he report to the next term of   this court.

P-299
> Alfred Shorter & E. Foster
>   vs
> Daniel Yarnell et al
> % %

The complainants by James A. Whiteside their attorney came and dismiss their bill and by agreement (Page 300) Samuel T ? Igow confesses

Judgment for the costs. It is therefore ordered by the court that the complainants bill be dismissed and that the said Samuel T. Igow pay the costs of this suit for which execution may Issue as at law.

P-300
> Joseph G. Smith
>   vs
> Anderson Skillern &
> Henry Miller

The complainant by his attorney James P. Thompson esq. came and directed his bill to be dismissed Whereupon it was ordered and decreed by the court that said bill bill be dismissed and that the complainant pay all the costs in this behalf

expended for which an execution may issue as at law.

P-300

James Parker? & William Parker)
        vs)
John C. Everett Benjamin R. King)
Elizabeth Rice & Charles B. Raines)
)

It appearing to the sat-
isfaction of the court
that at the March term
of the Chancery Court
held at Pikeville in the
year 1843 a decree was
had devesting the tittle

to the lands and town lots mentioned in said decree out of the defendant
and vesting the same in the complainants and no writ of possession having
been ordered to issue It is therefore ordered by the court that a writ of
possession of the land and town lots mentioned in said January decree.

P-300

Audley M. Martin)
        vs)
Thompson Gardenhire &)
Willie J. Gardenhire)
)

Be it remembered that this cause
came on to be heard before the
Honorable B. L. Ridley on this 9th
of Sept. 1845 upon the bill answers
replication proof and exhibits
when it appeared to the satisfaction of the court that complain-

ant as assignee of Black was entitled to the occupant claim as a mill site
in the Ocoe district , that complainant had erected her said Mill of said
quarter it being the the southwest quarter of section 1st fractional
township 1st Range west of the bases line lying in the south corner thereof
and upon which the mills are situated, the court being satisfied from the
proof that complainant entered (Page 301) a nother fraction through mistake
supposing he was entering the quarter on which the said Mills are erected
and it further appearing that defendants entered the same fractional quarter on which the complainant had built his mill and that defendants had no
legal right to enter the same as a general enterer upon the whole case the
court is of opinion that complainant is entitled to hold the quarter upon
which his mills are built and that defendants entry is illegal and void-
Whereupon the court doth order adjudged and decree that defendants grant
for said quarter be cancelled and delivered up and that the legal title to
fractional which the said mills are built be divested out of the defendant
and vested in the complainant and that complainant pay the costs of this suit
for which an execution may issue.

P-301

Weatherston S. Greer Administr vs John Kimmer deceased)
b vs John Shreah & Ambrose S. Shreak)
          &)
Chatten T ? Pollard)
        vs)
John Shreak & A. S. Shreak)
)

Bill &
Cross Bill

Be it re-
membered
that on
this 9th
day of

September 1845 before the honorable B. L. Ridley Chancellor & C the above
cause came on to be heard and delivered upon the report of the clerk and
master, which is unexcepted to, and it appears from said report of the rep
port of the clerk and master that he had in conformity with the decree

P-301   rendered in this cause at the last term sold the land mentioned
in said decree to Weatherston S. Greer for the sum of $ 310. Which   he
was permitted to retain in his own handsthe same being due to and coming
to him under said decree It is therefore ordered adjudged and decreed by
the court that the said sale and report be in all things confirmed and
that the title of the defendants in and to the land described in the decree
be divested out of the said John Shreak and Ambrose L. Shreak and vestedb
in the said Weatherston S..Greer his heirs and assigns forever and that a
writ issue to the sheriff of Bledsoe County to deliver to him the possession of the same. It is further ordered and decreed that the complainant
Weatherston S. Greer pay the costs of the suit in the first place (Page 302)
and that he have execution thereof over against the defendant except the
costs of the cross bill which is ordered shall in the first instance   be
paid by complainant Pollard and that he have execution therefor over,
against the defendant.

P-302

    Erasmus Alley Administr & C   )   On motion and because
            vs   )   it appears to the court
    The Heirs of Walter I ? Alley decd.   )   that James Peak the
      6 _)   guardian adliten?   of
                                        the minor heirs of
                                        Walter I. Alley decd
had not answered It is ordered by the court that this cause be remanded tot
the rules and that Alexander Alley be appointed guardian ad litem of said
minor heirs in place of the said James Peak.

P-302

    Jeptha Barber?   )   Be it remembered that the de-
        vs   )   murrer of the defendants to
    Green H. Pryor & Others   )   complainants bill came on for
)   argument, and the matters of
    _ _ _ _ _ _ _ _ _ _ _ _ _ _ _ _   demurrer being considered of by
                                the court , It is ordered ad-
judged and decreed by the court that said demurrer be overruled and that
the defendants be required to answer said bill.

P-302

    Martha Hatfield   )   This day came the complainant by
    by her nex friend   )   James A. Whiteside Esq and filed
    Marcellus Smith   )   a request in writing that this
        vs   )   suit should be dismissed. Where-
    Hyrom Hatfield & Others   )   upon it was ordered adjudged and
)   decreed by the court that this
    _ _ _ _ _ _ _ _ _ _ _ _ _ _ _ _ _)   suit should be dismissed and that
Marcellus Smith as the next friend of complainant pay the costs for which
let Fi Fa? issue .

P-303

Tuesday 9th Septr. 1845

P-303 John Skillern & Henry Miller)   On motion of Defts Solici-
        & Lawson Guthrie   )   tor & because it appears to
              vs   )   the court that more than
     Joseph G. Smith   )   two terms of the court have
)   elapsed since the last step
- - - - - - - - - - - - - - - - - -)   taken in the cause it   is
therefore ordered that the same be dismissed? as for more prosecution &
that complts pay the costs of the same for which let Fe Fa issue.

P-303
     Benj. R. King   )   It appearing to the court that this cause
         vs   )   has been set for hearing presentively?
     James & Wm. Park   )   it is ordered that the same be remanded
)   to the rules with leave to matire? the
- - - - - - - - - - - - -)   same for hearing and then the Chancellor
                               ordered the court to be adjourned, till
the regular term, which is done accordingly.

                                          Broomfield Ridley

P-303
State of Tennessee   )   November term of the of the Circuit Court
Bledsoe County   )   of Bledsoe County held at the court house in
)   the town of Pikeville on the 2 Monday of
- - - - - - - - - - -)   November 1845 the onorable John A, Cannon
                           presiding.

P-303
     George W. Hopkins and others   )   This cause being brought
              vs   )   into this court by the clerk
     Franklin Locke and others   )   and Master of the Chancery
)   Court at Pikeville by   an
- - - - - - - - - - - - - - - - - - -)   order (Page 304) of the
Chancellorpresiding (he being incompetent to hear and determine the same)
came the complainants by James P? Thompson their solicitor and suggested
the death of Andrew Jackson & Thomas Crutcher two of the respondants which
is not claimed?
     And then the court adjourned until court in course.

                    Monday March 9th 1846

State of Tennessee)
Bledsoe County   )   Be it remembered that at a chancery court opened
)   and held in the fourth chancery division at the
- - - - - - - - - -)   courthouse in the town of Pikeville on the second
                         Monday and ninth day of March 1846, there was
on the bench the honorable Broomfield L. Ridley Chancellor & C.

Robert Burke   )
      vs   )   Be it remembered hat on Monday the 9th day of March

John B. Groves &   )   1846 before the Honorable Broomfield L.
John Kirk   )   Ridley chancelor and C.   This cause
)   came on to be heard pro confesso--It
)   appears from the bill that Robert Burke

in 1841 visited the state of Mississippi for the purpose of looking after
the estate of his brother William Burke decd, that the respondant Kirk
informed complainant be held a note against the deceased Henry Peaton
and William Grubb secu ity dated 10th December 1839 due twelve months
after date for seven thousand five hundred and two dollars and thirty
five cents and that complainant being desirous to receive as much as
possible of his deceased brothers estate that Kirk responded to complainant if he could get his note complainant would then be enabled to
administer upon said estate in the place of Peaton who had administered
and who would resign accordingly complainant executed his three notes to
Kirk all bearing interest from date and dated 3rd day of March 1841 the
first for fifteen hundred dollars, and due six months after date, the second for three thousand and seventy dollars and thirty five cents due
eighteen months after date. The 3rd for three thousand and seventy
dollars and thirty five cents due two years after date all in consideration of the seven thousand five hundred and two dollars and thirty five
cents note in consideration of the three executed as above described but
that he failed to do so: but placed the same in the hands of Nye? to in-
stitute suit on the same against (P-305) Peaton and Grubb in the name
of Kirk which was accordingly done: but it further appears that at the
May term of the Circuit court for Yazoo county Mississippi in 1842 for
one of John Kirk, against Henry Peaton and William Grubb the securities in
said note, that the same had been paid and discharged, and that a verdice
was found in said cause for the defendants and it further appears, that
some time in March after the execution of said notes the defendant Kirk
was greatly embarressed unto? insolvency: and that the defendant Groves
was liable as a security in a suit or suits then pending in Mury county in
order to idemify the said Groves as security the said Kirk placed the third
note mentioned in this decree for the sum of $3070.35 as an indemnity or
collatteral security and that defendant Groves paid not one cent for the
nor received it in due course of tracts not sustained any liability upon
his securityship and it further appears that defendant Groves instituted a
suit upon said note against complainant in Roane county at the October
term of the circuit court for said county 1843 and obtained judgment for
the sum of three thousand seven hundred and fourteen dollars beside costs
and that an execution was issued on said judgment and was placed in the hands
of the said sheriff of Bledsoe county for collection that chancelor Williams
granted an injunction to stay said execution on the 24th of March 1845----
upon the whold case the court is of opinion and doth order adjudge and
decree that defendant Groves be perpetually enjoined from the collection
of said notes because the same were not received in the dur course of
tracts, not a bona fide consideration were paid for the same; but that the
same were fraudently obtained and defenda nt Kirk be perpetually enjoined
from Pattempting to collect said judgment-- And that the complainant pay
the costs in this behalf expended, and have execution over against the
defendants for the same.

P-306

Wednesday 9th March 1846

P-306

Thomas Robinson ( )
vs
Thomas White

Be it remembered that on Monday 9th day of March 1846 this cause came on to be heard before the honorable Broomfield L. Ridley Chancellor & C upon the being taken for confessed against the defendant when it appears from the alligations that in 1843 defendant sold complainant two hundred and fifty acres of land mentioned in the pleadings making a warrenty deed for the sum of two hundred and fifty dollars one hundred of which was paid in advance previous to the execution of the deed that the complainant executed his three several notes to defendant all dated the 17th of September 1842? for fifty dollars each payable in one two and three years thereafter It further appears that defendant at the time of the sale had no title to the land and that the notes were fraudulently obtained and ought to be canceled the sale set aside and declared null and void, The court doth therefore order adjudged and decree that notes outstanding for collecion be perpetually enjoined and that complainant have judgment against defendant for the one hundred dollars advanced and interest thereon from the 17th of Septr, 1843 the time of the advancement and that the complainant pay all the costs of this cause and have execution against the defendant for the same for all which execution may issue as at law.

P-306

Erasmus Alley ( )
vs
Samuel B, Mead

This day came the complainant by her solicitor James A. Whiteside and directed this suit to be dismissed whereupon it was ordered adjudged and decreed by the court that this suit dismissed and that complainant pay the costs expended for which an execution

may Issue as at law.

P-306

Valentine Spring & ( )
Samuel McReynolds Trustees ( )
of Clarinda J. M. Reed ( )
Petition exparte ( )

Be it remembered that this cause came on to be heard upon the report of the clerk and master heretofore ordered which being unexcepted to is in all things confirmed- from which it appears that the hire of the slaves together with the proceeds of the sale of the land and negroes heretofore ordered constituted a fund in the hands of the Trustees amounting to the sum of 1671.06 1/4 and that of that sum there had been applied by the trustee for the benefit of the said Clarinda J. M. Reed in the purchase of other lands and necessaries the sum of $ 1437.20 leaving in the hands of the trustees unappropriated the sum of $ 33. 86 and that said trustees are entitled for their services each to the sum of 36.77¢ whereupon it was ordered adjudged and decreed by the court th that the trustee pay the costs in this behalf expended out of the fund in their hand and the residue be applied to the payment of the trustees for their services.

P-307

P-307

P-307 Henry Griffith)
        vs)
    Robert N. Gillespie)
              ─ ─ ─ ─ ─ ─ ─ ─ ─ ─)

Came the complainant by his solicitor James A. Whiteside and directed this cause to be dismissed whereupon it is ordered adjudged and decreed by the court that this suit be dismissed and that the complainant pay the costs in this behalf expended for which an execution may issue as at law.

P-307
    Hazeltine Haddock & Co.)
           vs)
    Ephraim M. Evans)
    Jesse H. Standifer)
    Arthur Crozier &)
    Arthur T. Crozier)
)
         ─ ─ ─ ─ ─ ─ ─ ─)

Be it remembered that this cause being set down for hearing (after the death of Arthur L. Crozier was suggested and proved and complainant agreed that his suit abate? as to Arthur L. so fare as this suit is concerned) upon the bill ammended bill and pro confesso as to Arthur Crozier and the answer of the defendants Evans & Standifer replication and evidence . hen it appeared to the satisfaction of the court that complainants recover a judgment against the defendants Evans for the sum of $ 394.97¢ besides the costs of this suit on the 13th day of July 1843. That on the 20th of February 1844 an alias Fi Fa issued on said judgment and came to the hands of the Sheriff of Bledsoe County which was returned no property to pay and satisfy the same. And it further appeared that the defendant Evans purchased the 220 acres of land e mentioned in the pleadings at the sum of $ 1200 from his codefendant Standifer. But because the court is not satisfied as to the amount of money due defendant Standifer and because the Court is not satisfied as to the probate P-308 and registration of the title bond executed by Standifer to defendant Evans- Whereupon the ordered and decreed that the clerk and master of the court take and state an account of the balance of the purchase money dueto defendant Standifer and further that he take proof as to the probate and registration of the title bond mentioned in the pleadings and report to the next term of this court. All other mattersare reserved untill the coming in of said report.

P-308
    Ephraim M. Evans)
         vs)
    Alexander H. Montgomery)
    and others)
         ─ ─ ─ ─ ─ ─ ─ ─ ─)

This day came James P. Thompson esq. and suggested that since the last continuance of this cause Alexander H. Montgomery and Uphoma P. Story two of the defendants departed this life , which is not

denied.

P-308
    George W. Rice)
         vs)
    The Bank of Tennessee)
    and others)
         ─ ─ ─ ─ ─ ─ ─ ─ ─)

On motion of the complainant by his solicitor and because it appears to the satisfaction of the court that this cause was prematurely placed upon the hearing

P-308   dockett it is ordered by the court the same be demanded to the rules.

Samuel & Owen R. Bean)
vs)
Samuel B. Mead)

It appearing to the satisfaction of of the court from the report of the Clerk and Master made in this cause that the parties after having notice failed to attend, and that thereby no account could be stated. Thereupon it was ordered by the court that the decreetal order heretofore entered in this cause be received and that the clerk and master report upon the matters therein refered to the next term of this court.

P-308
Charles F. Kramer)
vs)
Thomas White &)
Charles Foster)

Be it remembered that on Monday the 8th day of March 1846 this cause came on to be heard before the Honorably B. L. Ridley Chancellor & C upon the bill being taken for confessed against the defendants from the obligations in the complainants bill it appears that defendant White sold to complainant 250 acres of land for the sum of $ 250 and that complainant paid the sum of $ 100. and executed his three several promisory notes bearing date the 17th of Sept. 1843 for fifty dollars payable in one two (Page 309) and three years, and it further appears that defendant White at the time of the sale had no title to the land and that the money and notes paid in consideration for the same were fraudulently obtained. It is therefore ordered adjudged and decreed by the court that said sale be set aside and declared null and void , that all of said notes be perpetually enjoined from collection , and it further appears that defendant Foster purchased one of said notes which has been surrendered to complainant upon condition that Foster should pay no costs It is further considered by the court that Complainant pay the costs in this behalf expended and have execution therefor against the defendant Thomas White together with the further sum of $ 100 advanced on the 17th of Septr. 1843 and interest thereon untill paid. for which executions may issue as at law.

P-309
Azariah Shelton & Others)
vs)
Henry A. Shelton et al)

Be it remembered that this cause came on to be heard upon the report of the clerk and master heretofore ordered and which being u unexcepted to is in all things c confirmed from which it appears h that the administrators were chargeable with $ 4709.64 that out of that sum the distributors have received $ 2961.36 leaving undistributed the sum of $ 448.28¢ that out of the sum remaining undistributed , there is in the office of the clerk and master in money and notes arising from the hire and sale of the slaves the sum of $ 886. And it further appeared that there was still in the hands of the administrators the sum of $ 862.28 and of that sum there was due to the defendant Anderson Jones in right of his wife the sum of $ 18.94 , and to the complainant Azariah Shelton $ 281.11 and to

P-309   William Johnson in right of his wife Malinda $ 281.11. And to
Crespin B. Shelton the like sum of $ 281.11 And it further appearing   to
the satisfaction of the court that Richard Waterhouse Henry Collins Henry
Griffith and Spills B. Dyer are the securities of the defendant Henry A.
Shelton and Sarah Shelton as administrator and administratrix of the said
Crespin B. Shelton deceased- Whereupon it is ordered adjudged and decreed
by the court that the aforesaid distributirs have each their execution
against the said administrators & (Page 310) their said securities for the
aforesaid sums so remaining in the hands of the administrators amounting in
all to the sums of $ 862.28 and it is further ordered and decreed that the
clerk and master proceed to clooect the note still due and unpaid for the
P-310   sale of the slaves and after paying all the costs expended in this
cause out of the funds in his hands that he pay over to the distributors tk
the residue in the proportions specified in said report and that the complainants have execution over against the administrator and administrators
and their said securities for the costs.

    The court adjourned untill tomorrow 8 oclock.

                                            Broomfield Ridley

P-310   Tuesday March 10th 1846

    Court met pursuant to adjournment present on the bench the Honorable
Broomfield L. Ridley Chancellor & C.

Thomas Brown &   )   On motion of the defendant by her sol-
Wm. F. Brown   )   icitor leave is given her to take the
     vs   )   deposition of her co defendant David
Elizabeth McCull &   )   McCull to read as evidence at the hear-
Others   )   ing of this cause subject to all legal
)   exceptions.

P-310
The State of Tennessee   )   On motion of George W.
by the Attorney General   )   Thompson one of the defend-
     vs   )   ants by his solicitor it
The Jasper & Pelham Turnpike Co) is ordered by the court
)   that he be permitted to
                                 withdraw the books of the
                                 company filed in this cause,
for the purpose of using them as evidence in certain causes pending in the
circuit court of Marion County and that said books be filed with the clerk
& Master of this court at or before the hearing of this cause.

P-310
Ann Thompson   )   By consent of the parties by their
     vs   )   solicitors and with the assent of the
Jesse C. Robinson   )   court this cause is continued and re-
)   manded to the rules.

P-311   Tuesday 10th March 1846

Alexander H. Montgomery   )   Came the defendants by their
            vs   )   solicitor and suggested the
Lewis Merriman and   )   death of the complainant which
others   )   is not denied , and it appearing
)   to the satisfaction of the court
)   that Thomas N. Frazier and James
                                      A . Tulloss are the executors of
the said A. H. Montgomery, whereupon by consent & with the assent of the
court this cause is reviewed? in the name of the said executors and it is
further ordered that the defendants be allowed four months to file their
answer.

P-311
Bird Thomas   )   This day came the complainant by his
            vs   )   solicitor and directed the appeal
Austin M. Hammer   )   prayed and granted to him in this cause
)   at the last term of this court to be
)   dismissed, whereupon it is ordered ad-
)   judged and decreed by the court that
said appeal be dismissed-- and that the defendant have execution against
the complainant for the costs in this behalf expended.

P-311
Samuel B. Mead admr.   )   By consent of the parties by their
            vs   )   solicitors and with the assent of
b Wiley Webb and others   )   the court this cause is continued.
)   Complainant is ordered to file his
)   letters of administration with the
                                      clerk and master of this court   on
or before the second rule day.

P-311
Jeptha Barbee   )   It appearing to the satisfaction of
            vs   )   court that the complainant had filed his
Green H. Pryor   )   order in writing directs this cause   to
)   be dismissed. It is therefore ordered
)   adjudged and decreed by the court that
                                      said suit be dismissed and the complain-
ant pay all the costs in this behalf expended.

Alexander H. Montgomery &   )   This day came James P.
Euphema I. Story Admrs. of   )   Thompson esq. and suggested
Samuel L. Story   )   to the court that since the
            vs   )   last continuance of this
Thomas Crutchfield & the other   )   cause the complainant
creditors of Saml. L. Story decd.   )   Alexander H. Montgomery and
)   Euphema I. departed this life
)   which is not denied.

P-312   Tuesday 10th March 1846

Bryan Heard Guardian of   )   Be it remembered came on to be
Martha Smith   )   heard this 10th day of March 1846
Petition Expartie   )   and upon complainants petition be-
)   ing red the honorable B. L. Ridley
)   Chancellor was pleased to order
)   adjudged and decree that the land

mentioned in the petition be sold by the said Heard guardian as aforesaid
after advertising the same fifteen days to the highest bidder on a credit
of 12 Months requiring the purchaser , to give bond & security retaining
a lein on the land untill the purchase money is paid & report thereof to
the next term of this court.

P-312

G. W. White Elizabeth Minton   )   Be it remembered that
M. G. Smith, Nancy Walker   )   this application came
Martha Smith & Selvana L. Smith   )   o n again to be heard
heirs at alw of David Smith decd   )   upon the coming in of
Expartie   )   this report of the
Application for partition of real   )   commissioner hereto-
estate   )   fore appointed to
)   partition and set apart
)   the real estate mention-

ed in the petition which said report being unexcepted to in all things confirmed , and is in the words and figures following towit-
    The undersigned being unconnected with the parties either by affinity
or consanguinity and entirely disinterested having met and been duly sworn
as a jury to alot and set off to G. W. Smith, Martha Smith, Elizabeth Smith
Maleijah Smith Nancy Smith & Selvana Smith , three parts out of the real
estate of David Smith deceased after having duly considered and fully understood the whole matter, we have made partition of said real estate among
and between the heirs at law of David Smith with as much equality as practi-
ble as follows--
    We assign to Elizabeth Smith lot No. 1 containing 26 acres more or
less bounded as follows towit beginning in the center of the wagon road
thence south 50 east 92 poles to a black oak and 2 post oaks, thence north
50 west 92 poles to a stake in the center of the waggon road at the mouth
of a lane thence South 10 west 65 poles to the Beginning also a tract of
Land on Cumberland Mountain known as lot No. 3 beginning at a Black Oak the
north west corner of lot No. 1 , hence south 26 west100 poles to a chestnut
tree. Thence south 45 east to a back line (Page 313) on the side of the
Mountain Thence with a line north 45 east to a stake the south west corner
of lot No. 1 Thence with a line of the same to the beginning containing
120 acres more or less--
P-313   We assign to Martha Smith Lot No 2 towit -
    Beginning at a stake in the line of a 180 acre tract thence south 33
west 62 poles to a point in a branch to a ash white oak Elm and sewwt gum
pointers thence down said branch as it meanders to A. B. Ewton's line thence
with his line north 33 east 62 poles to a spotted oak Thence south 50 east
89 poles to a pos t oak Thence north 14 east 35 poles to a post oak Thence
north14 east 35 poles to a black oak thence north 50 west 92 poles to a p
point in the center of the wagon road thence south 10 west 34 poles to said

P-313   spotted oak Thence north 50 West 18 poles to the beginning containing 22 acres more or less also one tract on Cumberland Mountain known as lot No. 6 containing 120 acres more or less as follows Beginning at a pine the north west corner, of lot No. 4 Thence with a line of lot No. 5 to a stake in the western boundry line thence southwardly and eastwardly with the old line to a stake corner of lot No. 4 Thence with a line of the same north 45 west to the beginning.

We assign to Selvana Smith lot No. 3 containing 21 acres more or less towit Beginning on a stake the beginning corner of lot No. 2 thence north 50 west 58 poles to a mulberry thence south 33 west 72 poles to a stake Houts line with a black gum pointer, thence with said line down the branch to the north west corner of lot No. 2 Thence with said line to the beginning-- Also one tract on cumberland Mountain Containing 120 acres more or less towit Beginning on a black oak the north east corner of lot no. 1 thence south 26 west 162 poles to a chestnut tree Thence north 45 west to the back line . Thence north eastwardly to a pine. Thence south east to the Beginning .

We assign to Macijah Smith lot No. 4 containing 35 acres more or less towit Beginning at a Mulberry. Thence north 50 west 31 poles to a stake thence south 11 west 14 poles to a stake. Thence south 56 west 32 poles to a Hickory bush Thence south west 27 poles to a pine stump thence north 41 west to a stump? in the widows dower of 2000 acres. thence with the line of the same west to 2 black oaks Thence south 70 east 98 poles to a stake and black gum pointer . Thence north 35 east 72 poles to the beginning--- Also a tract of land on Cumberland Mountain known as lot No. 5 containing 120 acres more or less, towit beginning on a chestnut tree the south west corner of lot No. 2 thence south 26 west 20 poles to a chestnut tree thence south 12 west 100 poles with a line of lot No. 4 the line continued to the western boundry line. Thence northwardly with the back line to a stake corner lot No. 2 thence with a line of the same south 45 east to th e beginning.
P-314

Tuesday 10th March 1846.

We assign to G. W. Smith lot No. 5 containing 40 acres more or less towit Beginning at a Hickory stump in the Hoots line thence south 10 west 45 poles to a black walnut sapling thence north 77 west 82 poles to a stake thence north 55 west 52 poles to a stake thence north 55 west 38 poles to a hickory bush thence a direct line to a black gum Thence along A. B. Ewtons line to a brased red oak thence with Hoots line his corner near the head of a spring thence a direct line to the beginning-- Also one tract on Cumberland Mountain containing 50 acres more or less towit beginning at a black oak thence north 45 west 80 poles to a black oak thence south 45 west 90 poles to a stake Thence north 45 east 90 poles to the beginning

We also assign to Nancy Smith lot No. 6 containing 40 acres more or less, towit beginning at a hickory stump . Thence north 70 west 72 poles to 2 black oaks the south east corner of a 28 acre tract thence with the line of the same westerly to a white oak so as to include the spring thence southwardly to a hickory thence southwardly to a maple, thence southwardly to a dogwood thence eastwardly to a spanish oak the north west corner of a 50 acre entry made by Elliot H. Boyd thence eastwardly along said Boyds

P-314   line to a hickory bush the north east corner of said 50 acre s thence south 53 east 38 poles to a stake thence south 77 east 52 poles to a black walnut saplin thence north 10 east 45 poles to the beginning also one tract of land on Cumberland Mountain known as lot No. 4 containing 120 acres more or less towit beginning at a chestnut tree corner of lot No. 2 thence south 22 west 20 poles to a chestnut thence south 12 west 100 poles to a pine thence south 45 east to a stake on the side of the mountain in the old line thence with the line of the same to a stake corner of lot No. 3 thence with the line of the same north 45 west to the begining which in our opinion constituted their equal parts of the real estate of the said David Smith deceased Given under our hands and seals.

Jacob Newman (Seal)
A. B. Ewton (Seal)
Phillip Hoots (Seal)
Wm. D. Rogers (Seal)

    It is considered by the court that the commissioners have the sum of $ 1.50 pr day and the surveyor be allowed the sum of $ 2.00 per day   as P-315   compensation for their services and that the petitioners pay the costs in this behalf expended for which execution may Issue.

P-315

The heirs at law of James Keeney and William Gardenhire vs Samuel Williams & Others	)))))

Came the defendants by their solicitors and suggested to the court Claibourn Gott a citizen of Marion County is the regular guardian of Calvin Williams   and Pleasant Williams minor heirs of George Williams deceased whereupon it is ordered that copy of the bill of revivor filed against said heirs together with a subpoena against said heirs to answer be served on said guardian instead of Samuel Williams who was heretofore appointed guardian ad litem for said heirs--- and upon motion it is further ordered that this cause and the original papers on file together with a certified copy of the record and proceedings had therein be transfered to the Chancery Court at Harrison to be further proceeded in, in persuance of the provisions of the late act of the general assembly directing such Transfer.

P-315

Smith Brown administrators of George Brown deceased vs John Cordell Jr. & Others	))))

Came the parties by their solicitors and by their consent and with the assent of the court this cause and the original papers on file together with a certified Transcript of the records and proceedings had therein are directed to be transferred

P-315   to be further proceeded in to the chancery court at Harrison as directed by a late act of assembly authorizing such transfer.

James Loyd Guardian
Expartie   )

Be it remembered that this application came on again to be heard upon the report of the clerk and master , and said report being unexcepted to is in all things confirmed-- from which it appears that the real estate mentioned in the petition had been sold by the clerk and master as heretofore ordered upon a credit of one and two years for the sum of $ 1075, and that there had been paid into the office of the clerk and master upon the first installment dut the sum of $ 200. It is therefore ordered and decreed that the clerk and master after deducting the costs in this behalf expended pay over the proceeds of the sale of said land to James Loyd the regular guardian upon his giving (Page 316) bond and security to manage and account for such funds as guardian.

P-316
James Loyd Guardian
vs
Nicholas Spring, Margaret A. Spring
and David H. Spring   )

Be it remembered that this cause came on to be heard upon the report of the clerk and master heretofore ordered and said report being unexcepted to is in all things confirmed from which it appears that the complainant Loyd had in his hands on the 5th day of March 1846, The sum of $ 2163.05 and out of that sum the defendant Nicholas A. Spring is entitled to the sum of $ 655.49, Margaret A. Spring to the sum of $ 449.98¢ and David H . Spring to the sum of $ 1057. 58--- Whereupon it is ordered adjudged and decreed by the court that the complainant pay the costs in this behalf exrended out of the funds in his hands. And that this cause upon the dockett as heretofore ordered.

P-316
Nason Swafford
vs
Thomas P. Kelly &
Thomas A. Lathan   )

Be it remembered that this cause came on to be heard on the defendants motion to disolve the injunction heretofore granted in this cause and because it appears to the courtthat the defendant answer fully meets and denies all the equity in complainants bill it is ordered that said injunction be dissolved, and because it further appears that Thomas Swafford is the security of the complainant in the injunction bond it is further ordered adjudged and decreed that the defendant Thomas P. Kelly have judgment over and recover againstbthe complainant and Thomas W. Swafford his security as aforesaid the sum of sixty seven dollars being the amount of the judgment enjoined together with the sum of $ 3.68 ¢ interest thereon acrued from the 10th day of July 1845 up to the 10th of March 1846,and that execution issue therefore as at law upon the defendants giving bond with good and sufficient securéty conditioned   to

P-316   refund the sum if it shall be so decreed upon the final hearing of said bill.

Eucled Waterhouse & Others)
        vs)
John Codley Ann Giss)
and others)

This day came the parties by their solicitor and the complainants unexcepted to the answer of John Cord- ley and Ann Giss (Page 317 filed in this cause being argued and considered by t

P-317   the court It is ordered that the first exception to said answer be sustained The second exception overruled and that said defendants have untill the third rule day to put in a full answer.

P-317
Stoddard & Wood)
        vs)
Jackson Pryor et al)

Be it remembered that this cause came on to be heard upon the report of the clerk and master-- from which it appeared that no account had been stated in this cause in consequence of the bad health of said clerk

whereupon it is ordered yb the court that the introductory decree order- ing an account in this cause be revived, and that Stephen Hicks be as- sociated with the clerk and master as commissioner to take and state said account and that the clerk and master and said commissioner report to the next term of this court

P-317
Jackson Pryor Administrator)
        vs)
Erasmus Alley & Others)

This day came the defendant Erasmus Alley and presented his Report as receiver in this cause which was accepted by the court and directed to be filed. And

it appearing tha t the account heretofore ordered in this cause had   not been stated. It is therefore ordered that the introductory decree directing said account be revived and that Stephens Hicks be associated with the clerk and master as commissioner to take and state said account and that said Clerk and master and the commissio ner report to the next term of this court----- And it is further ordered that the receiver Alley proceed to collect the claims in his hands as such receiver.

P-317
George W. Rice)
        vs)
The South Western Rail Road)
Bank at Knoxville)
----
exception being taken   by complainant counsel to the deposition of James Rankin which were sustained by the Clerk and Master and an ap- peal taken-- The court was

P-317   of opinion that said exceptions were well taken, and that the deposition ought to be suppressed because it was not filed on Saturday before court sat but was filed on Sunday before court and that it was taken
after the expiration of the time given in the order directing the same to
be taken.

P-318   Tuesday 10th March 1846

          George W. Rice   )   Be it remembered that this
               vs   )   cause came on to be heard befor
          The South Western Rail Road)   the honorable B. L. Ridley this
          Bank at Knoxville   )   10th of March 1846 upon bill
)   answer replication and proof wa
          ------------------------- --   when it appeared to the satis-
                                          faction of the court that on the
2nd day of December 1839 one Elijah Rice and others made a note for the
sum of $ 1800 and payable to the defendant at Knoxville four months after
date , which was signed by Elijah C. Rice, and procured the sum to be
discounted . And that the name of complainant was endorsed on said note
with others without the knowledge or consent of complainant either verbal
or written. And it further appeared that suit was brought on said note
against complainant and others about the 24th of March 1841, that complainant from sickness was prevented from defending said suit at law, by
reason of his failure to do judgment was rendered against him or about
the 22 nd of November 1841 for the sum of $ 19.79 besides costs of said
suit at law upon the whole case the court is of opinion that complainant
has a good and vallud defence against said note and that his name was
used without authority from him either verbal or written and should not be
obligatory on him and the court is further of opinion that a court   of
chancery have jurisdiction to relieve complainant against said judgment
Whereupon the court doth order adjudged and decree and it is accordingly
decreed that defendant be perpetually decreed that defendants be enjoined
from collecting said judgment of $ 1979.00 or any part thereof-- but that
complainant the costs of this suit and of the suit at law for which execution may issue as at law-- from which decree defendants prayed an appeal
which to them is awarded upon their giving bond and security on or before
the second rule day.

     And the court then adjourned untill court in course.

                                              Broomfield Ridley

P-318
     State of Tennessee   )   March term of the Circuit Court of
     Bledsoe County   )   Bledsoe County held at the court
)   house in tht town of Pikeville   on
     ------------------------- --   the second Monday of March 1846 The
Honorable Andrew J. (Page 319) Marchbank presiding.

P 319

George W. Hopkins & Others	)
vs	)
Franklin Locke & Others	)

This cause being brought into this court by the clerk and master of the Chancery Court of Pikeville by an order of the chancery presi'ding (he bing incompetent to have and determine the same) By consent of the parties and with the assent of the court this cause is continued the next term of said court.

Andrew J. Marchbank

Wednesday July 15th 1846

George W. Hopkins Mary French. Mary Campbell, Henry Roads , James H. Rowls Thomas J ? Roads Greenberry Roads John H. Roads Charles L? Roads Benj. F. oads, Nicholas Dalton , Mary Dalton, Thomas Labaune? Amy Labaume Emily Jane Knight Thomas C. Vaughn Hudson Vaughn Wm. Hopkins Robert Horsley Ann Horsley , James Bradford, Thomas Bradford, Martha Bradford, Edward Bradford, George Vaughn John Vaughn Florintha Vaughn Wm. P. Vaughn Daniel Green & Elizabet Green
vs
Franklin Locke, Newton Locke, Orville Paine, Elvira Paine, Willie H. Cunningham, Elvira Cunningham heirs at law of John Locke decd Andrew Jackson , Alfred Balch Thomas Crutcher Wm. B. Lewis Abraham Murry, Mary Murry Mecajah G. L. Claibourn Wm. F. Claibourn John Page? and Mary Page.

Be it remembered that this cause having been Heretofore certified to the circuit court , held for the County of Bledsoe and state of Tennessee from the Chancery Court at Pikeville The honorable Broomfield L. Ridley Chancellor presiding in said Chancery Court being incompetent, in conformity with the act of assembly in such case made and provided and now on this 15th day of July 1846 came on this cause (Page 320) to be heard before the ho norable George W. Rols one of the Judges of the corcuit court of law now presiding in said court for Bledsoe County Tennesseeto be finally heard and determined upon the original bill, amended bill, bill of revivor answer replication , proofs, judgment, pro confesso and the agreement of t the parties to read the deposition of Robert N. Gillespie & Ralph B. Locke as well as the agreement that there is a similar record of a judgment against the heirs of Wm. L. Lewis in the circuit court of Rhea County to the one on file in this cause- And because it appears to the satisfaction of the court that the last will and testament of William L. Lewis decd through which the complainants claim title to the land mentioned in the pleadings, confered no p wer upon his executors to sell said land and that the bond executed by William B. Lewis as agent of the executors of Wm.,L Lewis to Thomas Hopkins confered no title to the complainants -- And because it appears that there were two judgments rendered against the heirs of William L. Lewis decd in the circuit court of Rhea County , upon the lands mentioned in the pleadings and that the defendants ancestor John Locke became the purchaser at execution sale and took a sheriff decd regularly executed for the same. Which vested a legal and vallued? title in the said John Lockem that decended to his heirs and upon the whole case

p-320   the court is of opinion that complainants are not entitled to
the relief sought for in their bill . Therefore his honor thought fit to
adjudge and decree, and it is accordingly ordered adjudged and decreed
that the complainants original and amended bill be dismissed and that the
complainahts pay all the costs for which an execution may Issue as   at
Law From which decree the complainants by their solicitor pray an appeal
to the term of the supreme court to be held at Knoxville on the 2nd Monday
of September next which to them is granted upon this entering into bond
and security before the Clerk and Master of the Chancery Court at Pikeville
Tennessee written 40 days from the date.

                                                    Geo. W. Rowls
                                                    Spence Gadge ?

P-321   Monday Sept 14th 1846

        Be it remembered that at a chancery court opened and held, at the
court house in the town of Pikeville in the County of Bledsoe and State
of Tennessee. On the seconf monday and 14th day of September 1846, the Hon.
Broomfield L. Ridley Chancellor & C.

P-321
    James and William Park   )   This day came John C. Gaut solici-
              vs   )   tor for complainants and suggested
    John C. Everett   )   the death of William Park one of
    Benjamin R. King   )   the complainants which is not de-
    Elizabeth Rice   )   nied.
    Charles B. Rains   )

P-321
    Benjamin R. King   )   Cross Bill
              vs   )
    James and William Park   )   This day came John C. Gaut solicitor
    and others   )   for respondents James and William
)   Park and suggested the death   of
                                           William Park one of the respondants
                                           in this cause which is not denied.

P-321
    Ann Thompson   )   Came the parties by their solicitor
              vs   )   and for reasons appearing to the
    Jesse C. Roberson   )   satisfaction of the court from affi-
)   davit of the defendant this cause is
                                           continued and remanded to the rules
                                           so far as to permit the defendant to
take the deposition of James M. Roberson

    Bird Thomas   )
              vs   )   Came the parties by their solicitor and   by

Jeremiah Dorsey) consent and with the assent of the court the defendant is allowed untill the first Monday of November next to file his answer so as not to delay the trial.

P-321

Nason Swafford)
vs)
Thos. A. Latham and Thomas P? Kelly)

Came the parties by their solicitors and for reasons appearing to the satisfaction of court from affidavit of the defendants this

P-322 cause is continued untill next term of this court, upon the payment of all the costs accrued? in this cause up to the present term of this court.

It is therefore ordered adjudged and decreed by the court that the complainants recover of the respondants all costs in this behalf expended up to the present term of this court for which an execution may issue--- & that the injunction heretofore dissolved in this cause be reinstated.

P-322

The State of Tennessee by)
The Attorney General)
vs)
Geo. W. Thompson Geo. W. Rice)
John Kelley & Others)

This day came the state of Tennessee by Samuel A. Smith attorney general and suggested the death of John Kelly one of respondants in this cause which is not denied.

P-322

William Ford)
vs)
Rebecca Ford)

Be it remembered that this cause came on to be heard before the honorable Broomfield L. Ridley Chancelor on this 14th day of Sept. 1846 upon the bill taken for confessed and evidence--- When it appeared to the court that seven years ago the

petitioner was married to the defendant in the county of Bledsoe and State of Tennessee, where they have resided ever since that more that two years before the filing this petition the defendant Rebecca willfully and maliciously abandoned complainant, has continued absent from him, refusing to live with him ever since-- whereupon it is ordered adjudged and decreed by the court, that bonds of matrimony now existing between the complainant and defendant be dissolved. That compalinant be restored to the rights of a single man, and that he pay all the costs in this behalf expended for which an execution may issue as at law.

P-322

John Skillern)
vs)
Joseph G. Smith)

Came Samuel Turney solicitor for complainant, and suggested that since the last continuance of this cause. The complainant departed this life.

P-323   Monday Sept. 14th 1846

William McDonald David Ragsdale   )   Be it remembered that
and William B. Cozby   )   on this 14th day of
            vs   )   Sept. 1846 this cause
Saml. Worthington and Isaac Benson)   came on to be finally
)   heard and determined be
-----------------------------------)   fore the honorable B.
                                        L. Ridley Chancellor
on this 14th day of Sept. 1846 upon the petition filed in this application
when it appeared to the satisfaction of the court that John Kelley departed
this life intestate? in the county of Marion Tenn. in the Month of November
1845 that complainant was duly appointed his administrator, that he left
the distributors mentioned in the bill towit, Thomas B. Kelley James Kelley
James Hogue? and his wife Nancy , Wm. J. Kelley, Valentine M. Kelly, Alexander Kelley, Erasmus Alley and his wife Mary. Inatious Hall and his wife
Ester, Jane Kelley Thomas R. Rawlings & Martha L. Hogue- That his estate exclusive of the slaves does not exceed the sum of $ 255. And it further ap-
pears from said petition that John Kelley was indebted in his lifetime, to
a large amount as specified in the petition and that he left his affairs
in much confusion , and that he left the ten slaves mentioned in the petition . But because the court is not satisfied that it would be for the
interest of the said distributors that all of said slaves should be sold.
It is therefore ordered and decreed that the clerk and Master take proof
to that point and report instantly-- All other matters reserved untill the
coming in of said report.

P-324
                              Monday Sept. 14th 1846

E. M. Evans   )   On motion of the complainant by his sol-
     vs   )   icitor and it appearing that the death
A. H. Montgomery &   )   of the defendant had been suggested, It
Euphemy P. Story   )   is ordered by the court that a scien Fa
)   issue to revive this suit against these
---------------------)   personal representatives of said defend-
                          ants returnable to the next term of the
                          court.

P-324
Eucled Waterhouse Warner E. Colville   )
Vesta Colville George M. Smart   )   Amended Bill
and Ann Smart   )
          vs   )   Came the parties by
James A. Darwin Thomas Darwin   )   their solicitors and
James P. Collins & Robert Mitchell   )   it appearing to the
& James Blevins   )   satisfaction of the
)   court th at the mat-
---------------------------------------)   ters in controversy
between the complainants and the defendants to the amended bill in this

P-324   cause had been compromised and adjusted, that the complainants were to dismiss their suit amended bill, and pay one half of the costs expended thereon, and the defendants thereto go hence discharged. And that the complainants pay one half of the costs on said amended bill expended and the defendant James A. Darwin pay the other half of said costs for which execution may issue.

P-324

Anderson Skillern)
      vs)
Josephn G. Smith)
)
_ _ _ _ _ _ _ _ _ _ _ _ _ _)

Bill of Review?

Be it remembered that this cause came on to be heard , upon the defendants demurrer to the complainants bill, and after argument of council it appeared to the court that the defendants grounds of demurrer were not well taken, mIt is ordered adjudged and decreed by the court that said demurrer be overruled and that defendant untill the 3rd Monday in November next to file his answer, and that same is not to delay the hearing of the cause. And it is further ordered by the court that the execution of the decree in the original cause this seeks? to review? be stayed and enjoined unt ill the further order of this court.

P-325   Monday 14th Sept. 1846

The State of Tennessee by)
The Attorney General)
         vs)
Philip Bible , Christopher C. Bible)
and George Bible)
)
_ _ _ _ _ _ _ _ _ _ _ _ _ _ _ _ _)

Came the attorney General who prosecutes this bill and   on his motion and   it appearing to the court that the matters in dispute had been compromised under the provisions of a resolution of the legislature, and that the defendants had paid the costs of this suit, whereupon it is considered by the court that the suit be dismissed.

P-325

Fry Carpenter)
      vs)
Audley Martin)
Andrew Martin)
& C. T. Martin)
)
_ _ _ _ _ _ _ _ _ _ _)

Be it remembered that this cause came on to be heard before the honorable B.L. Ridley Chancellor on this 14th day   of Sept 1846 upon the bill taken for confessed against all the defendants when it appeared to the court that on the 9th day of August 1844 that defendants were indebted to complainant in the sum of $ 100 and to secure the payment thereof conveyed to the complainant the 50 acres of land mentioned in the bill as security or in mortgage that the defendants have failed to pay same or any part thereof that there is now due $ 100 with interest from the 9th day of August 1844 untill this time making in all $ 112 Whereupon the court doth order and decree that Clerk and Master sell said tract of land on a credit of 12 months after advertising the same

P-325   for 40 days at the court house in Jasper and atbtwo other public
places said sale to to be made at the courthouse door in the town   of
Jasper, said Clerk and Master taking bond and security for the payment of
the purchase money and retain a lein upon the land till the same is paid.
said sale to be made unless the defendant paynto the clerk and master
the amount of the complainants debt and the costs on or before the 1st day
of November next and report to the next term of the court, all other matters
reserved untill the coming i n of the said report.

P-325

      John Hazeltine   )   Be it remembered that this
      Wade B. Hazeltine &   )   cause came on to be heard e
      Daniel Hadock   )   before the honorable B. L.
            vs   )   Ridley Chancellor on this
      Isaac H. Standifer Ephraim M.   )   14th of September 1846 upon
      Evans and Arthur Crozier   )   the report of the clerk and
)   master (Page 326) heretofore
      ------------------------------   )   ordered which being unexcep-
                                              ted to is in all things

confirmed from which it appears that there is yet due the defendant Standifer
as purchase money the sum of $ 242 and that the title bond and the assignment
therein mentioned in the pleadings have never been registered in the county
of Bledsoe that the complainants recetered a judgment against t he defendant
Evans for the sum of $ 324. 92 besides the cost amounting to the sum of
$ 12.50 and also t e interest up to this time being $ 61.06 making the
whole of complainants debt the sum of $ 386.53 Whereupon the court doth
orderand decree that the clerk and master sell the tract of land mentioned
in the pleadings on a credit of nine months taking bond and security for
the purchase money & retaining a lein upon the land untill the money is
paid all to sold upon a credit except enough to pay the costs of this suit
and the suit at law said sale to be made on the premises after giving 40
days written notice at the court house in the town of Pikeville and two
other publicplaces in the vicinity of the land and report thereof to   the
next term the proceeds of said sale first to be applied to the payment of
the purchase money due defendant Standefer secondly to the costs of this
suit and the suit at law and lastly to the payment of the complainants
debt and interest.

P-326

      Edward Pankey And Smith Pankey   )   Be it remember-
            vs   )   ed that this
      Elizabeth White and Y. C. White administrators   )   cause came on
      and administratrix of J. White decd. et al   )   to be heard be-
)   fore the hon-
      ---)   orable B. L.
                                                                  Ridley Chan-

cellor upon the demurrer of the defendant Elizabeth and W. Y. C. White
and the same being set down for argument and was argued by council on both
sides. The court is of opinion that the defendants demurrer is well taken
and doth sustain the same and that the matters of law arising for the same
is fr the defendants whereupon the court doth order and decree that

P-326   complainants bill be dismissed and that they pay the costs of this
suit for which an execution may issue as at law.

P-326

    Alexander Kelley Administrator   )   Be it remembered that this
    Petition Expartie   )   cause came on again to be
)   heard upon the report of the
    ------------------------------------)   clerk and master heretofore
                      ordered which being unexcept-
ed to is in all things confirmed (Page 327) from which report it appears
it is manifestly to the interest of the creditors and all the distributors
of said estate that all the slaves mentioned in said petition be sold.

    Whereupon the court doth order and decree that the clerk and master
after giving 20 days notice in the Chattanooga Gazett and at the courthouse
door in the town of Jasper proceed to sell said leaves at the late residence
of the said John Kelley decd. upon a credit of 12 months taking bond and
security for the purchase money for all he may sell upon time and he is
authorised to sell for ready money so many of said slaves as shall be sufficient to meet the cash demand against the administrator, and report hereof to the next term of the court. And it is further ordered that in the
court the clerk and master should be unable to attend said sale the administrator is authorised to execute this decree by a sale of said slaves and
report to the next term, all other matters reserved untill the coming in of
said report.

P-327

    Erasmus Alley administrator of   )   Be it remembered that
    Walter J. Alley   )   this cause came on to
          vs   )   be heard finally upon
    John Humble, Mariah Humble   )   the bill answer replicat-
    Wm. Hardy Sarah Hardy Elizabeth Peak   )   ion , proof and exhibits.
    Polly Peak Geo. Peak , Wm. Puckett   )   When it appeared ot the
    Cornelious Maxwell, Jane Puckett   )   satisfaction of the court
    Nancy Maxwell, Alexander Ally   )   that some time in the
    ugh Shepurd Adaline Sheppurd   )   month of September 1840
    Tyler James, Nancy James   )   complainants interstate
    Martha Ally, Erasmus Ally,   )   departed this life leav-
    Harriett Ally, Erasmus Ally,   )   ing the complainant and
    Frances M. Ally   )   the defendants his heirs
    Elizabeth Ally, Marion Ally   )   at law That complainant
    James M. Ally Permelia Ally   )   administered on his es-
    Matthew Hailford   )   tate: that he had not
    Harriett Hailford Alfred Johnson   )   personal assets enough
    & Celia Johnson   )   to pay and satisfy all
    heirs at law of   )   the debts and demands
    Walter J. Ally deceased   )   against said estate.
)   And it further appeared
    ------------------------------------) --   that Walter J. Ally
                      decd seised and possed
of the land mentioned in said bill but because the court is not satisfied
or informed as to the state of the assets whether or not they have been
all exhausted in due course of administration the court doth order   and

P-327   decree that the clerk and master take and state an account of the assets of said estate and report whether it is necessary to sell said land to pay the debt against said estate & what sum is yet due and unpaid   and report Instantly

P-328

Alexander Kelley administrator on the estate of John Kelly decd. and Thomas L. Kelly James Kelley, Wm. J. Kelley Valentine M. Kelley. Alexander Kelley James Hogue and his wife Nancy , Erasmus Alley and his wife Mary Ignatious Hall and his wife Ester. Jane Kelley Thos. R. Rawlings and Martha L. Hogus heirs at law of Alexander Kelly deceased.

vs

Daniel Rawlings, Guardian for the minor heirs of Alexander Kelley deceased.

Be it remembered t at this cause came on to be heard before Honorable Broomfield L. Ridley Chancellor upon the bill and answer of the defendant by their guardian ad litern? - When it appeared to the satisfaction   of the court that some time in the month of November 1845 John Kelley departed this life intestate? that he left a personal estate supposed to be sufficient to pay all the debts of or against said estate that Alexander the administrator with the other complainants are willing to sell the land mentioned in the petition as well as the guardian for the minor heirs mentioned in the petition, but because the court wishes to be informed whether it would be to the interest of the heirs to sell or divide the line specified in the petition and it is ordered that the clerk and master take proof and report to the court whether the land aught to be sold or whether it would be the interest of said heirs for distribution to sell the land and report instantly.

P-328
Samuel Bean & Owen R. Bean   )
        vs   )
Samuel B. Mead   )
-------------------------------)

Be it remembered that on this 14th day of Septr. 1846 before the honorable Broomfield L. Ridley Chancellor & C.   the above cause came on to be further upon the report of the clerk and master and the same being unexcepted to is in all things confirmed and it appearing from the record in this cause and from said report that complainants testator Obediah Bean was was defendants security to Jacob Hise? and as such that a judgment was rendered against him jointly with defendant on the 16th of July 1838 in favor of said Hise In Marion Circuit Court for $ 396.61 whch with interest and costs amounted to $ 461.02 ¢ on the 8th of Jany 1840, that in order to indemnify Obediah Bean Mead placed in his hands sundry claims on individuals to the amount of 584.08¢ upon P-329   which the said Bean collected the sum of $ 563.27¢ including interest to the 8th of January 1840-- and that the said O. Bean paid over on said judgment the sum of ---------------429.54
To mead on his order to Allyy   34.80
To Mead himself 7th Decr. 1838   108.50

P-329   Interest on same to 8th Jany 1846 $ 6.78 $115.28
making in all paid to mead and for him the sum of   579.62
excluding the sum collected by Bean on Meads claim the sum of $ 16.35-- It
further appearing that in a settlement between complainant and defendant
after Obediah Beans death the returned to him uncollected, of the claims
received by O. Bean from Mead the sum of $ 62.60 and that about the 7th of
July 1843 Complainant executed to Mead their notes for $ 97.34 for   a
balance then supposed to be due him on said claims from their testator upon which they paid $ 3.87 on the 8th of August 1843, on which day Mead took
a judgment against them for $ 93 .85 ¢ - And it further appearing that
complainant injoined the collection of said judgment-- that at September
term 1844 of this court the injunction was disolved and on the 1st of Decr
1844 Mead collected of complainant , the sum of $ 106.10 on said Judgment
It is ordered adjudged and decreed by the court that complainant recover of
the defendant Samuel B. Mead and of Jackson Pryor his security in the refunding bond upon a dissolution of the injunction the said sum of $ 106.10
together with the further sum of $ 12.14 reported as interest thereon from
the time paid up to the time of stating the account towit the 12th of Septr.
1846 and that they recover of the said Mead the sum of $ 26.63 being the
amount overpaid by O. Bean with the amount paid by complainant on the notes
on the 8th August 1843 and interest thereon up to the time of stating the
account ..Making the decree against Mead and Pryor the sum of $ 118.24.
And against Mead alone the sum of $ 26.63¢ for which execution may issue
as at law.

P-330   Monday Septr. 14th 1846

Jackson Pryor administrator
of Thomas Burnett deceased   )   By consent of the
        vs   )   parties by their
Wm. A. Hargess Erasmus Ally and others   )   attornies and with
        and   )   the assent of the
Stoddard and Wood   )   court, the fore-
        vs   )   going two causes
Jackson Pryor administrator of   )   are consolidated and
Thomas Burnett decd, and Others   )   made to constitute
)   but one suit and on
)   this 14th day   of
                                                     September before the
Honorable Broomfield L. Ridley Chancellor & C. came on to be further heard
upon the report of the clerk and Master and Stephen Hicks special commissioner made in each case, and the same being unexcepted to is in all things
confirmed and it appearing from the report in the case first above named
that receiver Ally has still in his hands to indemnify him as Burnetts
security a large amount of claims due to the firm of Burnett and Hargess
It is rdered that he proceed with all reasonable dispatch to collect the same
and apply the proceeds to the extinguishment of the said debts for which
he is bound, so far as required for that purpose and that he account for and
pay over to the clerk and master any balance which he may receive after the
payment of said debts-- And it also appearing that receiver Hargess in the

P-330   same case has a large amount of the partnership effects in his
hands It is ordered that he in the first place and out of the first monies
in his hands over to the Clerk and Master of this court towards the costs
of this suit , the sum of fifty dollars and two special commissioners
Stephen Hicks for ading to state the account the sum of twenty five dollars and to Jesse C. Roberson a former receiver in the case the sum of
fifteen dollars and any balance in his possession to the payment pro rata
of the partnership liabilities as set fourth in the report- It also appearing that there is in the hands of Jesse C. Roberson receiver & C the sum
of $ 25.11 It is ordered that the same in addition to the $ 15.00 above
named be allowed him in conformity with the report-- It is further ordered
that receivor Hargiss proceed with all reasonable dispatch to close   the
business of partnership in his hands and he and receiver report (Ally) fully
what they shall have done with the (Page 331) effects in their hands res-
P-331   pectivelyto the next term of this court-- And it appearing from
the report in the case secondly anove named that there is a balance   in
the hands of Jackson Pryor, administrator of $ 528.87 including $ 365 due
for slaves slod by the Clerk and Master and which is not paid but in the
hands of Green H. Pryor the purchaser of said slaves -- It is ordered by
the court that the said administrator be released from any responsibility f
for the $ 365. and that the sum be under the control of the Clerk and Mas-
ter subject to the order of this court as to its collection and application
And it is further ordered that the sum of $ 50 be allowed the administr out
of the remaining fund in his hands as compe nsation for his services as
administrator and the further sum of $ 42.50 for attornies fee paid   by
him and also $ 18.88 for contingent expenses of his administration as ap-
pears from his account sworn to making the whole allowance to the administrator, the sum of $ 111.38 which being deducted from the assets still in
his hands leave the sum of $ 32.49 which he is directed to pay over to the
Clerk and Master of this court to be applied to the payment of the costs in
the case. It is also ordered that the Clerk and Master collect $ 25 of the
amount due for the slaves And pay the same to commissioner Hicks as compensation for stating the account in this cause- It also appearing from
said report that said Thomas Burnett decd seised and possessed of the following real estate to wit 80 acres of land on Tennessee River in Marion
County held by deed from John C. Everett, 33 acres lying in said County
held by deed from Haviron & Torbitt-- 200 acres in said county held   by
bond on John C. Everett, also the fee simple in lot No. 66 in the town of
Jasper held by deed from Geo. W. Rice - A life estate in which has been
assigned to Burnetts widow as dower and that it is necessary for the pay-
rent of debts, that the same be sold-- It is further ordered by the court,
that the Clerk and Master of this court after having given 40 days notice
of the time and place of sale, sell the same to the highest bidder on   a
credit of 12 months at the courthouse door in Jasper taking good personal
personal security and retaining a lein upon the land for the purchase money
and that he report hereof to the next term of this court . It is further
ordered that the question raised in the pleadings as to Green H Pryors
claim, to the sale of the negroes be reserved for the further consideration
of the court.

(NOTE) Pages 332 and 333 are missing from original copy.

                        Tuesday 15th Septr 1846

P-334   Opinion that complainant was prevented from making his defence at
law from his sickness and the conduct or remarks made by defendants council
and the court is further of opinion that the name of complainant was endorsed on said note without his knowledge or consent. And creates no obligation and on him. hereupon it is ordered adjudged and decreed by the court
that the defendant be perpetually enjoined from collecting said judgment
or that the injunction heretofore granted in this cause be made perpetual
and that the defendant pay the costs of this suit for which an execution my
may issue as at law.

P-334

        Nicolas A. Spring   )   Be it remembered that on this
        Rodolphus R. Davenport   )   15th day of September 1846. be-
                  vs   )   fore the honorable Broomfield L.
        James Loyd Guardian & C.   )   Aidley Chancellor and C the ab
)   bove causecame on to be heard
        - - - - - - - - - - - - - -   upon the petition answer and
                                            proof in the cause and because it
does not appear to the court that the division of the slaves as agreed on
between the parties and as set fourth in the petition , amongst the petitioners and David H. Spring a minor the word of defendant is just and equal
It is ordered that the matter be refered to the Clerk and Master with instructions to take proof and report thereon instantly--

        And the Clerk and Master having immediately taken proof and reported
that the division is fair and equal amongst the distributors and the said
report being unexcepted to, is confirmed--- Whereupon it is ordered adjudged and decreed by the court that of the said slaves there be allowed
to petitioners Nicholas A. Spring and his heirs as his separate property t
the slaves, John , Matilda, and Eliza--- And it appearing to the court
that petitioner Rodolphus R. Davenport has intermarried with Margaret Ann
formerly Margaret Ann Spring and that he is of lawful age It is ordered
and decreed that there be allowed to him and his said wife as their separate property and right the slaves, Reuben, Nancy Hannah and Rufus-- And
it further that there be allowed to David (Page 335) H. the minor and to
remain in the hands of the defendant as his guardian as his separate
property the slaves, Susan, Sarah James, Rebecca and Jordon, and further
that defendant deliver over to petitioners their said slaves as soon as the
time expires for which they are hired out, or so soon as he can get the
possession of the same accounting to petitioners their just portion   of
the hime (hire) -- It is further ordered that defendant pay over to petitioner Davenport the $ 449.99/100 admitted to be in his hands and interest
thereon from the 6th March 1846 untill paid, except the sum of two dollars
interest on cash in hands of guardian-- And further that defendant pay to
said Davenport whatever he may collect & when collected of the $ 19.38 ¢
due for slaves hire coming to Margaret Ann. And also one third of the $ 1075
proceeds of the sale of the realestate sold whenever collected deducting
expenses of collection-- It is further ordered that in like manner, defendant deliver over to Nicholas A. Spring the slaves allosed to him and account
to and pay him the hire to which he may be entitled for them, untill he re-
ceives them, and also the balance coming to him, of one third of the $ 1075
after deducting $ 123.69¢ already paid him on that account. It is further
ordered that the defendant pay the costs of this suit, and that apportion

the same amoingst his aid three words and retain one third thereof out of
the portion allotted to each of petitioners and the othere third out of the
funds of his word David H. the minor------

George C. Wheeler vs Alfred G. Cosby and Exra Ceizer?	Be it remembered that upon motion to disolve the injunction in this cause the court is satisfied that the defendants answer meets and denies the equity of the complainants bill whereupon it is ordered and decreed that the injunction heretofore granted in this caus be disolved and

becaus it appears to the court that the judgment recovered against the
complainant and John Thurman in the circuit court of Bledsoe county amounts
to the sum of $119.31 and that the interest thereon up to this time is $3.57 @ ad
and that John B. Murphey is the complainants security in the injunceion
bond whereupon it is decreed that the defendant Keizer recover of the complainant Geo. C. Wheeler John Thurman and J hn B. Murphey the sum of $122.88@
for which execution may issue upon his giving bond and security to refund.

Tuesday 15th Septr. 1846

P-336 Thomas Brown and Wm. F. Brown vs Mary A. E. McCull	Upon the reasons desolved in the affidavit of the defendants agent It is ordered that this cause be continued untill the next o court and that Benjamin B. Cannon be and is hereby apointed surveyor to run out the land by meeds and bounds and spedified

in the title bond executed by David as agent of defendant and which is on
file in this cause and also run the land according to the c lls of the
grant of Mary A. E. McCull and that he designate the   the direction and location at the time the contract of sale was made in 1840 and
expecially designate the fence or place where the fence then stood that the
eastern boundary of the Thompson lease showing in t isplot the direction said
fence runs from the river as proved by witnesses also designate the road or
roads on said and all tract of land at the time the sale was made any and all
remarks necessary to illustrate and make plain the true dividing line between
the Gellespie and McCull tracts of land. and designate the place where
Emrey and Milton were splitting wood to be shown b witnesses and also the
fence of Brown which is said to e over the line of Gillespie at or near his
north east corner and make any and all remark to explain and illustrate
said survey and designate all illegable places or locations for settlemens
and also the residence of Brown on the land in dispute--and it is furthere
order d that the defendants have leave to take the deposition and for the
purposes specified in their affidavit all to be taken and the survey to be
made within three monts and the complainants have three months to take rebutting testimony the surveyor will make his return showing the quantit?
of land called for in the bond and with the explantions and remarks above
indicated which when returned shall be eveidence in this cause also point
out the remarkable oak mentioned in the bill also report whether there are
any marked lines on the imaginary line run by Patty or laid down on Pattys
map and designate all the corner trees that c n be found and where the
sycamore and sweet Gum mwq now stand at the termination o" the imaginary

line on the river and likewise designate the corner tree at the lower
line or end of Gillespies land on the river towit, Gillespies western boundry
line, and make any and all remarks necessary to the understanding said
report and run the line of the eastern boundary of the Thompson leas till it
intersects and strikes the true line so as to shew how much of the Thompson
lease, will be cut off, if any that is where the funce run and stood in
1840 as heretofore set out----- and it is further ordered that the defendants have leave to take Thomas Gillespies testimony to shew that what
time and where he permitted complainants to fence in any of the disputed land
and what was the argument at the time-- And on motion of defendants council
It is further ordered that the injunction heretofore disolved and recently
reinstated by Chancelor Williams be again disolved and defendants have leave
to take out execution and proceed in the collection of their judgments at
law upon the defendants giving bond with sufficient security to refund said
money if upon the final hearing the same may be so decreed.

P-337

Jubel Dixon)
vs)
Green H. Pryor)
)
_ _ _ _ _ _ _ _ _ _ _

Be it remembered that this cause came on to
be heard upon the demurrer which was set
down for argument and after argument of
Counsil It is the opinon of the court that
the demurrer is not well taken and that the
matters of law arising therein is in favor of the complainant whereupon it
is ordered that said demurrer be overr uled and the defendant have leave to
file his answer on or before the second Monday of December next and the same
is not to delay the hearing..

Armstead Jones)
vs)
Green H. Pryor)
)
_ _ _ _ _ _ _ _ _ _ _

Be it remembered that exceptions taken to
the defendants came on to be argued before
the court and the same being seen and understood the court is of the opinion that said
exceptions are well taken and sustains the
same except the 8th 10t and 11th which are over ruled. And the
defendant is allowed until 1 the fourth Monday in November next to file a
full answer and the same is not to delay the hearing.

P-338

Anderson Skillern)
vs)
Joseph G. Smith)
)
_ _ _ _ _ _ _ _ _ _ _

Tuesday 15th Septr. 1846
Be it remembered that by argument of the
parties the final decree inaside and reserved and it is ordered that the clerk and
master take and restate the account between
the parties upon the original interductory
decree ordereing an account in said cause, and said Clerk restate said accouny
in said cause, and report to the next term of the court and it is further
ordered that Stephen Hicks be appointed a commissioner and associated with
the Clerk and Master, in said account and making said report--all other
matters are reserved untill the coming in of said report.

September term of court 1846

P-338

Thos. N. Frazier & James A. Tulloys   )   Came the complainants
Executors of A. H. Montgomery decd   )   by their solicitors and
         vs   )   on his motion and it ap-
Lewis D. Merriman & Others   )   pearing to the court
)   from answer filed by the
---)   defendants that there
                                                 are other parties who

should be made defendants to the bill. It is therefore ordered that the
complainants be allowed to amend their bill by making Allen B. Carrolton,
Wilson Saxton and his wife Evaline Saxton defendants to said bill-- And it
further appearing to the court that Lewis D. Merrimon, Owen Merrimon, Allen
B. Carrolton Wilson Saxton and Evaline Saxton defendants to said bill are
non-residents. It is therefore ordered that publication be made for 4 successive weeks in the Chattanooga Gazett a newspaper printed in the town of
Chattanooga in the County of Hamilton and state of Tennessee requiring said
defendants to appear, on or before the first day of the next term of this
court and answer said or the same will be taken for confessed and set for
hearing exparte as to them .

P-338

A. H. Montgomery & E. P. Story Admr.   )   It is ordered in this
         vs   )   cause that the money ,
The Creditors of Saml. L. Story decd   )   heretofore paid into the
)   office of the Clerk and
---------------------------------------)   Master by the said A. H.
                                                 Montgomery for the pur-

chase of the house and lots sold by a decree of this court be held by the
Clerk and Master subject to the further order of this court.

P-339

Samuel B. Mead Admr. of   )   Be it remembered that this cause
Jonathan Rucker decd   )   came on to be heard this 15th day
         vs   )   of September 1846 before the honor-
Willie Webb & Others   )   able Broomfield L. Ridley Chancellor
)   and C upon the bill answer replica-
-----------------------------------)   tion publication and proof in the
                                                 cause, and the solicitor by consent

waving an account and it appearing to the satisfaction of the court from
the articles of argument entered into, between Willie Webb and Jonathan
Rucker in his lifetime and the depositions in the cause, that they were
rental partners in the two acres of land and the mills erected thereon and
it being uncertain as to the value of said premises, the court doth order
adjudged and decree, that the clerk and master after giving the usual notice
proceed to sell the one half interest in said two acres of land on a credit
of twelve months taking bond and security for the purchase money retain a
lein upon said land and mill, untill the purchase money be paid and that
the clerk and master , state an account of the indebtedness of the said
estate. Collect all the proceeds arising therefrom in the hands of the administrator if any and report to the next term of this court.

P-339

    Euclid Waterhouse & Others   )
              vs   )
    John Condley & Others   )
    _____   )

answers of the defendants.

P-339

    George C. Wheeler & Others   )
              vs   )
    Beaty & Benson   )
P-340 _____   )

For reasons appearing to the satisfaction of the court from the affidavit of one of the complainants
This cause is remanded to to the
rules and leave is given complainants to file a replication to the

Be it remembered that this cause
came on to be heard upon the defendants Beaty and Benson demurrer
to the complainants bill which
having been seen heard and under-
stood by the court is of opinion that said demurers are well taken and that
the matters of law arising thereon are for the defendants Whereupon it is
ordered and decreed by the court that said demurrer be sustained and that
the complainants have leave to amend their bill on or before December Rules.

P-340

    Morgan Allison & Co.   )
              vs   )
    John Thomas & John Thurman   )
    _____   )

The Demurrer is this case- was
this day organized? before the
Chancellor, when the same was
overruled and Defts have untill 2
th Nov. to come, so as not to delay the hearing.

    It is ordered that all the causes heard and deposed of at the present
term be ever called except there cause, specially ordered not to be overruled.
    Court adjourned to the regular term .

                                                        Broomfield Ridley

P-340   Monday March 8th 1847.

    Be it remembered that at a chancery Court opened and held at the court
house in the town of Pikeville in the county of Bledsoe and state of Tennessee, on the seconday and 8th day of March 1847 when there was present on
the bench the honorable Broomfield L. Ridley Chancellor & C.

P-341
                    Monday 8th March 1847

    Alexander Kelley administrator,
of John Kelley deceased Thomas P. Kelley James Kelley Wm. Kelley V. M.
Kelley James Hoge Nancy Hoge E. Ally Martha Ally I. Hall Ester Hall and

P-341   Jane Kelley Heirs of John Kelley deceased
                              vs
        Thomas R. Rawlings, Susan Hoge and Nancy Kelley Widow

     Be it remembered that this cause came on again to be heard before the
honorable B. L. Ridley Chancellor on this 8th day of March 1847 upon the report of the clerk and Master, heretofore ordered in this cause, which report
being unexcepted to be in all things confirmed. - From which re port it appears that on the 18th of Novr. 1846 the Clerk and Master after advertising
the time and place of sale of all the lands mentioned in the pleadings proceeded to expose to sale at the court house door in Jasper Tennessee   four
of said tracts of land one containing fifty acres lying on the road leading
from Jasper to Chattanooga and amediately where said road crossed sequatchee
River including the tole bridge thereon , Another containing seventy five
acres adjoining the first described tract lying on the south east side of
sequatchee river, Another containing 300 acres lying on the north west side
of sequatchee river adjoining the first described tract on which the bridge
is situated. The fourth tract containing 160 acres lying on the south east
side of sequatchee river adjoining the second described tract as well as
the lands of E. Ally Rogers and others all being in the County of Marion
and State of Tennessee, which said four tracts were struck off to John Hoge
he being the highest and best bidder, at the sum of fifteen hundred dollars
of which sum he paid down fifty dollars and executed his note with Wm.
Kelley his security for the balance being $ 1450.00 payable twelve months
after date and it further appears that the remaining tract containing forty
acres lying in the Ocee district in Marion County in range C west first
fractional township and 25th section , being the south east corner of the
north east quarter of said section was also at the same time and place,
struck off to Alexander Kelley he being the highest and best bidder at the
sum of ten dollars for which he executed his note with A. M. Kelley his
security and that a lein was retained on the land untill the purchase money
is paid. Whereupon the court doth order a writ of possession to the purchaser and that this cause remain in court untill the purchase money is
paid and that the costs of this suit be paid out of the purchase money and
that the clerk deliver to A. Kelly the administrator the notes taken for
the sale of said land for collection, payment of debts and distribution.

P-342
                            Monday 8th March 1847

     Samuel B. Mead Administrator   )   Be it remembered that
     of Jonathan Rucker deceased   )   this cause came on again
                   vs   )   to be heard upon the re-
     Willie Webb & Thos. J. B. Rucker   )   port of the clerk and
)   Master heretofore ordered
     — — — — — — — — — — — — — — — — —)   in this cause which being
                                               unexcepted to is in all
things confirmed, from which report it appears that the Clerk and Master
proceeded to sell the undivided half of the two acres of land mentioned in
the pleadings on which is situated a grist and saw mill after advertising
said sale as directed in the decree, that said sale was made at the court
house door in the town of Jasper , Tennessee, on the 17th day of Nov.1846

P-342   and the said undivided half of said two acres of land including
sadd grist and saw mill situated at the head spring of Nickajack creek M
Marion County was struck off to the said Samuel B. Mead at the sum of
$ 260 he being the highest and best bidder who gave his note for the pur-
chase money with Daniel Candoin his security due twelve months after date,
and that a lein was retained upon the land untill the purchase money   is
paid Whereupon it is ordered and decreed that a writ of possession issue
to the purchaser thatthis cause remain in court untill the purchase money
is paid when a vesiture of title will be made out of the purchase money.

P-342

    Frey Carpenter   )
         vs   )
    Audley M. Martin   )
    Andrew R. Martin   )
    C. T. Martin   )

Be it remembered that this cause came
on again to be heard upon the report
of the Clerk and Master heretofore
ordered in this cause which report being unexcepted to is in all things confirmed from which report it appears
that the Clerk and Master after advertising the time and place of sale ac-

cording to the directions contained in the decree expose the fifty acres of
land specified in the bill to sale at the courthouse door in the town of
Jasper Tennessee on the 17th day of Novr. 1846 and which was struck off to
Y. W. Moon at thesum of $ 146 he being the highest and best bidder who
gave hsi note with David Rankin his security for the payment of the purchase
money due twelve (Page 343) months after date. Whereupon it is ordered and
decreed that the lein be retained on said land untill the purchase money
be paid that the costs of this suit be retained out of the purchase money
and that this cause remain in court untill the said purchase be paid when
title will be vested in the purchaser-- And it is further ordered that a
writ of possession issue to the purchaser.

P-343

    Erasmus Ally Administrator of   )
    Walter J. Ally deceased   )
         vs   )
    The Heirs of Walter J. Ally deceased   )

Be it remembered th
that this cause
came on again to be
heard upon the re-
port of the Clerk
and Master hereto-
fore ordered which

being unexcepted to is in all things confirmed from which report it appears
that on the 17th day of November 1846 the Clerk and Master proceeded to
sell the several tracts of land specified in the pleadings after advertising
the same as directed in the decree that said sale was made on the   one
hundred and sixty acre tract when the said tract was struck off to Erasmus
Ally at the sum of five hundred dollars he being the highest and best bid-
derwho gave his note with Walter J. Ally his security for the purchase
money due twelve months after date wherefore it is ordered adjudged and decreed thatthe legal to said three tracts of land be divested out of the defendants as heirs at law of Walter J. Ally deceased and vested in the purchaser the said Erasmus Ally and his heirs forever subject to a lein   for
a payment of the purchase money and it is further ordered that complainant

P-343   pay the costs of this suit out of the proceeds of the sales   of
said lands and that a writ of possession Issue and it is further ordered
that complainant proceed to pay the debts due by his intestate as reported
to the last term of this court. and the cost in discharge of the note
given for the purchase money.

P-343

    James and William Park   )   Came James P. Thompson
           vs   )   Esqr. and suggested that
    John C Everett Benjm R. King & Others)   since the last   con-
    and cross bill   )   tinuance of the original
    Benjamin R. King   )   and cross bill Benjm R
           vs   )   King one of the parties
    James and William Park & Others   )   there to departed this
)   life which is not denied.

P-344

Monday 8th March 1847

    Alexander Kelly Administrator   )
    of John Kelly deceased   )   Be it remembered that this
          Expartee   )   cause came on again to be
    Petition to sell slaves   )   heard upon the report of
)   the Clerk and Master here-
)   tofore ordered in this
)   cause which being unexcep-
ted to is in all things confirmed from which report it appears, that onnths
19th of November 1846 the clerk and master proceeded to execute the order
of the court by exposing to sale the slaves mentioned in the pleadings
after advertising the time and place of said sale it having been made   at
the residence of the defendant , where Andy, Vine and Jack were struck off
to Nancy Kellyshe being the highest and best bidder at the sum of $ 400,
who gave her note with Alexander Kelly as her security in 12 months. At
the same time and place , Zelphia was struck off to Jane Kelley at the sum
of $ 500 she being the highest and best bid who gave her note with Alexander
Kelley her security due 12 months after date. And at the same time and
place Bryant, Mariah Jeremiah and four children were struck off to Alexander
Kelley at the sum of $ 2335.00 he being the highest and best bidder and
gave his note with James Rankin and William I. Kelley his securities payable in 12 months after date. And at the same time and place Pheba on of
said slaves was struck off to James Hoge at the sum of $ 560 he being the
highest and bestbidder who gave his note with I. Hall as his security
payable in 12 months after date. Also at the same time and place Golding wa
was struck off to Erasmus Ally at the sum of $ 600 he being the highest
and best bidder who gave his note for the same with James Rankin his security payable 12 months after date. Also at the same time and place Caroline
was struck off to James Kelley at the sum of $ 375. he being the highest
and best bidder who gave his note for the same, with Wm. J. Kelley   his
security payable 12 months after date. Whereupon it is ordered adjudged
and decreed by the court , that the legal title to said slaves be divested

P-344   out ofmAlexander Kelley administrator of John Kelley deceased and
be vested in the purchasers as above specified and their heirs forever-
And It is further ordered and decreed by the court that the clerk and master deliver over to Alexander Kelley administrator of John Kelly deceased
the notes so taken for the purchase of sais slaves as above sepcified for
P-345   the purpose of clocection, paying the debts of the estate   and
distribuiton. And that the complainant pay the costs of this application
for which execution may issue as al law.

P-345

        Craven Sherill & Green J. Holding   )   Be it remembered that
        Admr. of Samuel Holding decd.   )   this cause came on to
                        vs   )   be heard upon the bill
        John W. Holding and others   )   taken for confessed
)   Whereupon the court
        _____)   thinks fit to order
                                                              the clerk & take an
account and report whether the complainants have exhausted in the payment
of bona fide debts of their intestate the whole of the personal effects
of said intestate which came to their hands to be administered, and also
to shew the amount of the debt mentioned, in the bill, as being due to the
branch of the Bank of Tennessee and report hereof to the next term of this
court.

P-345

        John Skillern   )   Came the paties by their solicitors and
                vs   )   on motion of complainants solicitor   and
        Joseph G. Smith   )   it appearing to the court that the death
            &   )   of the complainant has heretofore been
        _____)   suggested upon the record and that William
                                          Skillern is the execution pf the last
will and testament of complainant , he having failed his letters testamen-
tary. It is therefore ordered, that this suit be revived in the name of
the said William Skillern as executor of the said John Skillern deceased
and stand as at the death of the complainant and alotement thereof.

P-345

        George C. Wheeler   )   Came the parties b their solicitors
                vs   )   and on motion of the defendats and it
        Alfred G. Cosby &   )   appearing that five months had not elap-
        Ezra Reizer   )   sed since the filing of the replicat-
)   ion in this caus   It is ordered that
        _____)   the same be remanded to the rules--
and it is further ordered that the defendants be permitted to take the
deposition of Alfred G. Cosby one of the defendants subject to all legal
exceptions---

                        Monday March 8th 1846

P-345

Joseph G. Smith)
vs)
Anderson Skillern)

Be it remember d that this cause came
on to be heard upon the report of the
Clerk and Master, from which it (p-346)
appears, that the account ordered at
the last term of this court was not
taken and stated as required in the decretal order rendered in this cause,
Whereupon it is ordered and decreed, that the order to take said account
rendered at the last term of this court be revided and that the Clerk and
Master together with Stephen Hicks as commissioner proceed to state the
account as required by said decree, and report to the next term of this
court.

P-346

John Parham Executor)
of John Parham deceased)
Expartie)
for sale of slave)

Be it remembered that this cause
came on to be heard before the honorable B. L. Ridley chancellor
upon this 8th day of March 1847
upon the complainants petition,
when it appeared to the court that
on the 18th day of Octr. 1846 John Parham departed this life in the county
of Bledsoe and state of Tennessee having first made his last will and testament and apointed the petitioner executor thereof who has been duly
qualified and took upon himself the execution of said Will that amongst
other things in said will the said testator Bequeathed to his daughter
Elva Parham a negro boy named King about 25 years of age, to have said boy
during her life and at her death the prodeeds of the sale of said boy be
equally divided amongst the childrn of said Testator and It further appeared that since the death of said testator the said Elva Parham has departed
this life intestate and without issue and it further appears that the children
and heirs of the said John Parham are numerous and that a sale of said boy
King ouths to be had for the purpose of carrying into effect the will of
the testator Whereupon It is ordered adjudged and decreed by the that the
clerk and Master after giving 40 days notice in writing at the court house
door in the town of Pikeville and two other public places in he county of
Bledsoe, proceed to sell said negro boy King at the courthouse door in the
town of Pikeville to the highest bidder on a credit of twelve months taking
note and good personal security for the payment of the purchase money and
report here of to the next term of this court.

And then court adjourned till tomorrow morning 8 o'clock

Broomfield Ridley

Tuesday 9th March 1847

P-347
Court met persuant to adjournment present on the bench honorable B.
L. Ridley Chancelor and 6

March 9th 1847

P-347

Jackson Pryor administrator)
Of Thomas Burnett deceased)
vs)
Erasmus Ally and others)
and)
Stoddard and Wood)
vs)
Jackson Pryor and others.)

)

Be it remembered thatthis cause
came on again to be heard upon the report of the clerk
and Master hertofore ordered
in this cause which report being unexcepted tp is in all
things confirmed from which
report it appears that the
Clerk proceeded to advetise
the sale of the land mentiond

in the decree and on the 17th day of Novr. 1846? at the court house door in
the town of Jasper T4 nessee Three of the tracts of land mentioned in the
decree containing by estimation 318 acres more or less Were struck off to
William Steel at the sum of $5.50 he being the highexy and best bidder who
gave his note for the same with A. M. Kelley his security payable 12 months
after date and at the same time and place lot No. 66 in the town of Jasper
being the same mentioned in said decree was sold subject to a life estate
in the same to the widow of Thos. Burnett deceased and the same was struck
off to Eliza W. Burnett for the sum of $50 she being the highest and best
bidder and gave her note for the same with Westly Y. Burnett his security
due 12 months after date whereupon the court doth order adjudge and decreed
that a lein be retained upon said land for the purchase money after which
title will be vested in the pruchaser--- And it is further ordered that
writs of possession issue to said purchasers.

P-347

The State of Tennessee by)
The Attorney General)
vs)
George W. Thompson)
George W. Rice and others.)

)

Be it remembered that on this
day this 9th day of March 1847
the state by her a torney general came and suggested the deth
of Benjamin R. King which was
not denied and by consent that
this suit ab t3 as to the said
Benjamin R. King and John Kelly

whose death was suggested at the last term of this court. and on affidavit
of the attorney general it is ordered that the complainant have four months
to take proof generally in this cause and that leave is gra ted to the
complainant to take the deposition of David Rankin and Wm. L. Mooney to
be read as evidence in this cause subject to all just exceptions-- And that
P-348 the respondent file with the Clerk and Master of this court
all the books and papers of the Jasper and Pelham Turnpike company refered
to in their answers by the first ruly day and it is further ordered by the
court that notice served by complainants above upon George W. Rice and
George W. Thompson two of the respondents above.

P-348

Milley Ladd by her next friend)
vs)
George W. Thompson)

)

This cause came on to be
heard this 7th day of
March 1847 upon bill ans-
wer replication, proof and

P-348   the affidavit of J A Minnis? solicitor for complainant when it
appeared to the court from the answer of the defendant that Campbell Henley is a material party to this suit and from the affidavit of said solicitor that it is material to the justice of this cause that the bill as to
other defendants should be amend. It was therefore ordered by the court
that complainant have leave to amend said bill which amendment is to   be
filed on or before the second rule day and that said Campbell Henley   be
made defendant to this suit.

P-348

    Jackson Pryor Admr.   )
    of Thomas Burnett   )
          vs   )
    Erasmus Alley and Others)

Erasmus Alley a receiver in this
cause made a report to the court
which is ordered to be filed and
constitute a part of the record
in this cause.

P-348

    Thomas & Wm. F. Brown   )
          vs   )
    Mary A. E. McCull &   )
    David McCull   )

Be it remembered that this cause
came on to be heard ~~when~~ it ap -
peared to the court that Benjamin
B. Cannon who was appointed survey-
or in this cause at the last term
could not make the survey ordered
in consequence of the ill health of
his family till after the expiration of the time allowed nor have the depositions been taken to illustrate said survey. Whereupon it is ordered tht
the decreetal order made at the last term so far as the ordering the survey in conserwed be revived? and that Benjamin B. Cannon proceed within
four months from this day 9th of March 1847 to make out the survey as directed in said decree And in the court he should not be able to do so,
then Isaac T ylor of White County (Page 349) be and is hereby appointed in
his stead to make out the survey in the same manner as Cannon is directed
P-349   but not unless B. B. Cannon fails to do so and the defendants are
fully authorised to take the additional deposition of Edward Scott at their
cost by giving ten days notice of the time and place, and complainants of
William Johnson and Lewis Miller by giving the notice required by the rules
of this court and that defendants have leave to take rebutting evidence to
said Miller and Johnsons testimony and it is further ordered that said
Scott Miller and Johnsons deposition be taken in therr months from this date
the other depositions taken to illustrate and explain the survey be taken
after the survey is made and that defendants give five days notice to one
or both of complainants of the time and place of making said survey.   And
it is further ordered that said Cannon or Taylor proceed mak said survey
and return the same to the next court and that plots with the surveyor explanatory remarks be red as evidence in this cause and complainants have
leave to take rebutting testimony to the deposition of Edward Scott and also to the testimony explanatory of said survey upon giving notice   to
either of the defendants.

P-349 Myra Freeman) Be it remembered that this cause came
        vs   ) on to be heard this 9th day of March
      Felix M. Freeman) 1847 upon petition orders of publi-
) cation judgment upon petition taken
-- -- -- -- -- -- -- -- -- -- -- --) for confessed and proof-- from which
                                      it appearing to the court that the
petitioner and the said defendant intermarried in the state of North Carolina several years ago, that three years before the filing of this petition
said defendant wilfully and with out cause abandoned petitioner and that for
more that two tears before the filing of this petition and forever since
petitioner has been a citizen of Bledsoe County in the State of Tennessee.
It is therefore ordered adjudged and decreed by the court, that the bonds
of matrimony heretofore existing between the complainant Myra Freeman and
the defendant Felix M. Freeman be disolved
and she be restored to the rights of a free? sale and that the defendant
pay the costs of this suit for which an execution may Issue as at law.

P-350

    Noble Stone
         vs
    Wm. McMurry, Jacob Setton   ) Be it remembered that this
      Samuel H. Dixon Betsey Dixon) cause came on to be heard
    Richard Dixon & Sarah A. Dixon) before the honorable B.
) L. Ridley Chancellor &
-- -- -- -- -- -- -- -- -- -- -- --) C. on this 9th day of
                                      March 1847 when it appear-
                                      ed to the satisfaction of
the court that the defendant McMurry purchased of defendant intestate Wm.
L. Dixon 100 acres of land lying and being in Marion County Tennessee, for
the consideration of $ 232. And by his agent Leroy May agreed to make title
to the same said agreement is dated the 18th Novr. 18 31 that on the   5th
of Janry 1835, defendant by his letter agreed to said sale. It further
appeared that the defendant selton and McMurry by their covenant   of
warranty agreed to convey by deed to complainant said 100 acres of land as
described in this title bond dated the 18th of March 1845 and specified as
exhibit No. 3 in complainants bill.
        Whereupon it ordered and decreed that the legal title to said 100
acres of land be the same more or less be divested out of the Defendant
and vested in the Complainant and his heirs and assigns forever and that
the Clerk and Master make a deed to complainant in conformity with the a-
greement of said title bond or to his assigns. that the complainant pay
the costs of this suit in the first instance and that he have execution
over against the defendants.

                        Tuesday 9th March 1847

P-350

Samuel Worthington)
vs)
James J. Pope)
and)
Jonathan Clark)
)
)
)
-------------------------)

Be it remembered that this cause
came on to be heard upon the defendants motion to dissolve the
injunction heretofore ordered in
this cause and the court having
examined the pleadings is of
opinion that the defendants answer meets and denies the equity
of the bill . Whereupon it is ordered and decreed that the injunction be dissolved and that the

defendant Pope permitted to proceed in the collection of his debt upon
his giving bond with security aonditioned to refund the money collected if
upon the final hearing it should be so decreed-

P-350

Rouled Waterhouse and others)
vs)
John Condley Wm. L. Gass? and Others)
)
)
-----------------------)

For reasons appearing
to the satisfaction
of the court from
the affidavit of W.
E. Colville one
of the complainants
It is ordered by the

Tuesday 9th March 1847

That this cause be continued and the complainants be permitted to take
the depositions of Orville Pain and Samuel Craig--- and also testimony
P-351 generally Jefferson County teeoh!ng the validity of the title to
slaves mentioned in the pleadings set up by the defendant Gisaso that the
same are taken within three months and the defendants are permitted to take
rebutting testimony generally and notice to take depositions be served
upon Wm. L. Goss on part of the defendants and Warner E. Colville on part
of the complainants and it is further ordered that the complainants pay
the costs of all such depositions as they take under this order.

P-351

The Bank of Tennessee)
vs)
Samuel Lambeth)
)
------------------------)

On motion and it appearing that the
defendant is a nonresident It is
ordered that publication be made
for four successive weeks in the
Chattanooga gazett a newspaper

published in the town of Chattanooga Tennessee requiring the defendant to
appear on or before the next term of the chancery court to be held at Pikeville Bledsoe County Tennessee on the 2nd Monday of September next and answer
the complainants bill or the same will be taken for confessed and set for
hearing expartiee.

P-351 Burwell P? Evans) On motion of the defendants
         vs) by their solicitor and by
   Samuel Evans P. H. Williams) consent the defendants are
   and Jeremiah O. Evans) allowed untill the second
) rule day to file their ans-
) wer and the same is not to
) delay the hearing of the

cause.

P-351

   Bird Panky) This day came the complain-
      vs) ant in proper person and
   Elijah M. Hale Thos. N. Frazier) dismisses his suit and there-
   and James A. Tulloss) upon came the defendant
) Elijah M. Hale and confessed
) judgment for the costs. --

It is therefore ordered adjudged and decreed by the court that said suit
be dismissed and that the complainant recover of the defendant Eliajh M.
Hale all the costs in this behalf expended for which an execution may Issue.

P-351

   Bird Thomas) On motion and by argeement of the parties
      vs) by their solicitor It is ordered by the
   Jeremiah Dorsey) court that the Clerk and Master take and
) state an account showing in full all the
) partnership dealings between the parties
            in relation to the buying driving ans

selling hordes as set out in the (Page 352) pleadings including all accounts
advanced by each in the purchase of horses and defaying the expenses there
of, and that he show how the account stand between the parties upon a
final adjustment of their partnership dealings and make report thereof to
the next term of this court.

P-352

   Nason Swafford) Be it remembered that on this 9th day
      vs) of March 1847 before the honorable
   Thomas A. Lathan &) B. L. Ridley Chancellor & C this c
   Thomas P. Kelley) cause came on to be heard upon bill
) answers, replication and proofs and
) it appearing that the judgment for
) sixty seven dollars and costs in the

Circuit Court of Bledsoe County at July term 1845 in favor of Defendant
Lathan for the use of defendant Kelley was obtained on a note under seal
executed by complainant on the 7th of Novr. 1838 due one year after date
to respondent Lathan . And further that the consideration for which said
note was given had wholly failed before the transfer by delivery to Kelley
and before the distribution of the suit at law- It is therefore ordered adjudged and decreed by the court that the collection of the said Judgment
at law, be perpetually enjoined and that the defendants pay the sosts of

P-352   this suit and the suit at law to be taxed in this court for all
which an execution may Issue as at law.

P-352
          Ann Thompson   )   Be it remembered that this cause came
               vs   )   on to be heard before the honorable B.
          Jesse C. Roberson   )   L. Ridley chancellor & C. on the 9th
)   of March 1847 upon the bill answer, re-
     ___ ___ ___ ___ ___ ___ ___ ___)   plication and proof taken in the cause
                                               and it appearing to the satisfaction of
the chancelor that the note mentioned in the pleadings of one hundred dollars was given to defendant as a retaining fee to prosecute and adjust the
cause mentioned in the answer and it furhter appearing that the allegation
of usury and C. mentioned in the bill are false and many others subsequent
alligations. The chancelor doth therefore order adjudge and decree that
said bill be dismissed and that the complinant and her security pay the
costs of of this suit for which an execution may Issue.

P-352
          Ann? Floyd and   )   Be ir remembered that this cause
          George Brock   )   came on to be heard before the on
          Wm. Greger and John Haley)   honorable B. L. Ridley Chancellor
               vs   )   And C. on this 9th of March 1847
          George W. Rice and   )   upon the motion to dissolve the
          George W. Thompson   )   injunction heretofore ordered in
)   this cause When it appeared to
)   the court that all the continguent
     ___ ___ ___ ___ ___ ___ ___ ___)   liabilities happening in the deed
of trust made by George W. Rice to the complainants on the 25th of March
1843 to have expired by the successful prosecution of the suits in part
for which said deed was given and it is further from said deed of trust
that Ann Floyd was secured in three notes amounting in all to $1079 besides
interest occuring? upon the making of the trust which said notes where
transferred to the defendant George W. Thompson, whereupon it is ordered
and decreed by the court that said injunction be dissolved (P-353 and that
the Trustee proceed to sell the profits as required be the Trust Deed on
Bond and security being given as required by law.
          On motion and it appearing to the satisfaction of the court that
David H. Spring the minor heir of David Spring deceased has heretofore
been made a ward of this court and that since the last term of this court
James Loyd his regular guardian has depacted this life---Whereupon it is
ordered and decreed by court that the clerk and master of t is court act as
guardian to said word and that he take possession and control? of the
effects of said word that he make settlement with the executors of Loyd
the former guardian of said word and report to the next term of this court.

P-353
          William Skillern Executor)   Be it remembered that this cause
          of John Skillern deceased)   came on to be heard upon the
               vs   )   defendants demurrer to the com-
          Joseph G. Smith   )   plainants bill, which being
)   seen and understood by the court
     ___ ___ ___ ___ ___ ___ ___ ___)

P-353   and the court being of opinion that the matters of law arising upon the pleadings and for the defendant, and that the demurrer sustained
and that the complainant have leave to amend his bill, which is done by
stricking? all that part of the Bill which seeks as against of the partnership dealings same being the land speculated?.

P-353
    Juball Dixon   )   Be it remembered that this cause came on
        vs   )   to be heard before the honorable B. L.
    Green H. Pryor   )   Ridley Chancellor on the 9th day of March
)   1847. upon Bill answer replication and ex-
hibit when it appeared to the satisfaction
of the court, that complainant was   the
owner of the slave mentioned in the pleadings in November 1840. that   on
the 17th day of March 1840 defendant advanced by way of loan to the complainant the sum of $ 275. that on the same day complainant and defendant
entered into an agreement creating a mortgage on the two negroes as a se -
curity for said sum of $ 275. as manifested by exhibit A in defendants ans-
wer. Upon their whole case the court is of opininn that the complainant is
entitled to redeem said two negroes; but because the court is not satisfied
as to the amount of money advanced by the defendant Pryor at the request
of complainant for the purpose of preserving the trust property or whether
he advanced more than the $ 275 at the time of (Page 354) making the mort-
P-354   gagey nor how much trouble and expense the defendant was subjected
to by reason of taking the negroes off to Kentucky nor is the court satisfied as to the balance of the hire of two said slaves, if any thing since
they came to the hands of the defendant whereupon the court doth order and
decree that the clerk and master enquire and take proof as to the amount advanced by the defendant Pryor subsequent to the 17th of November 1840   at
the request of the complainant of for any monies legally advanced to the t
trust property, and enquire what the hire of the negroes are worth since
they came to the possession of the defendant, and in taking said account he
will allow defendant more? persecution for his trouble in passing the negroes to Kentucky and report hereof to the next term, all other things not
herein decreed , reserved till the coming in of said report, and the compla
lainant to pay the costs of this suit.

P-354
    Hazeltine Haddock decd   )   On motion of the defendant Jesse
           vs   )   H. Standifer by his attorney, it
    E. M. Evans Jesse H.   )   is ordered that the order at the
    Standifer and others   )   last term of this court to sell
)   the land mentioned in the pleadings
be revived , and that the Clerk
and Master be directed to sell   on
the terms and in the manner prescribed by said order so much of said land
as will be sufficient when collected to pay the decree in favor of the
defendant Standifer his purchas money, the interest thereon, and the
commission and costs of sale, and report hereof to the next term. And it
further appeared that since the last term by agreement between the complainants attorney and the defendant Evans . the sale ordered at the last

P-354 term was suspended, by the defendant Evans paying to the complainants the sum of $ 250, part of the complainants decree. And that by said
agreement the sale of the land was postponed for 12 months from the 12th
of Nov. 1846, that the balance due complainant to remain a lein upon the
land till said agreement expired. Whereupon it is ordered that the sale
of the land for the payment of complainants debt be postponed till the expiration of said agreement, but the same is to have no effect upon the
rights of the defendant Standifer, and that the Clk & M execute the decree
above so as to effect the sale of so much of the land as may be sufficient
to pay the debt of Standifer and costs & C.

P-354
    Armster Jones)
       vs)
    Green H. Pryor)

Be it remembered that on this 10th day
of March 1847, before the Hon. B.   L.
Ridley Chancellor, this cause came on to
be heard upon the bill answer Replication
exhibits and proofs in the cause and it
appearing to the court that the proof does not sustain the alligations in
complainants bill; It is therefore ordered adjudged and decreed that the
said bill be dismissed and that the defendant pa yone half of the cost of
this suit and the complainant pay the other half of the costs for all of
which execution may issue as at law. From which Decree? the complainant
P- 355 prays an appeal in the next Supreme court at Knoxville 2nd Monday in Septr. next which is granted in his executing Bond with security
as required by law and as before the May rules.

Court adjourned till tomorrow morning 9 o'clock

             Broomfield   Ridley

Wednesday March 10th 1847

Court met persuant to adjournment present on the ench the Honorable
B. L. Ridley Chancelor and C.

P-355
George C. Wheeler admr. of E. T. Wheeler Decd.
Bird Pankey in right of his wife Mary Pankey
and as next friend of Emily Story and Matilda A.
Story and on behalf of the creditors of the
estate of Samuel L. Story deceased.
        vs
John Beatty, Isaac Benson,
Thomas N. Frazier and James A. Tulloss executors
of A. H. Montgomery deceased and Daniel F. Cocke

Be it remember-
ed that this
cause came
on to be
heard before
the Hon. B.
L. Ridley
Chancellor
this 10th d
day of March

1847 upon the defendants Beatty and Bensons plea in abatement to the jurisdiction of the court when it appearing to the court that the demurrer of
the defendats Beatty and Benson to the complainants bill has heretofore
been sustained by the court and the complainants allowed to amend their

P-355   bill, and that the complainants had amended the same by striking
out all of the defendants except the defendants John Beatty and Isaac   C.
Benson, and it further appeared from the defendants plea, that the defendants Beatty and Benson are not citizens of this Chancery district and that
the law arising upon said plea was for said defendants Whereupon it is ordered adjudged and decreed that the plea be sustained, and the complainants
allowed to amend their bill, and it further appeared that the complainants
had again amended their bill by making Thos. N. Frazier and James A.
Tulloss executors of A. H. Montgomery decd. defendants thereto, and to which
there was a demurrer all of which being seen and understood by the court,
the court is of opinion that the law arising thereon is for the defendants
Whereupon it is ordered and decreed by the court, that the complainants
bill be dismissed. And that the complainants pay all the costs of this suit
for which execution may issue as at law (Page 356) It appearing from the
petition of F. A. Parham, that he had published in the Chattanooga Gazett,
the sale of certain land and negroes belonging to the estate of John Kelly
deceased, which hadd been ordered by this court. And also the sale of the
lands belonging to the estate of W. J. Ally decd which had been also ordered
by a decree of this court, and that he ought to be allowed a fee for   the
same over what is allowed by act of Assembly but because the court is not
satisfied what allowance should be made . The Clk. & Master is ordered to
take proof and report to the present term, and said report having been made
by the master, which is seen? and confirmed by the court, from which it appears that said Parham ought to be allowed for publishing the sale of the
slaves the sum og $ 10.50?, for the sale of Kellies land the sum of $ 19 and
for Allies land the sum of $ 10.50 as full compensation for the same Where-
upon it is ordered that the same be taxed in the bill of costs in each case.

P-356
     This day Thomas N. Frazier and James A.. Tulloss Exrs? of Allen Montgo-
mery decd. presented their petition asking for a confirmation of the sale
of the Houses and lots bought by their Testator? in his lifetime for reasons therein stated and thereupon Bird Pankey and others presented their
cross bill asking said sale to be set aside as null and void, for reasons
therein stated. Whereupon the Chancellor is pleased to order that all further proceedings in said Cause be suspended for the present-- that said
Cross Bill be received and filled and that Depts annul? the same by the
 August rules. All annulements will be ruled ? as heretofore except where
specially ordered to the contrary and then the Chancellor adjourned, till
the regular Term.

                                                      Broomfield Ridley

                          " THE END"

www.ingramcontent.com/pod-product-compliance
Lightning Source LLC
Chambersburg PA
CBHW081431270326
41932CB00019B/3166